1989

Violence

AN ELEMENT
OF AMERICAN LIFE

Violence

AN ELEMENT
OF AMERICAN LIFE

Edited by

KARL K. TAYLOR
Division of Communications
Illinois Central College

FRED W. SOADY, JR.
Division of Social Sciences
Illinois Central College

HOLBROOK PRESS, INC.
BOSTON

TO OUR PARENTS

Contents

Preface

Until we had worked for several months on the ideas that have resulted in this anthology, we were not aware of the massive, almost bewildering part that violence plays in our lives. Violence is one of those insoluble problems that will always perplex mankind. Man must have some of it in order to live. With too much, he will perish. The midpoint is difficult to find.

We have no intention of imposing a set hypothesis about violence in our presentations. We want to offer ideas for discussion and thought, set out interesting concepts, propose alternate routes to comprehension, and invite the readers to find some understanding of the nature and conditions of violence. We hope some proximate solutions for finding the midpoint will become possible by such study of the problems.

Many people have helped us as we gathered and selected materials for this reader: we thank the usual anonymous dozens for their aid. We especially appreciate the help of our colleague, Professor Samuel C. Jones; two of our students, Miss Janan Frank and Mr. Michael Muntner; and our typists, Mrs. Reva Poehlman and Miss Judy Brandow. We also thank our wives and families for understanding our preoccupation with violence for so many years.

K. K. T.
F. W. S. Jr.

East Peoria, Illinois

Violence
AN ELEMENT
OF AMERICAN LIFE

Introduction

Americans indulge in no more violence than do many other societies in the world, yet the existing violence seems to have a stronger effect on our lives. Its repeated use to adjust to the frustrations of life is so central to the development of the United States that it sometimes seems that without violence there would be no United States. Violence is an American fixation. It is an element in our character.

The people of the North American colonies and the early periods of our national existence found that violence cut down on Indian raids; expanded the boundaries of the country, opening more farmland, cotton fields, and mineral resources; and added spice to foreign relations. They felt that it was a "good thing to let off a little steam now and then." Violence was accepted as necessary for the "Manifest Destiny" of the United States.

Violence was also accepted as a means to effect internal change. Just as domestic disputes alter the relationships of a family, the violence among Americans achieved certain structural changes within the United States. The growth and development of most of the groups now operating within our society was accompanied by violence. Corpo-

1

rations rose above others through ruthless competition, rail-roads secured rights-of-way with "hooliganism," and labor organized through the strike. Many, especially those of minority groups, found wealth and acceptance through boxing and similar "manly sports." Today, the young have derived political considerations from a fierce application of threat and force. Just as internal family violence accounts for more injury to police officers than any other single cause, violence among some groups in our society often takes a greater toll of "innocent bystanders" than of participants. In any internal violence, the society may well be the greatest loser.

A society's attitude toward violence or aggression will dictate if and how violence will be used in that society and in relations between that society and another. For example, the American attitude toward violence affects how violence is used between elements in the United States and between the United States and other nations.

Most of the violence in the United States in the 1960's was directed at people living in the same society. From this can be drawn several possible conclusions. Perhaps one factor increasing violence is frustration, the exasperation brought about by the distance between the declared goals of a society and the actual conduct of its affairs—between what it wants to do and what it can do. Americans have always accepted some degree of frustration when unsuccessfully striving for goals. However, as the so-called generation gap illustrates, the goals of the older members of our society are not those of the younger members. Because the young have not experienced events under the same circumstances as their elders, they have different viewpoints. This difference creates frustration for both. People are also disoriented by their rapidly changing ways of living: neighborhoods change, work becomes more specialized and impersonal, religious concepts alter, and the like. Change creates a confused man, a "marginal man." He is no longer a part of the culture in which he grew up (since it no longer exists), nor is he really a full member of the new culture.

This identity conflict leads to confusion about the role the individual must play in the present society. What can he do? What can't he do? Despite his many material comforts, he is uneasy because he is not satisfied with what has been developed in the social order. When the individual discovers that he is unable to do what he wants to do, he reacts, sometimes violently.

Feelings of inability lead to even greater frustrations and feelings of inadequacy and unimportance. When a person is unable to cope with raising his children, for instance, he reaches for reasons—he looks for scapegoats to share the blame for his own presumed failures. Perhaps those who so casually blame Dr. Spock and the United States Supreme Court for permissiveness and lawlessness do so because they need to displace their own feelings of impotence in the face of the complexities of modern life.

Why do we hear so much about violence? According to Gore Vidal, "Americans are the only people in the world who make one word of 'sex and violence.' Now just think what that means. To an American, sex is as evil as violence, which means it's also every bit as exciting." Violence, though often a terminus to life itself, is also what makes life interesting. Many people have said that the news and entertainment media seem to dwell on violent acts. But perhaps these media only reflect the attitude and interests of Americans.

There are so many theories about the causes of violence that it is difficult to catalogue them all. Some people subscribe to psychological theories and findings. Violence is part of an adjustment pattern by each individual attempting to live in a society. Violent acts, then, may be the result of faltering or unsuccessful attempts to function in society. For instance, a child may find attempts to socialize him confusing and conflicting: he will react with violent tantrums or other forms of open hostility. Likewise, the new immigrant, seeking to assimilate a new role in a new culture, will sometimes strike at what frustrates him—a person or a symbol (whichever is immediately available) of what the immigrant dislikes or fails to comprehend. That act only adds to the confusion. Some persons, being deficient in social settings, have negative perceptions of the conditions that surround them. A few become disruptive, or even destructive, of social settings and react to rearrange or remove the conditions.

Violence will sometimes come as the result of an egocentric impulse—brawls are started in many instances because of challenges to an individual's sense of well-being. The violence becomes an adjustment or compensation for real or imagined threats or losses. Emotional appeals and open acts of violence bring about greater response than do reason or quiet requests to do something. An emotional outburst is a quick adjustment to personal needs and is sometimes an aid in venting an even more dangerous act. Banging on the desk for emphasis is considered more desirable than banging upon the head of the opponent. But often the first act does enough damage by itself to be of note to the onlookers.

Violence satisfies many needs. Since peer approval is one of man's more important needs, violence is more satisfying and enjoyable if done in a group setting. While most individual acts of violence are disapproved by the group, group violence is often sanctioned by the society. It is thus more rewarding than a single act committed in a dark alley. There may also be the desire for martyrdom—real or imagined—in taking up violence for a cause.

Others look for answers to the cause of violence in sociological studies, because in our society cultural factors condone violence. In some settings, violence is approved when it is open and aboveboard (for example, the police officer subduing the wild gunman shooting up a peaceful street). At other times, the subtle, covert forms are better understood and used (the business rival undermining the credit rating of a competitor). But the end result, damage or destruction to some symbol or person, is the same.

Many factors in our society, moreover, foster the emergence of violence. A society is based largely on the principle of trust; therefore, whatever causes that trust to be questioned is valued by dissident factions. Whenever a conflict exists over what role a person is to play in the society, violence may result from his sense of frustration.

Whenever a number of people are unable to cope with the norms of the established order, especially those that are socially rigid and offer no obvious alternatives, violence may result. When the society reacts against that violence, further violence may be brought about, for violence is most likely to develop in an atmosphere of repression and discrimination. In most situations, those who are violent represent only a small portion of the total population, but they are likely to represent a majority of those who feel the grievance.[1]

Persons who use violence have different thresholds for committing overt acts, but most employ it only after they have tried other approaches. Violence begins with an awareness that something will be more satisfying if altered in some way. A level of apprehension is reached before antagonism becomes noticeable. Frustration and antagonism lead to anxiety and anger, which in turn become aggression. Failure to resolve the problem or find alternatives to overt violence will result in attack on the symbol or on the offending party if the need remains strong. It may be that when manipulation fails, violence results.

[1] Though not an American example, the centuries-old dispute between Protestant and Roman Catholic residents of Ulster (Northern Ireland) has become, since 1969, a prime example of continued tension and violence. In that circumstance, both individual and group acts have been committed throughout the range of violence, but have fallen short of open warfare.

1

The Atmosphere of Hate

"Tell Me All About Yourself—Your Birth, Your Parents, How You Grew up, Your Hopes, Your Plans—and the Best Way for Us to Kill You"

[Haynie in the *Louisville Courier-Journal*.]

ABOVE THE DESK OF A PSYCHOLOGIST COLLEAGUE IS A MOTTO printed in bold black letters on a bright red card. "*Support Mental Health,*" it proclaims. "*Or I'll kill you.*" The small card satirizes violence as an attitude, one with a long and dignified, even sanctified, standing in many of the world's societies. Violence in American culture is ironic—we both condemn and condone it. For the majority, violence represents a threat to the establishment; for the minority, violence frequently represents the ultimate solution for society's ills. The irony of violence is explained by the Geis article that follows.

Like every society in the past, America attempts to solve intense problems brought by changing conditions. Social change is often accompanied by violence. The amount used depends on how much the cultural norms will tolerate. Carley and Gottschalk raise the proposition that we may not be as violent as we once were. Most of the violent solutions were temporary measures at best and few were of lasting value to the society. They occurred because internal strain and external stress finally impelled the society to try to solve the difficulties with domestic disorder and war against its outside enemies. Our problems are probably not so different today.

While it seems to worry some of us that others in our society propose to use violence once again, we do not completely repudiate violence. We hold tightly to the adage "might makes right" even as we challenge its truth. (Hofstadter, Spiegel, and the *Time* essay explore this idea as they discuss the historic precedents for violence in this country and throughout the world.) While we challenge the validity of the conventions of the past, we are still bound by them. When frustrated, we become aggressive and violent. We react as did the ancestors for whom the violent act was an "only salvation," using the same ways of settling disputes that have proven so destructive and shortsighted for generations. We believe that we must "git 'im before he gits us!" We have a legacy—an historical atmosphere of hate.

*"Bah—I just don't know what the youngsters are coming to
these days."*

The Future of American Violence

RICHARD HOFSTADTER

On the cover of the June 30, 1969, issue of *New Left Notes*, the organ of the Progressive Labor faction of Students for a Democratic Society, there is a large woodcut illustration which must surely be one of the minor signs of the times. Two young men, one white, one black, are seen crouching on a rooftop above a city in flames. Both are armed with automatic rifles, and both wear, Mexican-fashion, the criss-crossed bandoliers of the rural insurrectionary or *bandito*. They are revolutionaries, urban guerrillas. Alongside them is the legend: "We are advocates of the abolition of war, we do not want war; but war can only be abolished through war, and in order to get rid of the gun it is necessary to take up the gun." One must, I think, pass by the resemblance of this promise of a war-to-end-war to other such promises in the past; one must pass by also its hauntingly perverse echo of the words of the American officer in Vietnam that "In order to liberate the village we had to destroy it," to consider its larger meaning for American political culture.

There is in America today a rising mystique of violence on the Left. Those who lived through the rise of European fascism, or who have watched the development of right-wing groups in this country over the last generation, or have fully recognized the amount of violence leveled at civil-rights workers in the South, are never surprised at violence cults on the Right. They still see them in action in such crank groups as the Minutemen, and hear their accents in some uninhibited passages in George Wallace's speeches. What has been more arresting is the decline of the commitment to nonviolence on the Left, and the growth of a disposition to indulge or to exalt acts of force or violence. What was once the Student Nonviolent Coordinating Committee has taken the "Nonviolent" out of its title. Frantz Fanon's full-throated defense of the therapeutic and liberating effects of violence has been one of the most widely read books of our time. During a summer of exacerbated rioting, *The New York Review of Books*, one of the most influential and fashionable periodicals on the American campus today, elected to feature on its cover a set of instructions, complete with diagram, for making a Molotov cocktail. In its columns, a widely read leftwing journalist, Andrew Kopkind, has told us that morality comes out of the muzzle of a gun. The Weatherman faction of SDS has made a primary tactic of violent encounters with the police. A young leader of the Black Panthers rises at the 1969 summer convention of the SDS to taunt the white delegates with the boast that the Panthers have "shed more blood than anyone" and that white Leftists have not even shot rubber bands. Dotson Rader, a young veteran of Columbia's wars, informs the readers of the *New York Times* in its correspondence columns that the justice the New Left seeks will be won by "fighting in the streets." Some, no doubt, are reminded of the Paris Commune. Others will be reminded of the promises of Mussolini.

Certain ironies in the new cult of violence are inescapable. The sidewalk Sorels who preach violence know very little about it, and sometimes prove pitifully ineffectual in trying to use it. Those who practice it with the greatest effect—the police and the military—find preaching superfluous. The new prophets of violence are almost certain to become its chief victims, if it becomes general and uncontrolled, especially when their own romanticism carries them from the word to the deed. Historically, violence has not been an effective weapon of the Left, except in that rarest of rare circumstances, the truly revolutionary situation. Under normal circumstances, violence has more characteristically served domineering capitalists or trigger-happy police, peremptory sergeants or fascist hoodlums. And even in our day, I think it should be emphasized, the growing acceptance of violence has been unwittingly fostered from the top of society. The model for violence, which has rapidly eroded the effectiveness of appeals to nonviolent procedures, has been the hideous and gratuitous official violence in Vietnam. And after having created and made heroes of such a special tactical force as the Green Berets, we should not be altogether surprised to find the Black Panthers wearing *their* berets and practicing close-order drill. It may be childishly irrelevant to cite the example of Vietnam as an answer to every reproach for domestic acts of force or violence, but there is in that answer a point of psychological importance that we should not overlook: now, as always, the primary precedent and the primary rationale for violence comes from the established order itself. Violence is, so to speak, an official reality. No society exists without using force or violence and without devising sanctions for violence which are used to uphold just wars and necessary police actions. But the frequency and the manner in which official violence is used is of signal importance to the legitimation of the civic order. Any liberal democratic state is in danger of wearing away its legitimacy if it repeatedly uses violence at home or abroad when a substantial number of its people are wholly unpersuaded that violence is necessary.

Neither establishments nor revolutionary movements can do without sanctions for violence. What any man sees as a just war or a necessary police action will, of course, depend upon his situation and his politics; but only a few pacifists quarrel with the idea that just wars are conceivable, and only a few utopian anarchists are likely to deny that under some circumstances authorities have to use force or violence to keep order. The right of revolution is itself an established and sanctified rationale for violence. It can hardly be banished from the established sanctions in a country like America that was born in a revolution. One of our most sacred texts lays down the circumstances under which revolutionary resistance becomes legitimate. "Prudence," it also remarks (there *were* revolutionaries for whom prudence was a consideration), "will dictate that governments long established should not be changed for light and transient causes. . . . But when a long train of abuses and usurpations, pursuing invariably the same object, evinces a design to reduce them under absolute despotism, it is their right, it is their duty, to throw off such a government, and to provide new guards for their future security."

In our own time we have no difficulty in thinking of some tyrants against whom the right of revolution was or could have been justifiably invoked, and responsibly so when the circumstances warranted hope of success. Unfortunately, in this age of verbal overkill, the epithet of tyranny can be hurled at any regime that is intensely disliked by a morally self-confident minority, and the prospects of revolutionary success may seem astonishingly good to those who gull themselves with their own miscalculations and fantasies.

The classic rationale for revolution is now widely used to sanction piecemeal violence against democratic regimes in which no shadow of a revolutionary situation exists. The word "revolution" has been distended to apply to any situation in which there is rapid change or widespread discontent. Hence acts of forcible or violent adventurism can be given a superficial legitimacy by defining any situation one pleases as a "revolutionary situation." One radical thinker, Barrington Moore, Jr., who cannot be accused of lack of concern for the oppressed or of hostility to revolutions, has deplored the current disposition "to cast some vague universal cloak of legitimacy upon violence—even upon violent resistance to oppression," and has warned against occasions when "revolutionary rhetoric outruns the real possibilities inherent in a given historical situation." Today, in America, "talk about revolution is . . . pure talk with potentially dangerous and tragic consequences."

One of the essential difficulties in justifying violence is that its success is an ingredient in its justification, and such success is usually a matter of chance. There *are* some blunders that are worse than crimes, and among these are the blunders of those who, even in a good cause, precipitate violence without reasonable grounds for believing that violence will serve its purpose or that it can be contained within bounds that will be proportionate to the ends in view. No doubt it is tempting to think of putting a final end to some grave and massive social evil by a quick, surgical, limited act of violence. But the dfficulty lies in being reasonably sure, before the event, that the evil will indeed be ended and not exacerbated or succeeded by some equal or greater evil; that the violence can really be limited both in time and in the casualties it inflicts, and that the reaction will not be more harmful than the surgery. For this reason all politicians, revolutionary no less than establishment politicians, must work with a terrible calculus in human misfortune.

In order to justify the use of violence as a means toward the accomplishment of some humane and "progressive" end, one must first believe that he knows, roughly at least, two things: first, that so-and-so much violence is in fact necessary to achieve the end; and second, what the countervailing human cost of the violence will be—that is, where its repercussions will stop. There are, of course, many people who imagine that they have this kind of command of the future; but some of us are not so sure, since we are not even sure that we can judge the necessity or usefulness of *past* violence in many cases where all the returns seem to be in hand.

But let us not deceive ourselves. Current credulity about the benefits of violence is rarely based upon a careful concern about when and how violence can be justified, or upon sober estimates of its past role or its prospects of future success. We are not living in a period of moral casuistry or measured calculation but in one of robust political romanticism. The protest politics of the 1960s threatened at times to break with the historic politics of liberal American reformers—who aimed to persuade a wide public, had scruples about methods, were willing to compromise, to move patiently from one limited end to another. For a decisive but now perhaps waning segment of the Far Left, politics has become all too much a matter of self-expression and of style, and such efforts as its more extreme exponents make at calculations and casuistry seem feeble as compared with the full-blown bravado of their actionist creed. There are moments when the aim of the political act seems to have become little more than the venting of a sense of outrage, and there have been activists more concerned with their freedom to carry the Vietcong flag in a peace parade or to use four-letter words than with their ability to persuade. There is less hope that any particular foray will yield visible results or affect public policy, more desire to get a sense of emotional satisfaction out of a mass happening. The demand for programmatic achievement has become less fixed, that of self-assertion central. The distinction between politics and theater has been systematically blurred by activists in politics and activists in the theater.

In the new politics, force or violence has a new place: for some it is satisfying merely to use it, but others have devised strategies to provoke counterviolence to show up the Establishment, as they put it, for what it is. In any case, violence has come to have the promise of redemption. "Violence alone," writes Frantz Fanon in *The Wretched of the Earth*, one of the canonical works of the new politics, "violence committed by the people, violence organized and educated by its leaders, makes it possible for the masses to understand social truths and gives the key to them." Fanon, writes Sartre in presenting him, "shows clearly that this irrepressible violence is neither sound and fury, nor the resurrection of savage instincts, nor even the effect of resentment: it is man recreating himself. . . . No gentleness can efface the marks of violence, only violence itself can destroy them."

Violence, then, is not only useful but therapeutic, which is to say indispensable. It seems natural enough for those who have been victims of a great deal of violence, or simply of the constant threat of overwhelming force, to conclude that they can restore their dignity only when they use violence themselves. But the restorative power of violence, if indeed violence can have that power, must surely depend upon its being used successfully. The unsuccessful use of violence, ending in defeat and fresh humiliations, may in fact intensify the original malaise. It is hard, for example, to imagine that the survivors of the grim massacre of the Indonesian Communist party in 1965-66 would have the same enthusiasm for the restorative power of violence as the victorious Algerian rebels. And this is why the existential mystique of violence, which tries to circumvent the rational calculus of tactical probabilities, will not do: its claims for therapy or sanctification through violence rest upon an arbitrary assumption of success. There is no satisfactory refuge from political calculation in psychology or metaphysics.

But of course there *are* examples of success in our time—examples set by Mao, Castro, the Algerian rebels, Ho Chi Minh and the Vietcong. The circumstances in all these cases have a special quality: the successes have been among "backward" peoples with a firm territorial base and a history of colonial exploitation. It is now suggested that violence can be equally successful in modern industrial countries, that guerrilla action suitable to the Sierra Maestre or the terror and sabotage that won in Algiers can be adapted to New York, Chicago, Oakland, or even, it appears, Scarsdale. A good deal of tactical ingenuity has in fact been stimulated, but the chief intellectual consequences have been pathetic: many young blacks have begun to think of themselves as being a colonial people, and of their problems of liberation as having exactly the same characteristics.* The psychological similarities are, of course, there— and a book like Fanon's *The Wretched of the Earth*, the work of a psychiatrist, argues its case largely in psychological rather than in social structural terms. American blacks may have the psyches of other victims of colonialism but they lack all the essential features of the true colonial situation: a terrain suitable to guerrilla action, the prospect of becoming a majority, territoriality, and the promise

---

* Since so much has been accomplished by strategic minorities, it may not matter for the future of violence in America that the black militants have not yet converted a majority of Negroes. In *Newsweek*'s 1969 poll, 63 per cent (as against 21 per cent) thought that Negroes could win their rights without violence. Overwhelming majorities also repudiated separatism in response to questions about integrated schools and integrated neighborhoods. (*Newsweek*, June 30, 1969.) The appeal of militant ideas, however, is much higher among the young.

of integral control of the economy after the colonial power has been expelled. Except for these indispensable elements, the comparison is excellent, and therefore we may indulge ourselves in the fantasy that Watts is just like Algiers.

But in the end one must give the prophets of violence their due: violence *is* pervasive in human experience and has been pervasive in American history, and however it repels us, we must see it as an instrument of common use. The creed its proponents put before us is simple but forceful: Violence has been all but universal in the past. Violence changes things and nothing else does. Violence is therefore necessary. "Violence," said Rap Brown in what must surely remain one of the memorable utterances of our time, "is necessary and it's as American as cherry pie." Presumably he did not expect his listeners to be so uncritically patriotic as to think that violence must be good because Americans have so often used it. No doubt his hope was that if a decent respect for the normality and inevitability of violence could be instilled in the minds of his contemporaries, they would be less censorious about the violence supposedly necessary to black liberation. And one should grant all that is sound here: certainly violence that would in fact lead to a full realization of the rights of blacks would have a great deal to be said for it, and would stand in quite a different moral position from the violence, say, that many lynchers used for their own entertainment and for the edification of their children. Here, as always, however, one encounters the latent, the unexamined assumption: violence *will* deliver that which is expected of it. It is an assumption shared more and more among the very young, black or white: justice will be won by "fighting in the streets." Fighting in the streets as a revolutionary technique—it is one of the few old-fashioned ideas still alive.

Certainly world history yields plenty of cases in which some historical logjam seems to have been broken up by an eruption of violence, which is then followed by a period of peaceful, gradualist improvement. It is always possible in such cases to argue (though difficult to prove) that the violence was a necessary precondition of the peaceful change that followed. The trouble is that there are so many other cases in which violence has decided issues in ways we are less likely to applaud. American experience with the large-scale violent resolution of fundamental crises is mixed. The Revolution and the Civil War pose an interesting antithesis. The question of American independence was settled by violence, and, as historical issues go, settled with considerable success. But one of the keys to that success may be found in the minimum of gratuitus violence with which the Revolution was carried out. There could be no regicide and there was no terror. There were frequent incidents, but there was no wholesale mobbing of dissidents. Few loyalists outside the ranks of the British army were killed, though many were terrorized, may went into exile, and many lost large properties. Even the military action did not characteristically go beyond what we would call guerrilla warfare. Most important, the revolutionaries did not turn upon each other with violence or terror. The Thermidor, if the adoption of the Constitution can be correctly called that, was equally mild, and in part simply nationalized and embodied in institutional form some of the principles set forth in the Revolution itself. Not only was independence secured and the political life of the American states markedly democratized but some social reforms were given a strong impetus. In spite of the difficult questions of national organization that were not settled, and in spite of the tumultuous passions raised by the political issues of the Federal era, the episodes of domestic violence that followed the Revolution—and there were quite a number of them—were in a relatively low key and proved eminently controllable. The early rebellions mounted by Daniel Shays, the Whiskey rebels, and John Fries, though of much political consequence, were, as episodes of violence, kept at the level of skirmishes, and their leaders were afterwards treated with judicious consideration. The Revolution was followed by relative peace: on the whole, the era from 1790 to 1830, though far from violence-free, was one of the least violent periods in our domestic history.

The Civil War stands in marked contrast. Again, it did settle historical issues, the issues of union and of the legal status of slavery. But it was preceded by a decade of searing civic violence and climaxed by a war that cost 600,000 lives, and it left an extraordinary inheritance of bitterness and lethal passion that has not yet ended. The legal liberation of the slave was not followed by the actual liberation of the black man. The defeated states became less rather than more democratic. The violence of the war was followed by the resounding and horrifying episodic violence of Reconstruction, and the Thermidor in the South went on for a full generation after the guns were stilled. The war seems in retrospect to have been an intensely cruel and wasteful way of settling—if that is the right word—the issues that gave rise to it. I do not agree with the categorical form or exaggerated rhetoric of Barrington Moore's pessimistic world-historical estimates that "violence has settled all historical issues so far, and most of them in the wrong way," but in the considerable list of historical cases that could be drawn up to support his judgment, the Civil War would surely rank high.

If we look at the use of violence in social situations of less profound consequence than those which led to the Revolution and the Civil War, we can find instances when violence in the United States appears to have served its purpose. And it has been, on the whole, the violence of those who already had position and power. Many vigilante movements, for example, achieved their limited goal of suppressing outlaws. Lynching clearly added a note of terroristic enforcement to the South's caste system. For years employers used violence and the threat of violence against labor with success: in the main, the outstandingly violent episodes in industrial conflicts were tragic defeats for labor, although there were occasions when violence initiated on behalf of employers became too blatant for public acceptance and boomeranged. Labor has used violence less often than employers and with only rare success. There was, to be sure, one very effective series of extralegal actions by labor—the sit-downs of the 1930s. However, in these instances the workers, though using illegal *force*, were using a tactical device that tended to avert rather than precipitate acts of outright violence. This may explain why they won considerable sympathy from the public, which was at the same time becoming acutely aware of the violence, intimidation, and espionage used by employers in many industries. In any case, the sitdowns were a transient tactic which labor leaders abandoned as soon as collective bargaining was achieved, and it is difficult to imagine the sitdowns repeatedly successful as a standard device.

In sum, violence can succeed in a political environment like that of the United States under certain conditions. Those who use it must be able to localize it and limit its duration. They must use it under circumstances in which the public is either indifferent or uninformed, or in which the accessible and relevant public opinion (as in the case of vigilantes and, usually, of employers in the nineteenth century) is heavily biased in their favor. If violence is accompanied by exceptional brutality (lynching, employer actions like that at Ludlow), it must be kept a local matter, and one must hope that it can somehow be screened from the attention of the larger polity. The conditions for its success, in this respect, seem to have become more problematical in the age of mass communications, where the most vital tactical problem is to set the stage so that the onus for violent action can be made to seem to rest entirely upon one's adversaries.

If violence sometimes works, it does not follow that nothing but violence works. Most of the social reforms in American history have been brought about without violence, or with only a marginal and inessential use of it, by reformers who were prepared to carry on a long-term campaign of education and propaganda. The entire apparatus of the welfare state, from child labor laws, wage-hour regulation, industrial safety laws, and workmen's compensation to legally regulated collective bargaining, social security, and medical care for the aged, is the achievement of active minorities which, while sometimes militant and always persistent, were also patient and nonviolent. Ours, however, is an age that cannot wait, and it is doubtful that young militants, black or white, are taking much comfort from the example of such predecessors in the tradition of American reform. The activists, according to their temperaments, will argue either that earlier reforms, being props to the Establishment, were of little or no value, or that they were all a generation overdue when they came. The first response is simply inhumane, but the second has much truth in it: such reforms were indeed long overdue. However, it does not follow that the use of violence would have hastened their coming. Under some conditions the fear or threat of violence may hasten social reforms, yet if actual outbreaks of violence were the primary force in bringing reform, one might have expected social-welfare laws to come in the United States before they came to such countries as Great Britain and Germany where there was less industrial violence. The important element seems to have been not the resort to violence but the presence of powerful labor movements with a socialist commitment and the threat of sustained action through normal political channels.

But the confrontationist politicians of our time seem to have hit upon an approach to violence that surmounts one of the signal disadvantages under which social dissidents have labored in the past: they have learned the value not of committing violence but of *provoking* it. It remains true today, as it has always been, that most political violence is committed by the agents of authority. In the past, for example, labor often got the blame for violent outbursts that were primarily the work of police or other agents of employers. Hence one speaks of "labor violence" but not of "capital violence." Today, however, a technique has been found to put official violence to work in the apparent interests of dissent. A small cadre of determined activists, enveloped in a large crowd of demonstrators, can radicalize a substantial segment of public opinion by provoking the police into violent excesses—if necessary by hurling objects, but better still by hurling nothing more than verbal abuse. The activists have correctly gauged the temper of the police, who are often quite ready to oblige by lashing out indiscriminately against both those who have offended them and those who have not—orderly demonstrators, innocent bystanders, reporters, cameramen. Young radicals have thus found a way to put the police and the mass media to work for them, as the public sees a hideous spectacle of beating, kicking, and clubbing by officers of the law against unarmed demonstrators and witnesses. Outrage becomes the more blatant to those who are aware of and attracted by the milky innocence of the majority of young demonstrators.

Whether the larger public effect of such confrontations will actually work to the ultimate advantage of the activists is problematical. What they can see with their own eyes at the moment of conflict is that many persons, hitherto vaguely sympathetic, become, at least for a time, energized and activated out of indignation. What they choose to ignore is the other, less visible but usually larger public, which puts the full blame on demonstrators and backs the police and the authorities. (The behavior of the Chicago police during the Democratic Convention of 1968, one of the most flagrant police actions of this era, was approved by a sustained majority of the public.) Still, activist leaders are aware of *their* converts, and converts there usually are. Why not rejoice in the converts and dismiss the backlash? Hence the ubiquitous New Left agitator, Tom Hayden, has called for "two, three, many Chicagos," and the young activists interviewed by Jerome Skolnick's researchers for the National Commission on the Causes and Prevention of Violence show a shrewd if limited understanding of the implications of such tactics. The purpose of confrontations, they argue with striking candor, is to educate the public by staging spectacles of repression. "Direct action is not intended to win particular reforms or to influence decision-makers, but rather to bring out a repressive response from authorities—a response rarely seen by most white Americans. When confrontation brings violent official response, uncommitted elements of the public can see for themselves the true nature of the 'system.' " The activists also believe that such experience lowers the "cultural fear of violence" natural among young middle-class radicals—a fear that is "psychologically damaging and may be politically inhibiting," and thus prepares them for a serious commitment to revolution. To some degree they have already been proved right: the "damaging" inhibitions against the use of guns, bombs, and arson have begun to break down.

Can this breakdown be extrapolated into an indefinite future? No doubt most Americans are more curious about where our penchant for violence is taking us than they are about a more precise explanation of its pattern in the past. But here prognosis is as hazardous as anywhere. In the past our violence has always been cyclical, and it is possible to believe that the 1960s will some day appear on the charts of the sociologists as another peak period, rather more pronounced than many, which is followed by relative calm. As the young never tire of reminding us, we live

in a situation that is new and in some decisive respects un-
precedented. (I sometimes think that *all* American experience is a series of disjunctive situations whose chief con-
necting link is that each generation repeats the belief of its
predecessor that there is nothing to be learned from the
past.) In any case, our social violence is not a self-contained
universe that holds within itself all the conditions of its
future development. In fact almost everything depends upon
external forces which no one dares to predict: the tempo
at which we disengage from Vietnam, the national and international response to our undisguisable failure there, and
our ability to avoid another such costly venture.

Who can really believe that he knows what to expect
of the future of American violence? It is easy to draw up
two plausible scenarios for the future, one apocalyptic, the
other relatively benign though hardly exhilarating. Apocalyptic predictions are conventionally in order—indeed they
have become so conventional that they constitute a kind of
imperative intellectual fashion. But in them there is more
of omniscience than of science, and their function seems
more psychological than pragmatic. In a magical gesture
one predicts evil in order to ward it off. Or worse, in moments of terrible frustration one threatens one's audience
with some ultimate catastrophe by way of saying: This is
what you will all get for not having followed the social
policies I have prescribed for you. However, over the past
generation the visions of the future that have prevailed
among the most modishly apocalyptic intellectual circles in
this country have been so largely wrong that they could almost be used like odd-lot buying in the stock market as a
negative indicator of future realities. Perhaps the most co-
gent reason, aside from the perverse element of self-indul-
gence inherent in it, for not yielding too easily to the apocalyptic frame of mind is a pragmatic one: apocalyptic
predictions, repeated too often and believed too automatically, could at best reduce men of good will to a useless

passivity and at worst turn into self-fulfilling prophecies. Pragmatic wisdom argues for assuming that our difficulties are manageable, so that we may put our minds to thinking about how in fact they can be managed.

Still, it requires no remarkable ingenuity to see how some of the recent trends in American society, continued and magnified, could bring about the eclipse of liberal democratic politics. The danger is not that the alienated young and the militant blacks will wage a successful revolution. The United States is basically a conservative country, and its working class is one of the anchors of its conservatism. Its overwhelming majority is not poor, not black, and not in college. College activists, themselves only a fraction of the college population, command so much attention from the mass media that the actual state of mind of the American young has been obscured. Almost three-fourths of those in the 17–23 age bracket do not go to college, and their political direction is quite different from that of the college activists. Their responsiveness even to the cruder forms of backlash sentiment may be measured by their votes in the 1968 election; in which George Wallace had proportionately somewhat *more* support among white voters in the age groups 29 and under than in the age groups 30 and over.*

In a nation so constituted, the most serious danger comes not from the activities of young militants, black or white, but from the strength of the backlash that may arise out of an increasing polarization of the society. The apocalyptic scenario spells itself out rather easily: an indefinite prolongation of the war in Vietnam, or a re-escalation, or the launching of yet another such provocative and disastrous foreign undertaking; a continued unwillingness or inability to make adequate progress in accommodating the

* An American Institute for Public Opinion national sample showed that Wallace had the following support in four age brackets: 21–25, 13 percent; 26–29, 18 percent; 30–49, 13 percent; 50 and over, 11 per cent.

demand for racial justice; an intensification of confrontation politics in the colleges and on the streets: a heightened
alienation of the intelligent young; violent scenes, vividly
reported on TV, of provocative conduct by demonstrators
and brutal responses by police; a continuing polarization
of the political public into Right and Left which shuts off
just such political and social efforts as might relieve the
crisis; the formation of numerous armed groups of black
and white citizens, highlighted perhaps by a few mass gunfights in the big cities; the breakdown of one or both of
the major parties; the capture of the Presidency and Congress by a nationwide movement dedicated to political
repression at home and a hard line in foreign policy.

　　Not altogether impossible, one must say, though to
me it somehow fails to carry conviction. The particular
forms of violence that flourished in the 1960s seem now to
be on the decline: ghetto riots have been tapering off, and
the crest of violence touched off by campus protest may
have been reached in the years 1967 to 1969. Black militancy is certain to be with us for an indefinite future, and
it is a sobering thought that the one major breakdown of
the American political system came in association with an
unresolved problem of race; but black agitation tends to
grow more selective about methods and goals, and it is by
no means clear that it must involve large-scale violence or
mass casualties. Student activism too seems likely to outlast
the American withdrawal from Vietnam, since it rests on
a profound cultural malaise that goes beyond any political
issue, but it may work at a lower level of emotional intensity. An end to the war would bring about a political and
economic climate in which the effort to relieve urban
blight and poverty and to come to terms with the demand
for racial justice can be resumed under far more favorable
conditions than those of the past five or six years. It is a
rare thing in our experience to be centrally preoccupied
with the same problem for two successsive decades, and it

is quite conceivable that even a persisting and relatively high level of violence in the 1970s will come to be regarded as a marginal rather than a central problem. At some time in the near future the destruction of the environment, and the problems attendant upon pollution and overpopulation, are likely to take the center of the historical stage and to have such a commanding urgency that all other issues will be dwarfed. The styles of thought, the political mood that will be created by such problems, as well as the political alignments they will bring about, may be so startlingly different from those of the 1960s, that the mentality of the 1960s will seem even more strange by 1980 than the mentality of the 1950s has appeared during the past few years.

When one considers American history as a whole, it is hard to think of any very long period in which it could be said that the country has been consistently well governed. And yet its political system is, on the whole, a resilient and well seasoned one, and on the strength of its history one must assume that it can summon enough talent and good will to cope with its afflictions. To cope with them —but not, I think, to master them in any thoroughly decisive or admirable fashion. The nation seems to slouch onward into its uncertain future like some huge inarticulate beast, too much attainted by wounds and ailments to be robust, but too strong and resourceful to succumb.

QUESTIONS FOR DISCUSSION

1. *According to Hofstadter, which political faction—the right or the left—has been the most open in its use of violence in the past?*

2. *Does the author believe that violence has been "an effective weapon of the left"?*

3. *What "model for violence . . . has rapidly eroded the effectiveness of appeals to nonviolent procedures"?*

4. *What does Hofstadter mean by the following statement?
"Any liberal democratic state is in danger of wearing away
its legitimacy if it repeatedly uses violence at home or
abroad when a substantial number of its people are wholly
unpersuaded that violence is necessary."*

5. *Hofstadter admits that violence is justified in some cases
to change conditions, but does he feel that much of the
present violence is justified?*

6. *What are the author's two conditions for the use of violence?*

7. *What does the author mean when he says, "In the new
politics, force or violence has a new place: for some it
is satisfying merely to use it, but others have devised
strategies to provoke counter-violence to show up the Establishment, as they put it, for what it is"?*

8. *What does Hofstadter mean by saying that violence is
therapeutic?*

9. *On what grounds does the author question the validity of
Blacks' using violence to improve their lot in America?*

10. *In what way does the author feel that violence was a success during the American Revolutionary War?*

11. *Does he feel the same way about the violence used in the
Civil War?*

12. *What are examples cited by the author to illustrate other
times when violence was successful in improving social
situations?*

13. *Does Hofstadter believe that violence is the only way to
change our society? What examples does he cite to illustrate that patient, nonviolent reformers have been successful in our society?*

14. *What does the author mean when he says that "confrontationist politicians of our time . . . have learned the
value not of committing violence but of provoking it"?*

15. *What factors does he feel are necessary for promoting
more violence? Does Hofstadter believe that we are
headed for more violence in the future?*

The Tradition of Violence in Our Society

JOHN R. SPIEGEL

I have to begin with a definition because the word violence is used so loosely and so many different ways and if you're going to do some scientific work, you have to make your own definition and stick to it. That doesn't mean that everybody has to agree with our definition but this is the one that we are using now.

We say that violence is the extreme pole of a spectrum of behavior which is called aggression and that aggression means the use of force of some kind in order to make another person conform against his will to required behavior —to behavior that is being instituted by one person or organization over against another.

When we talk about violence, then, we are talking about the extreme pole of this whole spectrum of aggressive behavior which requires the use of force. We define its nature as the use of force in order to injure or destroy so that makes it a very specialized form of aggressive behavior.

In addition, there is a second characteristic to what we call violent behavior. Not only is it directed against

Dr. John R. Spiegel, "The Tradition of Violence in Our Society," Copyright *Washington Star*, October 13, 1968.

persons, objects or organizations with the attempt to injure, to destroy, but it also has an explosive quality. It's a very simple thing, the difference between setting my hands down on this table gently or my pounding the table.

In other words, the explosiveness in relation to the behavior being shown in an all or none form is a very important part of what we're calling violence. I mention this only because the word is used in so many different ways including an attempt to use the word violence to cover all forms of sin, injustice, cruelty, exploitation, deprivation. I don't think this is good and I think we should make an effort to straighten out our thinking so that, when we call something violence, when we speak of violence, we know what we are talking about.

MANY FORMS

There are many forms of violence. I'm not going to make an attempt to cover all these forms, to define them or to assess where the United States stands in relation to them. I'm not going to be saying anything about individual violence, for example, the thing that is of great concern today, such as the various types of violent attacks that occur in the streets. I'm not going to talk about war. I'm not going to talk about conspiracy. I'm not going to talk about a great many things that really ought to be known and assessed in order for us to reach a reasonable assessment of how violent the United States is.

I'm going to be talking only about the forms of collective violence in the city, the urban disorders, because this is where we have centered our attention. And, in trying to present to you a model—a conceptual model—of what it is that brings about this type of violence, I think one thing that's important at the outset, and that is for all of us to realize, is that the United States, ever since it was founded, has been characterized by repeated cycles of violence.

We are a peculiar people, it seems to me, in that we have an image of ourselves as quiet, peace loving and rational beings. The United States citizen thinks of himself and his country ordinarily as governed by democratic, rational, peace loving instincts.

But the fact of the matter is otherwise.

That is, we have always been a violent country and, in our country, there have been repeated cycles of violence, cycles of rioting, which we tend to forget about. That is, as a nation, we suffer from historical amnesia and it's easy to see why this happens; because these particular episodes in our past certainly don't fit into our self image as being so peace loving and so rational.

So we have forgotten about the Shays rebellion, for example, of 1786, when a group of hard-pressed poor farmers in the western part of Massachusetts, resentful about the tax laws in the Massachusetts State Legislature, simply seized the law courts and wouldn't let any justice be transacted, scaring the daylights out of the legislature to the extent that the tax laws, which these farmers so much resented, were modified. You might say that's a prototype of what has happened ever since with respect to the uses and functions of violence.

The Forgotten Riots

We've forgotten about the anti-Catholic riots—the anti-Irish riots—of the 1840s and the 1850s with a particularly bloody outbreak in the city of Philadelphia, the city of brotherly love, in 1844.

We've forgotten about the Civil War draft riot of 1863, in which in a period of five days, almost 2,000 people were killed. We have had nothing like that in the current series of urban disorders.

We've forgotten about the anti-Chinese riots on the West Coast in Los Angeles and San Francisco in the 1870s which were extraordinarily cruel.

We've forgotten about the labor uprisings, the whole series of episodes in the course of labor attempting to gain permission to organize itself and conduct collective bargaining which began seriously in the 1890s and was seen in such bloody affairs as the Homestead strike and the Pullman strike just south of Chicago in the 1890s. In the Pullman strike I don't think any of us remember the nation had to mobilize 16,000 federal troops to contain the disorders that spread so rapidly throughout the country.

And finally, we've forgotten about the anti-Negro riots of 1919, 1920, post World War I—the so-called race riots, which is an improper name for them because they were almost exclusively characterized by the activities of whites attacking black people.

So when we come up to the current cycle that we're now engaged in, of urban disorders in black communities and on college campuses, this is obviously seventh of a number of cycles that has characterized our country and I have left out a lot.

I haven't talked about the slave uprisings of pre-revolutionary times, I haven't talked about the Doctors Riot in the city of New York in the early part of the 19th century.

FIVE PRECONDITIONS

In talking about the conceptual model we are currently using to explain why collective hostile outbreaks occur, we are saying that in order for a riot to break out there need to be five preconditions. These are universal. They always need to be there. Or another way to describe these preconditions is to say if you're going to try to design a riot, this is the prescription, this is the way you bake the cake.

First, there must exist a very severe value conflict, a polarized conflict of basic values.

Second, there must exist a hostile system of beliefs— what we call a hostile belief system—in the minds of the adversaries involved in this basic value conflict. To illustrate, you will recall that the civil war draft riot of 1863, particularly the very bloody one that broke out in New York City in July of 1863, was characterized by a problem of injustice and grievance in the minds of the people who were rioting because of the way the draft had been set up.

President Lincoln's draft, you will recall, was a universal one with the exception that those who had $300 could buy their way out of the draft. Obviously this was not fair, did not conform to our basic democratic values. Rich people profited from it. Poor people suffered from it. And this was the value conflict. And in terms of this value conflict in the minds of the poor people, particularly those who were Irish and Catholic and therefore already felt exploited by the Protestant establishment, it was a sign that this establishment was out to get them, was out to exploit them. So this is the way a hostile belief system is generated around a value conflict and then is widely circulated and maintained in the minds of the aggrieved parties.

Third, there must be inadequate communications with respect to the hostile belief system. And this is where the media of any time and age are implicated in the preconditions that are behind the collective disorder. By inadequate communication I mean that both sides, both adversaries, both contending parties involved in the value conflict and the hostile belief system do not know enough about the other. In the 1863 draft riot for example, Republican party officials were almost completely ignorant of the resentment that existed in the minds of the poor people until the riot broke out. Then they began to get the message. But why did it require a riot to deliver this information to those who had power? Because it simply wasn't being taken up by the existing media of that time.

Fourth, there must be a failure of social control, such that those responsible for social control . . . the police and other non-military law enforcement agencies either function too much or too little. That is, there is either overcontrol or undercontrol. Law enforcement personnel either overreact, respond too repressively, too cruelly as we saw on the streets of Chicago, for example, or they stand around or don't appear at all, and do very little. That's encouraging transgressions of the law.

What's required is a firm presence of law enforcement agencies without either overresponding or underresponding. Now I recognize that it's very easy on the basis of hindsight, especially for those not involved in the particular conflict— such as a researcher like myself—to say "you underresponded" or "you overresponded" and I would have done it differently.

Enforcement Tough

I recognize that those responsible for law enforcement have a hard time, as we all do as a matter of fact, in almost all kinds of human occasions in knowing where that middle ground is, that appropriate ground.

But nevertheless, even though it's easy as an afterthought to see where the troubles were in overresponding or underresponding, law enforcement agencies could do a great deal better to get to this middle ground by anticipating, by planning and by informing themselves as to what types of problems they're going to be dealing with.

Finally, the fifth precondition is a triggering episode, a precipitating episode that gets the whole riot process started. In our current series, of course, we know that many of these precipitating episodes have been an unfair arrest or at least an arrest that is seen as unfair by an aggrieved party, some failure on the part of the city to do something it has promised to do.

The precipitating episode in itself is quite often not a very remarkable occasion. It becomes a precipitating incident because it fits so neatly into the four other preconditions—that it is representative of the value conflict. It is an item already predicted by the hostile belief system circulating in the minds of the people. People in black communities now, for example, feel in accord with their hostile belief systems that the police are going to be brutal and cruel in their handling and often, of course, they are.

I should say that when I talk about a hostile belief system, I don't mean a paranoid system. I don't mean a made-up set of beliefs, but I've followed a system in order to indicate that the items that exist in this set of thoughts are so systemized that the individuals can make no discriminations.

In Civil War times, for example, the poor people thought all Republicans were cruel. The life of a Republican wasn't safe on the streets at that time because no distinctions could be made. So it is that many people of black communities today believe that all white people are out to repress them, to suppress them, or to deal with them in an unjust fashion. In other words no distinction could be made.

It is in this sense that the hostile belief system functions badly but it is not to be said that the hostile belief system is not related to reality, because many of the items it contains are true and these are things that will happen. And whether they will happen or not, of course, is intimately related to whether a triggering occasion will occur.

Now there's much more to be said in terms of particular outbreaks of violence in the cities that we've seen and on college campuses in terms of these four preconditions, but I'd rather put that aside and let it wait for the question period because I now would like to talk about the substance of the value conflict.

I think this is the least misunderstood part of the problem of collective disorder that we're now all experiencing. That is, there is a trouble in the minds of all of us in proper appreciation, of realistic appreciation of what the value conflict is that we're all now caught up in. I don't think it's new.

I think that this country, ever since it was formed, has been caught up in a very severe struggle between the authoritarian, aristocratic principles that the American Revolution was designed to overthrow and the democratic set of values, the egalitarian values that the revolution was designed to institute in the new political procedures of the United States.

This conflict was never resolved at the time the country was formed. It was seen in the arguments between Thomas Jefferson, for example, and John Adams, and it has been going on in a sort of subterranean, underground way every since.

When our country was formed, it was formed as a limited democracy, limited by six structural principles. That is, it was like a democratic island floating in a sea of authoritarianism. In order to be on that democratic island and to participate in the power of our nation and in its decision-making process, you had to be:

1. White, which meant that all reds, yellows and blacks were out.

2. You had to be Anglo-Saxon or some related species, i.e., some Northern European country, which meant that all Mediterranean, orientals, Middle Easterners and so forth were out.

3. You had to be middle class or better, which meant that all poor people and working people, those who didn't hold property and so forth were out.

4. You had to be Protestant, which meant that all Catholics, Jews, Moslems and people of other religions were out.

5. You had to be adult, which meant that all young people were out or were exploited at that time.

6. Finally, you had to be male, which meant that all women were out, simply not included in the decision-making process.

All those who were out were regarded as inferior beings. This is a function of an aristocratic authoritarian system.

The history of the riot cycles that I described at the beginning was a drama of the efforts of the excluded to get up on this island, to get out of this sea of authoritarianism, to break down the barriers that the elite had put up against them, to be included in the democratic system.

Each age has had its time—the time of ripeness—when one or another of the excluded groups was ready to get in, and at this point the violence became quite acute and was characterized by a long, continued riot cycle.

The anti-Catholic riots of the 1840s and 1850s for example were the time of ripeness for the Catholics and the Irish to get into the system, and they were opposed by the American party and later by the Know-Nothing group.

APPLYING LABELS

I would love to talk about the type of violence that clusters around the effort of any particular group in its historical time to break down the barriers and get up on that democratic island.

Let us call those who are trying to break down the barriers the Reconstructivists for their time.

Let us call those who oppose their getting through the door or even getting a foot in the door the Nativists, generalizing from the native American party.

If this is correct, then every riot cycle has been characterized by the activities of Reconstructivists trying to get in and of Nativists trying to push them off, or hold them off, or keep things at their most ideal—that is their most Nativist ideal—to carry the country back to its origins, to be the sort of society the country had at the time of the American Revolution, or perhaps before that.

If this is correct, then we can discuss some of the psychological characteristics of the Nativists as opposed to the Reconstructionists [sic]. Reconstructivists, then, are not only the people who are trying to get in, break down the barriers, get into the democratic decision-making process, but to bring them with their culture, whatever the new group is—Irish, Italian, Jewish, Catholic, black, young people.

Whatever that new group is, it's trying to broaden and restructure American society to bring in its language, its ideals, its culture, its humor, its art, its songs and so forth.

The Nativists, on the other hand, are those who feel threatened by this attempt to broaden and restructure the democratic American society. They feel threatened by the new cultural items which to them seem to be corrupting, to diminish rather than to enrich the quality of American life. To the Nativists, America means a certain thing, and, therefore, un-American means something very different and that has to be kept out.

This is one important difference between Reconstructivists and Nativists; but another has to do with the type of violence or mode in which violence is used because violence will always occur with respect to the Nativists-Reconstructivists problem.

By and large there are exceptions to this proposition, but if violence is going to break out, Reconstructivists use it against property and things for the sake of disrupting the system or a part of the system, just as in Shay's Rebellion in 1786. Those poor farmers seized and occupied the law courts so no legal transactions could take place. So it has been ever since, particularly in terms of labor struggles.

ATTACK AND BURN

Where those attempting to organize a union, or to install a union in a particular industry or a particular plant, would seize a plant, occupy or obstruct the industry or workings of that plant until they were recognized or until they were given permission to have their union and carry on their activity.

So Reconstructivists do this. They obstruct. They attack property and they burn. Often they destroy, as machinery was destroyed in the course of the labor struggles. They occupy the seats of power, so to speak, as the students of various campuses occupy the administration building. Sometimes burning and other very serious types of property destruction takes place. Ordinarily the attacks are not against people.

Nativists, on the other hand, if they are going to be violent, and they frequently are because of the violent interaction, will direct their violence against persons. The attempt is to intimidate, to scare, to drive off the leadership or to destroy the movement, to make this whole problem of those who are knocking so loudly at the door go away. The best way to make a problem like that go away is to kill off a few people or to injure them in some way so that they are scared to continue doing what they're doing.

Now I don't want to emphasize this too much because we need to qualify, any generalization needs to be qualified, and there are exceptions to this generalization. But so it has gone in the course of our history and with respect to these riot cycles.

Reconstructivists have won all the major battles, although at a particular time they may be seeming to move backwards, because they've lost some temporary struggles, but over time, these barriers for most groups have been broken down. But some of them at different rates and some of them without violence.

For example, women were able to break down the barrier against them without the use of violence. True some of them chained themselves to trees, monkeyed around with mail boxes and acted in various disagreeable ways. But perhaps for biological reasons and perhaps for other reasons, including the fact that women always knew where the enemy was—and their patience—they were able largely to accomplish a remarkable reversal in the structuring of our society. When you consider that in 1800 a woman didn't have the right to vote, to hold property, to conduct a law suit, just didn't have control of her life. She wasn't able to get these things without struggle. But over a period of 100 years, by 1920, the vote at least was established.

UNEQUAL STATUS

Women's status, with respect to men, is still not equal. And I make this point to show that some of these Reconstructivist struggles are very drawn out, very attenuated. And this struggle will not be over until we have many women in high office in our country as well as at the head of other organizations such as business organizations. But I would say it is three-quarters completed.

Now another point with respect to the continuation of the Reconstructivist-Nativist struggle, is a very interesting process that I call a conversion process. The Reconstructivist[s] of one season become the Nativists of the next season. So that now the Irish-Catholics, for example, who had to struggle so hard to get into the system, are among those who are resisting the hardest the entry of new groups, such as blacks, into the Nativist system and the entry of youth into the system.

I think it is particularly striking in the case of labor. One would think that the working man, having had to suffer so much trouble from the Nativists in order to get the right to strike—and remember the word strike includes the violence in its very name but it's been institutionalized, it has been legalized, so now it's legal, it's all right and the working man has forgotten what he's gotten by his violence and is included in large numbers of people now who are screaming about law and order and permissiveness and troubles of the youth and so forth and are taking the traditional Nativists orientation.

This must be put down, and these people must be put in their places. The whole clock must be turned back to where it was before.

Why does this happen? Why do Reconstructivists convert into Nativists? This is a research problem and I can't answer it now. I mean some things are quite obvious. The latest arrivals are the most insecure and, being the most insecure, will try to keep the new arrivals away. But the degree to which the conversion process is to me so intense as to pass understanding, and I really don't understand it yet.

Now, finally, the role of the media.

I think the media are implicated to some extent in the conversion process itself. The media are implicated all through all these preconditions and are highly involved in the value conflict. There is much to be said about this which I won't attempt to outline because the hour is late. But I think three ways in which the media function with respect to this whole problem of violence as allocated to one or another Reconstructivist group trying to break in can be stated.

One is the failure on the part of the media to study and

distinguish the whole process, the process that I tried to outline in terms of the preconditions—particularly the triggering aspect of the process.

Reporters and television people in general do not do their homework with respect to any particular episode. They too readily take police handouts, or other handouts from city hall without taking the effort to find out what it is that really happened. They too often go along with the current confusion between a non-violent provocation and a violent response so that sitting in or occupying university buildings and so forth tend to be described in the media as part of the violence when obviously that is not part of the violence. That is part of the struggle but not in itself violence. That is the Reconstructivist struggle to disrupt.

Media Careless

If we confine violence to the definition I gave, that certainly cannot be talked about as violence. But it's usually mentioned in that context so in the minds of people as a whole all [t]his activity in the universities and in the streets —students demonstrating and so forth—is just generally labeled as part of the violent scene. So my complaint is that the media boys have not been careful to distinguish various steps, phases and parts of the whole process.

Second, and perhaps this is where an organization such as this, the UPI, comes in, and related to my first point, the spot reporting that one sees and one picks up the newspaper and reads a little one-paragraph or two-paragraph account that rioting has broken out in some school in Arizona or wherever it is, it's just a statement, really, with a very few descriptive facts and no interpretation and it allows no one reading it to get any real sense of what was going on there in Arizona so it just adds up in the minds of the public in whom a lot of information is fed and more of this law and order stuff.

Third, there is an absence of the historical perspective with which I began. One hardly ever reads anything about this in the press and any commentator and any columnist and any editorial. Most of the tone of editorial comments are on the line of we cannot condone, we must not put up with, we will not put up with violence. The fact is our country always has put up with violence.

So this is a ritual. It's merely a cold statement that registers the feeling of being ill at ease because our violence doesn't fit with our self-image, our self-concept. But, if editorial comment takes this tone—we will not condone, we will not put up—it not only violates historical reality, but it means that the country stops thinking. Literally it stops thinking about what this problem is, what the basic value concepts are and where new groups such as blacks and youth fit into a long historical process that's been characterized by these repeated cycles.

So I would hope that there would be a renewed attempt, or a new attempt on the part of those that are involved in giving information to the public to report about these matters in a more thoughtful way and to put them into the perspective I think they need to be put into.

Following are two of the questions and answers after Dr. Spiegel's talk:

Q. *Has your data so far revealed any model that might give us some specific ideas for a kind of social reporting that doesn't take place at the time of crisis or after crisis but a kind of preventive social reporting?*

A. There are a lot of things that can be done, including simply better information delivered to whites about what goes on in ghettoes and vice versa. The amount of misinformation is simply staggering in the minds of whites about what black people are like, what black communities are like and in the minds of black people and black communities the amount of misinformation about whites is absolutely staggering.

STRENGTH GREAT

In talking to kids from the south side of Chicago, for example, who are members of the Blackstone Rangers, we found that since they never see a white man, these kids have the idea that the black people of Chicago were about 80 or 90 percent of the population. Their strength was tremendous. They were Gargantuan. This was their complex. With regard to preventive reporting, there needs to be a lot more digging out of misinformation. It's up to the press to find out what these misconceptions are and to correct them, not to always be responding to the latest threat.

Q. *Where do you think we currently are in terms of incitement?*

A. We may be at the peak or we may be just below the peak. I do think that the form of the struggle now is going to be changing, both in black communities and on college campuses, in that the generalized explosion which seems so unprogrammed, so without a particular goal, will be seen less and less frequently.

The violence that we will see and the protest that we will see in the future will be directed more at specific targets, schools, police, welfare, organizations in the community. And this is to the good.

I think the same thing will be seen on college campuses. The complaints will be more specific. There still may be violence. But it will not be on such a broad scale. This is not to say that there might not be other episodes of violence directed particularly at the police. We have seen some evidence of that here and there because of the tremendous load of resentment and grievance the people have toward the police. The police are in danger. It would be wise if all police organizations, with the help of the public, gave more thought to the prevention of confrontation and shootouts which they are likely to get into. These are the two major developments.

QUESTIONS FOR DISCUSSION

1. How does Spiegel define "violence"?
2. What is the second characteristic of violence? Why does the author feel it is important?
3. What does Spiegel mean when he says that we suffer from "historical amnesia"?
4. What are some examples of violence our country has experienced over the years, according to the author?
5. What are the five preconditions for a riot?
6. What does the author mean by the following statement? "This country . . . has been caught up in a severe struggle between the authoritarian, aristocratic principles that the American Revolution was designed to overthrow and the democratic set of values, the egalitarian values that the revolution was designed to institute in the new political procedures of the United States."
7. What are the six principles by which our democracy is limited? What is the relationship between these principles and the riot cycles that Spiegel pointed out earlier?
8. Who are the "Nativists" and the "Reconstructivists"? Are they both, on occasion, violent? Which one of the two groups has won the most battles?
9. What does the author mean when he says, "The Reconstructivists of one season become the Nativists of the next season"?
10. What are the three ways by which the media function with respect to the problem of violence?

Violence & History

"Your poor country," sympathized a Japanese diplomat, speaking to a friend in Washington. "I had thought that after Dallas this could not happen again. There is enough misunderstanding about you abroad. This will make it even worse. How could this happen?"

The King assassination and the subsequent riots have reinforced a world image of America the violent: a vast, driving, brutal land that napalms Vietnamese peasants and murders its visionaries along with its Presidents. It is an image that has been persistently built up not only by bloody fact but also by fiction—in books, films and television—all the way from the westerns through the gangster stories to the more recent outpouring of sadomasochism that seems to demand a new legal definition of obscenity as cruelty. When new events put exclamation points behind the impression, and Negro Militant H. Rap Brown says that "violence is as American as cherry pie," heads nod in agreement around the world.

As ever, shocked foreigners seem to overlook conditions elsewhere. U.S. violence has never matched the Japanese rape of Nanking or the massacre of 400,000 Communists in Indonesia. Watts and Detroit were tea parties compared with assorted mass slaughters in India, Nigeria, and Red China. What country has the world's highest homicide rate? El Salvador, with 30.1 deaths per 100,000 people. In comparison, the U.S. rate stands at around 5.

And yet foreigners can and should expect the U.S. to rise far above its present status as the world's most violent advanced country. Among industrialized countries, Canada's homicide rate is 1.3 per 100,000; France's is .8; England's only .7. Within the U.S., the rate typically surges upward from .5 in Vermont to 11.4 in Alabama. In some Northern ghettos, it hits 90, just as it did some years ago in the King murder city of Memphis. Texas, home of the shoot-out and divorce-by-pistol, leads the U.S. with about 1,000 homicides a year, more than 14 other states combined. Houston is the U.S. murder capital: 244 last year, more than in England, which has 45 million more people. And murder statistics hardly measure the scope of U.S. violence.

Paradoxically, the first fact to be faced is a happy one: there is much evidence suggesting that violent crime in the U.S. has—at least until recently—not been increasing relative to the population. Although the FBI reports a 35% total increase during the 1960s, many experts argue that this figure overlooks population growth, improved police statistics and the new willingness of the poor to report crimes that used to go unrecorded. On the whole, Americans are now more apt to settle their arguments through legal redress, or at least nonviolent cunning, rather than with fists, knives and guns. Organized crime has shifted from blatant violence to financial infighting; today's juvenile gangs are more talkers than fighters; very few labor-dispute slayings have occurred since the 1950s.

Whereas the South once accepted public lynchings as a community sport, the white racists who still kill Negroes are now increasingly prosecuted and punished. In three decades, the U.S. incidence of murder and robbery has decreased relative to the population by 30%. Says Sociologist Marvin Wolfgang, president of the American Society of Criminology: "Contrary to the rise in public fear, crimes of violence are not significantly increasing."

THE POWER OF FEAR

Unfortunately, that very fear has a way of increasing violence. Fearful citizens ignore the victim's cry for help; by shunning parks and other public places, they free muggers to attack isolated pedestrians. The U.S. mind is haunted by wanton multiple murder—16 people killed by a sniper in Austin, eight nurses slain by a demented drifter in Chicago. It is hard to convince the fearful that 80% of the U.S. murders (half involve alcohol) are committed by antagonistic relatives or acquaintances, not strangers.

Now, above all, there is white fear of Negro attacks. While the Negro arrest rate for murder is ten times that among whites, most of the violent crimes committed by Negroes are against other Negroes. Of 172 Washington, D.C., murders in a recent two-year period, for example, only twelve were interracial. Yet fear that Negro riots are leading to some ghastly racial holocaust is fueling a vast, scandalously uncontrolled traffic in firearms that has equipped one-half of U.S. homes with 50 million guns, largely for "self-defense." All this is rationalized by virtue of the Second Amendment "right of the people to keep and bear arms." In fact, the right clearly applies to collective defense, as in a state militia. But Congress and most state legislatures refuse to regulate the gun craze, partly in fear of the political power of the 700,000-member National Rifle Association, which often seems to view America as still being Indian country. Only New York requires permits to own household pistols; only eight states require permits to buy them. Guns figure in about 60% of all U.S. murders; since 1900, they have killed 800,000 Americans (excluding wars).

Today's fear of violence is rightly aimed at the terrifying anonymity of the big cities—of which 26, containing less than one-fifth of the U.S. population, account for more than half of all violent crimes. But this fear can be localized: violence is overwhelmingly a ghetto phenomenon; it is the slum dweller who suffers most and cries out for better police protection. In Atlanta, for example, the violent-crime rate in neighborhoods with incomes below $3,000 is eight times that among $9,000-income families.

Who are the violent? Primarily youth: the fatherless Negro boy aching to prove his manliness, the school dropout taunted by TV commercials offering what he cannot have and often incited by what he has learned about the Mickey Spillane brand of violence. Adding to the slum kid's anger is all the middle-class hypocrisy about violence. "Good" people utterly delegate society's dirty work to overworked white cops, few of whom are inclined to be Boy Scouts. The middle class denounces violence but wants the police to use it, and is then shocked when hordes of young hooligans respond in kind—vividly teaching irresponsible elders (most sharply disapprove) that looting is a handy way to grab the possessions they lack.

OF MEN AND RATS

The fearful middle class, Negro as well as white, can no longer afford to ignore violence, a phenomenon from which no human being is exempt. Freud held that man has a death instinct that must be satisfied in either suicide or aggresion against others. Many modern psychiatrists disagree. Dr. Fredric Wertham, famed crusader against violence, argues that violence is learned behavior, a product of cultural influences such as violent comic books. The violent man, he says, is the socially alienated man.

Konrad Lorenz, the Austrian-born naturalist, believes that human aggressiveness is the instinct that powers not only self-preservation against enemies but also love and friendship for those who share the struggle. Overcoming obstacles provides self-esteem; lacking such fulfillment, man turns against handy targets—his wife, even himself. Polar explorers, deprived of quarrels with strangers, often start to hate one another; the antidote is smashing some inanimate object, like crockery. Accident-prone drivers may be victims of "displaced aggression." The once ferocious Ute Indians, now shorn of war outlets, have the worst auto-accident rate on record.

Lorenz points out that men and rats share the dubious distinction of being the only carnivores with no innate inhibitions against attacking members of their own species. Early man was too weak to do so. But as he developed weapons, he learned to cherish the "warrior virtues" of truculent masculinity and pleasure in dominating others. Though he also developed moral restraints against killing, these are not natural and tend to collapse under stress. Seeking a really nonviolent community, anthropologists point with hope to the peace-loving pygmies of the Ituri rain forest in the Congo. Unlike other men, those "primitives" have no male-warrior hangup; they retreat from power-seeking neighbors—and hugely enjoy the sensual pleasures of eating, drinking, sex and laughter.

Modern man is often at his noblest in small-unit war, a caveman hangover. But peacetime culture bars such outlets, and when men fail to achieve the virility substitute of money, power or meaningful work, they can explode in violence. Not that man has a killer instinct; he simply does not fully realize the effect of pulling a trigger and blowing off another man's head. Modern long-range weapons further blunt his sensibilities. Mussolini's son extolled the bombing of the Ethiopians: "I dropped an aerial torpedo right in the center of a cluster of tribesmen, and the group opened up like a flowering rose. It was most entertaining."

In a moral sense, violence is not power but an act of despair, an admission of failure to find any other way to gain a goal. By definition, every society is committed to nonviolence; the violent are suicidal, for society must repress acts against law and order. Yet realistically, one cannot gloss over the fact that violence often pays off. In the violent subculture of a juvenile gang, the nonviolent are considered cowards, and violence produces not guilt but status.

As a Force for Reform

It is undeniable that all through history, violence has been the chief means of social reform. Even primitive Christians, proclaiming love, destroyed pagan temples to dramatize their cause. The Boston Tea Party had the same purpose. The 13th century King John's Magna Carta illustrated the oldest inducement for social reform: fear of "revolution or worse." To his credit, Marx argued against violence until societies were really ripe for change; most Western European labor terrorism disappeared as a result. But in romantic countries, including the U.S., revolutionary violence often became a mystique for purging feelings of inferiority. Explains Brandeis University Sociologist Lewis Coser: "The act of violence commits a man symbolically to the revolutionary movement and breaks his ties with his previous life. He is, so to speak, reborn."

At first glance, group violence may not seem to be the U.S. paradigm. Individualists claw their way through the unrelieved shootings, stabbings, rapes and lynchings of American fiction; lone duelers against fate people the works of writers as various as Melville, Fitzgerald, Hemingway and Saul Bellow. James Fenimore Cooper's Leatherstocking and his numerous up-tight descendants—the Western marshal, the private eye—are solitary scouts strewing the wilderness with dead Indians and renegades. Still, the singular misfits who tamed the frontier with bile, brawn and bowies were also members of often hostile groups—cattlemen v. sheepherders, for example. Indeed, U.S. history roils with political violence, much of it self-defense by countless groups against what they considered majority injustice.

The Revolution, a prime example, was followed by farmer uprisings over debts and taxes—the Shay and Whisky rebellions. In the mid-1800s, the nativist Know-Nothings fought rising Irish political power by killing Roman Catholics, burning churches and ultimately controlling 48% of the House of Representatives. In 1863, the Irish, fearing that Negroes would take their jobs while they were drafted into the Civil War, conducted a frightful race riot in New York City that killed an estimated 2,000 people and injured 8,000. The Civil War killed 500,000 soldiers—the equivalent of 3,000,000 in today's U.S. Afterward, the supposedly defeated white South defeated Reconstruction with a guerrilla war in which the Ku Klux Klan and other whites killed thousands of would-be Negro voters, imposed segregation, and infected the North with the very racism that the Civil War supposedly ended. Over the years, a dozen or more major Northern race riots followed the same pattern: whites invading black neighborhoods and killing scores of Negroes.

Some experts see a possible direction for Negro protest in the history of the once brutally violent American

labor movement. In the late 19th century, depressions triggered virtual revolutions when employers cut wages, im-
ported scabs, tried to break unions. Strikes were then bitterly repressed by company cops or state militia; federal
troops were called in often. The bloody railroad strikes of
1877 killed 150 people; the Rocky Mountain mining wars
at the turn of the century killed 198, including a Governor.
In Pennsylvania, a secret band of Irish miners called the
Molly Maguires assassinated bosses in a Viet Cong-style
attempt to win better working conditions. The Wobblies (Industrial Workers of the World) lauded and used terror
tactics and in many areas were in turn murdered and muti-
lated. All in all, several thousand people died in labor disputes before the movement finally won its point in 1935,
when federal law forced employers to recognize unions and
engage in collective bargaining—dramatic proof that the
U.S. can create a legal system for resolving even the most
desperate havenot grievances.

Unfortunately, Negroes lack the organization and specific grievances that make labor disputes negotiable within
a framework of rational group conflict. The basic Negro
grievance is emotional: the white attitude toward Negroes.
King tried to shame whites by nonviolence, by Negro suffering. The tragedy is that his remarkable success also produced white backlash, black militancy and a kind of moral
vacuum in which hapless white police are left to cope with
mindless ghetto explosions.

One ground for optimism is the remarkable effect of
the President's riot commission report, which, ironically if
necessarily, taught many police to be nonviolent and hence
more effective in handling the post-King riots. Yet this advance also has the very disquieting effect of seeming to
condone looters; and violence rewarded would seem to
promise more of it, especially among the guilt-free kids who
take it as a lark. Even grimmer is the psychological import

of the King assassination: his killer, however twisted his mind, clearly felt that he had a mandate for murder. The appalling result suggests that all too many unstable Americans unconsciously identify with a kind of avenging Western hero, and believe that one man with one bullet can and should change history.

Help the Other Fellow Survive

The U.S. must utterly reject this grammar of violence—just as it must urgently enact effective laws against the dangerous, absurdly outdated sale of firearms to all comers. If Americans seriously hope to pacify their own country, they must also do nothing less than abolish ghettos and what they breed: the hopelessness that incites violence. Above all, the U.S. must provide the jobless with the most elemental source of self-respect—meaningful work.

Beyond the ghetto, though, there will probably always be violence—out of anger, greed, insanity—until people are taught as children how to master the art of diverting pent-up aggressions into constructive action. At this stage of human knowledge, every school in the land ought to be teaching psychology as one of its most crucial subjects. Today, every parent who cares about peace ought to be guiding his children to militant enthusiasm for some humane cause, the most beneficent outlet for aggressions.

And every American who abhors violence should start talking to the very people he fears and hates. Attitude is the important factor. When people grow up with one another, work together, learn to know one another, one group will be less likely to fear and hate the other. If there is any way to curb violence, it is for man to study man and start fighting for the other fellow's survival.

QUESTIONS FOR DISCUSSION

1. *According to this essay, what besides the Martin Luther King assassination and the subsequent riots has led foreigners to believe that our country is violent?*

2. *According to this essay, is "violence as American as cherry pie"?*

3. *Compared to the riots in other countries throughout history, how violent is America? According to murder statistics, how violent is America?*

4. *What evidence does* Time *give that "violent crime in the U.S. has—at least until recently—not been increasing relative to the population"?*

5. *According to the article, does the public feel that violence is increasing or decreasing? In what way does this fear influence the amount of violence that we may be having? the amount of weapons owned in this country?*

6. *For the most part, where does violence take place? Who are the violent in our society? What segment of our society detests violence most, but wants the police to use it to stop further violence?*

7. *What did Sigmund Freud believe about violence? How do the views of Dr. Fredric Wertham and Konrad Lorenz differ from those of Freud? According to* Time, *where do the members of a nonviolent society find enjoyment? Is violence an act by which a man can express his virility? What are substitutes for violence?*

8. *To what extent has violence been necessary to achieve social reform? What evidence from American history does* Time *give to support this notion?*

9. *What did President Johnson's riot commission report tell us about violence? What effect may it have on future riots? What does Martin Luther King's murder say about his assassin? How does the assassin apparently feel about violence?*

10. *According to the* Time *essay, what are the things we must do to pacify our country? What can schools and parents do? Why should we talk to people we fear and hate?*

Violence in American Society

GILBERT GEIS

On Easter Sunday, 1967—as on other days in recent times
—thousands of young persons gathered at points spanning
the country, to participate in a contemporary version of
Christian ritual. In Los Angeles' Elysian Park an estimated
6,000 "hippies," many of them carrying flutes and tambo-
rines, came together for a "love-in," the men wearing East
Indian robes or American Indian blankets, the girls dressed
in miniskirts, their legs painted psychedelic colors. Children
and oldsters, according to a local newspaper, "danced on
the grass like Pans in a rite of spring." In New York City,
on the same day, some 10,000 young persons gathered in
Central Park for what they called a "be-in." An observer
commented: "They sang love, shouted love, and lettered
love on their foreheads in pink paint."

Meanwhile, other persons were attending more traditional Easter services. Both the "hippie" and the "square"
gatherings, tranquil and almost transcendental in nature,
were counterpointed by events which provide a fundamental
key to the ambiguous role of violence in contemporary

Gilbert Geis, "Violence in American Society," *Current History*,
June 1967, pp. 354–358.

58

American society. At the Easter religious services in Los Angeles, for instance, pickets paraded the circumference of the Hollywood Bowl, bearing signs with messages such as "Would Christ Drop Napalm?" Near Elysian Park, where the younger generation was romping, one of their number, wandering from the main body, was set upon by a gang of children aged 10 to 12. The gang boys threw rocks and bottles, and flailed the "hippie" youth with clubs, sending him to the hospital in critical condition, with a threatened loss of his right eye.

The duality between peacefulness and passivity, on the one hand, and aggression and violence, on the other, is one that has continuously permeated American life. Both forms of behavior are at times rewarded, both are encouraged, and both at different times are denigrated and denounced. It has been said that it is cowardly not to fight, that if you *don't* throw your weight around people will ignore you, that subtlety is more effective than force, that women may be weak and "nice" but that boys should be strong and aggressive. These, with similar bits of folk wisdom, constitute the variegated and confusing indoctrination regarding violence that is transmitted in the United States. From it emerge diverse amalgams of violent behavior, some of them sanctioned and praised, others of them deplored and interdicted by the criminal codes under names such as murder, manslaughter, assault and battery, rape and robbery.

It is important to keep clearly in mind which element of an act of violence is being stressed in discussions of the subject. Is it the inherent nature of the act itself, is it its overt manifestations, is it its social or legal definition, or is it its consequences?

Take, for instance, the matter of consequences. It is evident that unprovoked physical attacks by gang members on passers-by are deplorable because innocent people are unreasonably maimed or killed; fear of similar attacks impairs the freedom of movement and sense of well-being of an untold number of other citizens. It seems obvious that street violence of this kind should be outlawed and that persons who commit it should be put out of circulation or otherwise convinced that they must behave in a fashion acceptable to society.

There are, however, many other things which also maim and kill innocent people that are tolerated and even approved. If, for instance, governors were placed on automobiles, permitting them to travel at speeds not greater than 40 or 50 miles an hour, perhaps 10,000 fewer persons would be killed in highway accidents each year and untold numbers of others would be spared injury. Fast driving, within speed limits, is perfectly permissible, however, and persons who bring about accidents under these conditions normally are not considered to be "violent." Their victims are written off as sacrifices to an ethos that prefers to move rapidly from one place to another rather than to keep alive thousands of driving casualties. It cannot, therefore, be only the lethal consequences of violence which make it abhorrent.

Infringement of freedom of movement, another outcome of unchecked street violence, may also be produced by numerous other situations. It is sadly true that residents in cities such as New York are likely to be fearful about venturing forth after dark, particularly in certain neighborhoods. But it is equally true that a much greater number of persons are much more seriously circumscribed in the freedom of their movement by actions bearing upon them that, while less direct and physical in their manifestation, are equally efficient. Lack of money and absence of adequate transportation, for instance, are but two such circumstances. It cannot, therefore, be only the restrictive consequences of violence which make it abhorrent.

It would seem, in such terms, that it is only in part the results of violence which contribute to concern regarding it. More important probably is the degree of directness involved—the fact that we may readily identify the per-petrator, and thus blame him, and that we may easily view and pinpoint the immediate wounds brought about by the particular violent act. It is much less easy to maintain with certainty that quietly vicious parents have produced a mentally ill, frightened child, or that a remote landlord, charging exploitative rents in a slum district, has produced a defeatist, alienated member of a minority group. It is quick, direct violence that we primarily attend to, undoubt-edly in large measure because it is so much easier to do so.

VIOLENCE VERSUS CUNNING

Physical violence need not be the most devastating form of aggression. Stab wounds heal and victims of beatings recover. Violence directed against enemies may prevent greater social and personal harm, though the remoter ef-fects of recourse to force to combat force is an arguable—and much argued—proposition. Violence in the form of athletic contests may tend to inculcate self-reliance and a will-to-succeed which in their turn can be personally and socially enabling. Without threat of violence, human beings may succumb to apathy and inertia, making them vulner-able to more overwhelming assaults, though perhaps, given the proper conditions, they will use energy no longer con-sidered necessary for self-protection for more constructive ends.

Each of these propositions requires a much more care-ful delineation and appraisal before a flat declaration of the value of violence for a social system and for an individual can be reached. They merely indicate that violence is not necessarily despicable.

Many early societies, weighing the matter, placed more severe penalties upon offenses involving guile than upon those involving physical aggression. A citizen, they reasoned, had some possibility of protecting himself from direct attack, but few resources with which to cope with superior cunning. Today, covert and wily forms of aggression may be replacing frontal expressions of anger and hostility as self-control becomes a more valued trait. It is moot, however, whether this change is an improvement.

Consider, for example, the pattern of child-rearing that is said to be fairly characteristic of middle-class American families. Themselves perhaps resentful of their own upbringing, contemporary parents tend to eschew spanking and similar physical attacks on their offspring in favor of tactics of deprivation. Deprivation generally involves a delicate determination of precisely those things which a child cherishes, such as a particular televison show. Then, in the face of misbehavior, the parents cut off the treasured "privilege."

The outcome of deprivation may be much less desirable than the consequences of violence by parents against children. For one thing, hitting has a certain cathartic effect for parents. They will, despite their infuriating (to the child) claim that it hurts them more than it hurts the child, usually feel a good deal better afterwards. For another, the matter usually ends there, the air much purified. The difficulty is the same as with any expression of physical violence; it conveys to its recipient the vivid lesson that physical strength is the fundamental resource to be employed to resolve difficulties, especially when a weaker object can be found. In its extreme form, parental maltreatment has been found to be the most significant experience of murderers for whom "remorseful physical brutality at the hands of parents had been a common experience. Brutality far beyond the ordinary excuses of discipline had been perpetrated on them; often, it was so extreme as to compel neighbors to intercede. . . ."[1]

[1] See Glen M. Duncan, Shervert H. Frazier, et al., "Etiological Factors in First-Degree Murder," in Journal of the American Medical Association, 168 (November 22, 1959), pp. 1755–1758.

Deprivation punishment, for its part, may bring in its wake equally formidable difficulties. For one thing, the clever child soon learns to conceal his pleasures from the parent, knowing that otherwise they may be taken away in the event of misbehavior. Finally, as the contest of wills proceeds, the insecure child, with few other resources to sustain him, may find that his only protection lies in developing no attachment to or fondness for anything. Failing this, he is apt to be desperately hurt by the withdrawal of valued things. As an adult, such a child is likely to become a flat, emotionless individual, often particularly liable to exploit others because he has developed no fellow feeling for them or for anything else.

In such terms, it must be stressed that single-minded ideas about violence being good or bad, desirable or undesirable, preferable or outrageous, all must be carefully reviewed in regard to the available alternatives and *their* consequences and in regard to the total context in which the violence occurs.

THE CRIMES OF VIOLENCE

Little enlightenment on the amount of violence involved in the categories proscribed by the criminal law is apt to be gained from scrutiny of official tabulations. Fashions play altogether too great a role in compilations of official crime statistics to allow them to be taken very seriously. For one thing, public confidence in a police department will condition the amount of crime reported to it. For another, the efficiency of a department will itself influence the volume of crime coming to its attention so that, paradoxically, a very good police department may look quite bad in terms of the amount of crime in its jurisdiction when compared to a poorer department which neither discovers nor solves most crimes within its realm. For a third thing, intramural recording procedures may vary from year to year, conditioning the level of crime reported by the police. For instance, a 72 per cent increase in crime in New York City was recorded in 1966—virtually all of it traceable to changes in the manner in which violations were tabulated.

Crime itself is mediated by so many factors that it is usually far-fetched to jump from statements about its prevalence to judgments about the nature of the society at any given time. High rates of some forms of crime may even reflect improved social conditions. Take, for instance, the question of race relations. In earlier periods in the history of the United States, with a stabilized racial etiquette, there was comparatively little (though a good deal more than most persons realize) interracial disturbance. With enhanced freedom for Negroes came expanded visions, greater disappointments and deeper frustrations. Additional violence grew out of such circumstances, but few persons would be apt to rate a social climate stressing an unrealized but emerging democratic spirit as less admirable than a social climate preempting freedom and emphasizing subservience and absence of opportunity for persons in certain preordained castes.

Violence in the United States is also probably as much a matter of perception as one of reality. Daniel Bell, the sociologist, for instance, has pointed out that the breakdown of class barriers has alerted many Americans to violence that was always present but rarely seen by them.[2] Residents of the suburbs may now view on television screens acts of violence formerly cushioned by their remoteness, in the manner that the slaying of former President John F. Kennedy directly involved the emotions and thoughts of so many citizens. Better forms of public and private transportation mean that today persons traverse more and different kinds of territory than they did in earlier times. Thus, it is not unusual for such persons to view people and things that their forebears never encountered.

[2] See Daniel Bell, "Crime as an American Way of Life," chapter 7 in *The End of Ideology* (Glencoe, Ill.: The Free Press, 1960).

The often artificial foundation of attitudes regarding violence is shown by a recent study conducted in Roxbury, a high-delinquency area adjacent to the city of Boston.[3] In interviews, Roxbury residents complained bitterly about the crime rate, the danger of setting forth at night, and about uncontrolled violence in the neighborhood. A group of detached workers was assigned to work with gang members. Careful records kept of their accomplishments showed that the detached workers were unable to make any impress on the amount or kind of delinquency occurring in Roxbury. Nonetheless, when interviewed later, a large number of the neighborhood residents then maintained, despite the factual evidence of which they were unaware, that they felt safer, that they were certain there was less crime and that they believed it was the new program which had brought about the improved conditions.

What is it then that may be said with certainty about crimes of violence in the United States? We can report with some assurance that, compared to frontier days, there has been a significant decrease in such activities. It also seems likely that during the past decades, and particularly since World War II, violent offenses in the United States have been increasingly committed by younger people. This situation is undoubtedly the product of an almost ubiquitous precocity that has marked youthful activities. Youngsters marry younger, learn more earlier, and are freer (in urban settings conducive to such activities) to get into and to create their own difficulties.

For particular crimes of violence, the pattern is erratic, and this erraticism highlights the difficulty of placing faith in broad generalizations. Murder, for instance, has not increased much, if at all, in recent decades. Expanded employment of competent medical examiners in place of bumbling coroners has enabled us to designate as homicide

[3] See Walter B. Miller, "The Impact of 'Total-Community' Delinquency Control Project," in *Social Problems*, 10 (Fall, 1962), pp. 168–191.

many deaths previously listed as natural. But, on the other hand, medical advances, such as the discovery of sulpha drugs and the newer techniques of surgery, save innumerable persons, who, only a few years ago, would have been added to the roster of murder victims. Such items, some tending to raise the count of murder, others tending to decrease the total, make definitive evaluations almost impossible.

Other crimes of violence are equally mecurial when we try to pinpoint their numerical character and to determine their variation over time. Criminal assault is probably much more apt to be reported to the police today than in earlier times, particularly as American women come to regard regular beatings less as a sign of husbandly duty and affection and more as an untoward insult. Rape too has been very responsive to changes in the moral standards of the society. Increased amounts of premarital sexual behavior, for instance, may be encouraging many more intricate near-seduction situations which (rather than the stereotyped lurking stranger) now account for the largest number of sexual assaults.

VIOLENCE AND THE MASS MEDIA

A popular assumption is that the uninhibited portrayal of violence by mass media in the United States transmits an image of aggression that is apt to be duplicated by those continuously exposed to its message. Literary violence is not, of course, a new phenomenon. Satirists are fond of dissecting the classic stories of childhood and pointing out that they are indeed a grim and gory collection. There is Captain Hook, his arm waving a spiked hook at Peter Pan, and there are Hansel and Gretel, on the verge of fiery immurement in the ugly witch's oven, after a frightening night in a dark and evil forest, having been abandoned to their fate by an indifferent father and a wicked step-mother.

Such portrayals of violence, given their extraordinary longevity and appeal, may be bereft of serious behavioral implications for children. Nobody, at least, has been able to demonstrate that children raised on such a bedtime diet are destined to reproduce similar grisly events in later life. Neither, it should be recorded, has the contrary been proved, nor is it apt to be.

There is no gainsaying, however, that the mass media in the United States often reflects patterns of violence differing in degree and intensity from those found elsewhere in the world. Viewers of television, for instance, are apt to be impressed by the ritualistic manner in which violence is portrayed. Stories, in which events appear to be reasonably true to life and well within the realm of the possible will suddenly present fight sequences defying credence, with individuals inflicting punishment on each other that no one could conceivably survive for more than a few seconds. In rapid order, chairs bashed over heads will be ignored, punches that would fell elephants will be casually shrugged aside, and kicks ferocious enough to finish off any mortal will be greeted with no more than a momentary grunt on the part of the hero. The pummeling will proceed resolutely for perhaps a minute or more until (perhaps from the tedium of it all) the villain succumbs.

It is easier to caricature such proceedings, however, than to assay their importance and influence, however tempting such moralizing may be. This involves an intricate kind of research. Results to date, while far from conclusive, tend to point in the direction of culpability on the part of the media for their inordinate and disproportionate stress on violence.

THE VIOLENT MALE?

It is vital to appreciate the fact that man does not possess an inborn instinct for violence; expressions of violence represent matters learned after birth in a social context. Konrad Lorenz' *On Aggression*, a book considered to be the most important contribution on the subject in this century, points out that among the carnivores only rats and men have no innate inhibitions against killing members of their own species. It has been noted in this respect that the Latin proverb *homo homini lupus*—man is a wolf to man— represents a libel on the wolf, a quite gentle animal with other wolves.

Anthropologists have filled out the biological portrait drawn by Lorenz with ethnographic studies of preliterate tribes that find no pleasure in dominating other persons or in hunting and killing. All such groups ask is that they be left in peace, a state they can achieve in the midst of power-seeking neighbors only by retreating to inaccessible territories. To Geoffrey Gorer, a prominent anthropologist, the most common distinguishing trait of the peace-loving tribes is an enormous gusto for sensual pleasures—eating, drinking, sex and laughter. Gorer has also found that these tribes make little distinction between the social characteristics of men and women. In particular, they have no ideal of brave, aggressive masculinity. No child grows up being told that All men do X" or that "No proper woman does Y."[4]

Appraisal

For Gorer and others who have studied the matter, it is here that the key to the riddle of violence lies. Violence that warps and destroys will be controlled, they believe, only when societies no longer insist that virility and similar masculine status symbols be tied to demonstrations of aggression and violence. Some observers suspect that the "hippies," those Easter celebrants noted at the outset of this piece,

[4] See Geoffrey Gorer, "Man Has No 'Killer' Instinct," in *The New York Times Magazine*, November 4, 1966, pp. 47ff.

may in some manner sense this. Sex roles seem blurred among them and it is sometimes difficult to distinguish the girls from the boys. The use of drugs by juveniles also represents withdrawal from combat, a disinvolvement from matters physical and forceful.

The paradox of course is that the United States is not an inaccessible territory and its citizens are not likely to be able to survive without some display of traditional masculine-style truculence and aggression. Abhorrence of violence presumably will either have to become universal or the violent will prevail. The alternative, asking for violence to be expressed only toward real enemies, but to be inhibited in regard to one's fellows, is an achievement that no society has yet been able to realize.

QUESTIONS FOR DISCUSSION

1. *With what facts does Geis back up his statement that "the duality between peacefulness and passivity, on the one hand, and aggression and violence, on the other, is one that has continuously permeated American life"?*

2. *How does Geis compare street violence with violence on the highways? How does our ability to identify the person causing violence contribute to concern regarding it?*

3. *How does the author support the notion that violence "is not necessarily despicable"? According to this article, how in our society has violence changed, particularly in the raising of children? Why may covert or subtle violent behavior be less desirable than the more overt or open violence? How may parental maltreatment of children affect their later development?*

4. *What are three factors that may affect official tabulations of violent crimes? What evidence does the author offer to illustrate that "high rates of some forms of crime may even reflect improved social conditions"? In what way is violence in the United States probably "as much a matter of perception as one of reality"?*

5. *According to the author, what may be said with certainty about crimes of violence in the United States? Why are more and more crimes committed by the young? Why have we recently had fewer murder victims? In what way may social climate affect crimes of violence and the recording of them?*

6. *According to Geis, what evidence do we have that violence in the mass media has behavioral implications for children?*

7. *What does the author feel is necessary in order for our country to be less violent?*

How Violent Are We?

WILLIAM M. CARLEY
EARL C. GOTTSCHALK, JR.

Mounting violence seems to suggest that America is a "sick" society, and Arthur M. Schlesinger Jr., the historian, says we are "the most frightening people on this planet."

Just how violent is America?

More so, it would appear, than Britain, Japan, Australia and a number of other nations. But less violent than Colombia, Indonesia, Burma, Mexico and many other countries. And noticeably less violent than the United States of several decades ago.

By the most visible measurements of violence—homicides, insurrections, riots and strikes, political terrorism and civil war—the U.S. falls behind several score other nations. Ted Gurr, a Princeton University political scientist who ranked 114 nations on overall violence for the years 1961 through 1965, placed the U.S. 42nd.

Among the 50 nations that Mr. Gurr classed as functioning democracies (thus ruling out of the comparisons those authoritarian states where violence is checked by repression), 15 were ranked more violent than the U.S. in total

Carley and Gottschalk, Jr., "How Violent Are We?" *Wall Street Journal,* June 1968.

strife. But Mr. Gurr thinks a new study might put America among the top few democratic nations with regard to domestic violence. He attributes the change to agitation over the racial and Vietnam issues.

OVERSTATING THE PROBLEM

Social scientists acknowledge that it's difficult to measure all the activities that might indicate violence, but they concur in saying that America may be indicting itself too severely. "I'm not persuaded that society is morally decayed, that kids are any worse than they used to be, that the U.S. has any special gift for violence," says Marvin E. Wolfgang, professor of sociology at the University of Pennsylvania and an authority on criminal statistics.

He does say that the annual homicide rate in America, 5.6 per 100,000, is eight times that of England and Wales and four times that of Japan, Australia and Canada. But he notes that Colombia's announced homicide rate is 34 per 100,000, Mexico's 30 per 100,000 and Guatemala's 12 per 100,000—even with erratically collected statistics in those nations.

The Federal Bureau of Investigation said yesterday that serious crimes rose 17% in the first three months of 1968 over the like period of 1967. But some experts say improved reporting by citizens and better bookkeeping by officials make the increase seem greater than it is. Ronald Beattie, chief of California's Bureau of Criminal Statistics, maintains the U.S. has had "no substantial increase" in crimes of violence such as robbery and rape in recent years.

In one category, labor violence, the U.S. is dramatically less violent than it was in the past. One hundred and fifty persons died in the railroad strikes of 1877. The Rocky Mountain mining wars around the turn of the century took

198 lives. Twenty-one persons died in the 1934 national cotton-textile labor dispute, and in 1937, 10 men were killed in a strike near the South Chicago plant of Republic Steel Corp. There is no comparable labor strife now.

The Past Was Worse

"When you take a nation that has discriminated groups," says Mr. Gurr of Princeton, "you find higher levels of violence." With 20 million Negroes in the population, plus other minorities among the 30 million or so Americans considered below the poverty line, few would contest that inequities in the treatment of minorities persist in the U.S. Nowadays minority group agitation often merges with the antiwar movement to produce domestic unrest.

The Lemberg Center for the Study of Violence at Brandeis University counted 43 civil disorders in the U.S. during the first three months of 1968, compared with 4 in the same period of 1967. But, harking to the past, Dr. John Spiegel of the center says, "In terms of people hurt and killed, the violence we're seeing today doesn't even compare to the 1860 draft riots." The Irish draft riot in New York at that time resulted in nearly 2,000 deaths and 8,000 injuries in about a week.

No American can ignore the chronicle of violence that has attended the civil rights struggle in recent years. Riots in the cities have taken many scores of lives. Premeditated slayings such as those of Martin Luther King Jr. and the three civil rights workers slain near Philadelphia, Miss., have shocked the nation. But recent racial violence, however horrific, pales by comparison with the past.

In 1871, the Ku Klux Klan had a membership of more than 500,000 and a Congressional investigation in that year disclosed thousands of lynchings, shootings, whippings and mutilations in the South. The commanding general of Federal forces in Texas reported; "Murders of Negroes are so common as to render it impossible to keep accurate accounts of them."

THERE IS HOPE

Mr. Gurr believes that the racial upheaval isn't qualitatively different from past crises. "Other societies have gone through violent phases and have gone on to rebuild and reestablish democratic traditions," he says. "There's no reason to say that our present turmoil over the race issue won't pass as labor violence and Irish violence came and went."

The scholars suggest that some forms of violence, common elsewhere, are alien to present-day America—all-out civil war or insurrection and political coups, for instance. And some types of domestic violence that horrify Americans also are common elsewhere. Statistics suggest that it might be more accurate to speak of a violent world than a violent U.S.

"That violence isn't unique to the U.S. is an assertion that needs no more than a few illustrations to support," says Mr. Wolfgang. His cases in point:

"The tortures in French Algeria, the Stalinist terrors in Russia, the mob violence and riots between Pakistan and India, the current Nigerian civil war, student and union violence in France today, the violence of Colombia for nearly 20 years that resulted in an estimated 200,000 deaths up to 1967, the confused cultural revolution in Mainland China and the horrendous, little-publicized massacre of 400,000 persons in recent years in Indonesia."

Since 1945, more revolutions, guerrilla wars and coups d'etat have taken place around the world than national elections. Between 1961 and 1967, some form of civil strife took place in 114 of 121 nations and colonies studied by Mr.

Gurr of Princeton. Going all the way back, the scholars point out that an analysis of European states from 500 BC to 1925 AD shows that, on average, each state had only five peaceful years for each year in which major political violence took place.

Most dismaying to Americans at large, and most perplexing to students of violence, is this country's history of political assassinations. Presidents Lincoln, Garfield, McKinley and Kennedy were assassinated; attempts were made on Presidents Jackson, Theodore Roosevelt, Franklin D. Roosevelt and Truman.

A Secret Service report released in January shows a startling increase in arrests of persons accused of threatening the President. Eighty such arrests were made in 1963, but the figure for 1967 was 425.

However, the increase may stem partly from greater diligence by the Secret Service in recent years. And, again, the phenomenon isn't confined to the U.S. Since 1945, world-wide records excluding Europe show 66 assassination attempts on heads of state in 28 nations. Ten heads of state besides President Kennedy have been slain. There have been 80 assassination attempts on high government officials other than heads of state in 40 nations.

Who are the assassins, and the would-be-assassins, in the U.S.? Why are they impelled to violence? Gresham Sykes, a sociologist on the staff of the University of Denver law school, says, "Such violence may be of two kinds. There is violence caused by mental aberration, and there is violence stemming from ideological motives."

Mr. Sykes considers the ideological assassination much more disrupting and disturbing in its implications" for society as a whole. While psychiatrists and sociologists suggest that a climate of violence and political tension may provoke a potential assassin to act, there is general agreement that the American assassins have been in the category of deranged, aberrant individuals.

Dr. Donald W. Hastings, a psychiatrist at the University of Minnesota medical school, has studied those who killed or attempted to kill eight American presidents. "With one exception (the two Puerto Ricans who shot at Truman), none of the murders, actual or attempted, was the result of foreign or domestic intrigue," Dr. Hastings says. "Rather, each was the product of one man's disordered mind." (However, historians consider the Lincoln slaying the result of an elaborate conspiracy.)

The assassins and would-be assassins all had schizophrenia, usually of the paranoid type that involves delusions of persecution Dr. Hastings says. The causes of schizophrenia aren't known, but he says it often is associated with parental rejection, broken homes, lack of a strong male figure with whom a boy can identify and other emotional stresses severe enough to prevent a developing child from dealing successfully with his environment.

DISADVANTAGED ASSASSINS

Dr. Hastings says that the father of John Wilkes Booth, Lincoln's assassin, was an itinerant actor who died when his son was 14. The father of John Schrank, who shot and wounded Theodore Roosevelt, died when the boy was seven; the mother soon abandoned the child to an uncle and aunt.

Giuseppe Zangara, who shot at Franklin Roosevelt, was put to work by his father when he was six, a fact he bitterly resented. Lee Harvey Oswald's father died just before his son was born.

The psychiatrist asserts that almost all the assassins and would-be assassins demonstrated symptoms of mental disturbance, such as failure to hold down a job, inability to form friendships, a seclusive personality and resentment of authority. Some also demonstrated delusions of grandeur, hallucinations or a conviction that they were carrying out the will of God.

Dr. David A. Rothstein of the Medical Center for Federal Prisoners, Springfield, Mo., has interviewed 27 prisoners who threatened Presidents within the last several years. They tended to have much in common, he said—youth, unhappy home environments and, typically, an upbringing by a dominant mother while an ineffectual father stood aside.

Their threats were directed at men, but Dr. Rothstein believes the underlying object of resentment was the mother. Anger at the mother, he says, "is only later displaced onto male authorities," then to the Government and finally to the President, "the embodiment of the U.S. Government."

Sociologist Wolfgang says it may be difficult to identify the potential assassin. "There will always be some segment of the population on the brink of psychopathic manifestation," he says, "but I don't think it's fair to indict the entire U.S. population because of what one assassin does."

Mr. Gurr doesn't believe political assassination is a "permanent part of the style of American politics." Outrage following the slaying of Sen. Robert F. Kennedy and restrictive gun legislation should have healthy effects, he suggests.

Also, says Mr. Gurr, if the assassins of Sen. Kennedy and Mr. King are prosecuted successfully "by conventional legal means," it should "reduce the likelihood that this will happen in the future."

QUESTIONS FOR DISCUSSION

1. *According to the statistics compiled by Ted Gurr, how violent is America today, compared to America of the past or compared to other countries today?*

2. *Compared to the homicide rates of other nations, how high is the U.S. homicide rate? What has been happening to our rates of crime involving robbery, rape, and labor?*

3. *In what way does the existence of discrimination in a country affect its level of violence?*

4. *Even though civil disorders have increased recently, how do these disorders compare to the 1860 draft riots? How does the number of Ku Klux Klan members relate to violence?*

5. *Do some countries experience types of violence that are not common to the U.S.? Do we have types of violence that are common only to the U.S.?*

6. *What evidence do the authors supply indicating that violence has increased recently, not only in the U.S., but also in the world? Have all the nations had an increase in the number of political assassinations? How do the authors account for the increase? Are most assassins deranged? From what do they suffer? What are its causes? What examples do the authors supply?*

2

What is Violence?

"He's not happy unless he's in the great outdoors killing something."

VIOLENCE IS A BASIC HUMAN REACTION TO ENVIRONMENT. It is also an end, the extreme form of aggression. Violence has so many shades of meaning that it seems, like beauty, to be "in the eyes of the beholder." Each discipline, each researcher, each society, each person places his own interpretations upon the word. Some people consider violent behavior natural, legitimate, acceptable, desirable, and defensible. Concurrently, others consider it deviant, unnecessary, unwanted, and abhorrent. The authors of the selections in this section seek to both define and explain the conditions contributing to violence. Scott gives insight into recent animal behavior studies; Dancey suggests that we deliberately establish the conditions that cause violence; and Menninger considers the consequences of some people's apathy toward violence, coupled with others' apathy toward seeking its prevention.

In this changing world, man is seeking identity. By trying to answer the riddle of American violence, we are also probing the larger question, "What is an American?" At first glance, violence seems similar in all societies—all people have disputes at both personal and group levels; all societies have criminal elements that resort to acts of violence to achieve their ends; and all nations will turn to open warfare when other methods fail. It follows that there should be some universal yardstick for violence.

But there isn't. Each society must be judged upon its own standards. Violence in the United States seems to have unique qualities in addition to those shared with the rest of the world. We taught the world that people could successfully use violence to achieve democracy for themselves. Over the years, the use of violence to gain some political goal has become ingrained in Americans. Violence has become patriotic; the "Nativists" of the 1840's, the "Know-nothings" of the 1850's, and a series of similar super-patriotic organizations like the John Birchers and Minute-men of our own time have used or seemed to advocate violence to defend "100 percent Americanism." While they are the first to condemn violence in those who oppose them, the super-patriots will propose violence to eliminate that opposition. Their patriotic behavior is echoed by the actions of the Black Panthers, Weathermen, and similar dissident elements that use the same means to accomplish a similar end: political and social change.

The American philosophic position toward violence has made folk heroes of the bounty hunter, the cattle rus-tler, the bank robber, the "vigilante," the bootlegger, and many other people practicing unlawful or shady occupa-tions that trade in violence. (Who but Americans could have created the terror of a *lynching*?) The result of this attitude is that Americans are frequently aggressive in their dealings with other people, both at home and throughout the world. We force our policies and practices on others because we feel they have worked well for us.

To define violence we need to know the difference be-tween it and aggression. We must realize that aggression leads to violence, and that one can be aggressive without becoming violent, as Scott discusses in "The Anatomy of Violence." Overt violence is the actual commission of some act that damages in some fashion the target of aggression or frustration. In one of the following readings, Wilson raises several theories about violence and its recurrent nature. Ranly, in a more humorous way, classifies the basic stances toward violence, and Hahn profiles some elements of violent behavior in urban settings.

Perhaps the message is that violence is bad for us—unless we use it successfully. Is that hypocrisy? Or is it a practical way of looking at the real needs of changing circumstances?

"Loved the show!"

[Drawing by Edward Koren; © 1968 The New Yorker Magazine, Inc.]

The Anatomy of Violence

JOHN PAUL SCOTT

A boy murders an old woman because she will not give him 50¢, or a stranger is set upon and beaten by a crowd of unemployed youths. Crimes are committed in public in the presence of onlookers who refuse to become involved even to the extent of calling for help. These occurrences are alarming because we cannot easily understand them as the acts of human beings. Is some mysterious animal or primitive drive toward violence beginning to spread through human populations?

While crime is an old phenomenon, its scientific study is relatively new, and the study of the basic causes of violent behavior is newer still. One set of answers is being given by the study of fighting and aggression in lower animals, from which an intriguing picture of normal animal social life is emerging. For example, wolves have been traditionally pictured as bloodthirsty slavering beasts, but the field studies of Adolph Murie in Alaska show that the home life of a pack of wolves is a delightful affair, the group cooperating

John Paul Scott, "The Anatomy of Violence," *The Nation*, June 21, 1965, pp. 662–666.

peacefully to obtain food, feed their young, and keep off other predators. Wolves reared by hand under proper conditions make delightful pets, better behaved than many dogs. Wolves can indeed be extremely destructive of livestock, and the pack may mercilessly attack and drive off a strange wolf, but the traditional slinking, slavering and treacherous animal of fiction corresponds only to the behavior of a wolf that has been recently trapped and is extremely frightened.

The behavior of wolves is mirrored in their relatives, domestic dogs. The pet dog behaves as if the human family were his pack and its house his den. Within the family he is peaceful and cooperative, but unless trained otherwise he will attempt to attack and drive out any strange person or dog that enters the yard. Hence the frequent difficulties of postmen and other visitors. In a neighborhood with many dogs, the area around each house with a dog is recognized by every other dog as a territory, not to be entered except by permission, and this arrangement results in generally peaceful behavior. However, if a dog owner disturbs this organization by attempting to lead his animal into the territory of another, a serious dog fight is very likely to occur. The human being has introduced the element of social disorganization by leading his pet to break the bounds of territories.

I have studied the way in which peaceful behavior develops in a litter of puppies. Starting early in life, they begin playful fighting, biting and chewing on one another, and occasionally barking and threatening. Sometimes this develops into a serious fight; the puppies are too small to do much damage, but the result is a dominance relationship. In any conflict, the former winner of a fight has only to threaten the other pup, who responds by rolling on his back and yelping, thus indicating that he is subordinate. As the animals grow older these gestures may be reduced to a point where almost no overt aggression is seen.

Similar peaceful relationships can be developed between puppies and their human handlers. Indeed, puppies provide a model for the development of social control of aggression. In one experiment in which I participated, we raised more than 500 puppies from birth to maturity. For theoretical reasons we never punished them, yet I was bitten only once—a slight nip from a mother who resented my handling her newborn offspring. On every occasion these animals appeared to be extraordinarily submissive, but we achieved this without any overt repression. Instead, we started to pick up the young puppies and carry them from one place to another soon after they were born, and we continued the practice as they grew older. If we ever wished to control the behavior of a dog, all we had to do was to pick him up; we could even stop a dog fight in this way. The basic method was gentle restraint, beginning early in life, and it appeared to be enormously effective.

The means for the social control of aggression differ from one kind of animal to another, but common methods, as seen in wolves and dogs, are the development of dominance and subordination, and of territoriality. The results of a breakdown in social control have also been observed in many kinds of animals, and one of the most striking examples comes from the lower primates.

The behavior of baboons was first seriously studied by Zuckerman in the London Zoo. He described a situation in which a large number of strange males and a small number of females were confined in an area about the size of a small city lot. Then a large group of strange females was introduced, and the males began to fight with one another for the possession of the females. Sometimes females were torn to pieces, and during the three years that Zuckerman studied the group only one infant animal survived. The picture was one of unrelieved brutality and senseless violence. One could conclude that this is an analogue of man's primary nature, kept in check only by civilization.

But some time later, Washburn, De Vore and Hall began to study baboons under natural conditions and found that the behavior of the animals in normal, well-organized social groups on the African plains presented an entirely different picture. There was almost no serious fighting. The males were organized in a dominance order and kept their distance from one another. As a result, the younger and more subordinate males stayed on the outer edge of the group where they were most likely to come first into contact with predators. When a cheetah or other dangerous animal appeared, an alarm cry was given and the males all combined to attack and drive off the intruder. The females and young, far from being attacked as in the disorganized zoo society described above, traveled inside the protection of this outer circle. If a juvenile baboon played so roughly with an infant that it began to cry, the mother or one of the senior males immediately came to its rescue and drove the older one away. When a female was ready to mate there was little excitement and no fighting. Rather than compete for her, the males waited while she chose a male, who might be, but was not necessarily, the most dominant animal. She could also pass from male to male with no disturbance.

In a baboon society, peaceful behavior is developed in many ways. One of the most important is the formation of strong habits of acting peaceably toward other members of the troop, which begins early in life and is enforced by the older members. Second, the formation of a dominance order establishes habitual modes whereby each baboon relates to every other member of the troop. Another important factor is undoubtedly the simple necessity of spending a great deal of time in the search for food. This peaceful and constructive activity makes it difficult to find leisure for destructive action, and tolerance in the course of time becomes a strong habit.

We can conclude that the social animal is capable of maturing into a peaceful and cooperative individual within a well-organized society, but that he is also capable of developing destructive and violent behavior under conditions of social disorganization. In short, the major cause of outbreaks of destructive violence in animals is acute social disorganization.

We can no longer put the blame for irrational and destructive human behavior on man's "animal nature," for animal nature appears to permit a high degree of perfectibility. There is every reason to believe that our human ancestors, even before they developed language and a verbal culture, had evolved and developed similar mechanisms to control aggression through basic social organization. Whether culturally derived or not, territoriality is a common human device for control of aggression. Indeed, in our society, violation of territory is considered a serious crime. Dominance and subordination relationships are developed between every parent and child, as well as through quarrels among children on playgrounds. However, these primitive methods of social control all depend upon the ability of individuals to recognize one another and thus determine what behavior is appropriate—something much easier to do in a small group of lifelong associates than in the large crowds of a modern city.

One of the appealing characteristics of an urban community is that within it one may escape from the petty restrictions of a closely organized village society. On the other hand, almost all the examples of senseless human violence come from large cities, and it may be that one price that must be paid for freedom from meddlesome scrutiny is the danger of violence from unknown hands.

Accurate figures are difficult to obtain, but it is clear from FBI crime reports that the incidence of most crimes of violence is correlated with the size of the city. In a recent year, the rate of aggravated assault (including all attempts to injure another person physically) was twice as great in cities as in suburban and rural areas, and the rate in cities greater than 250,000 was more than four times that in rural areas. This is the class of crime most likely to include acts of senseless violence. Robbery and forcible rape follow similar patterns, with an almost perfect correlation between city size and crime rate.

Crimes resulting in death follow a different pattern. The rates for murder and negligent homicide are high in rural areas, low in small cities, and jump again in cities of more than 100,000. The safest place with respect to any class of violent crime is in a town or city smaller than 10,000. Violence also occurs here, but the crimes are understandable: husbands beating wives and wives shooting husbands; have-nots stealing from the haves. Furthermore, in a stable village community the author of a crime is almost always apprehended because everyone knows everyone else.

It is hard to determine whether or not crimes of violence are actually on the increase. FBI figures report greater total numbers of crimes over the past few years, but this may in part be caused by better methods of reporting. These figures also show increasing crime rates, but those relating to violence are concentrated in the large cities. Cases of aggravated assault actually decreased in the ten years from 1953 to 1963, except in cities of more than 100,000, and murder similarly dropped except in cities of the very largest class.

The figures may be misleading also because they are based on the total population rather than on age groups. The baby boom following World War II has produced a tremendous increase in the relative numbers of young people. This could cause an increase in per capita crime rates because a larger proportion of the population is now in the age bracket which commits most of the crimes.

Who are the criminals who commit apparently purpose-less violence? Frequently they are lost in the anonymity of a large and partially disorganized city community, but when they are apprehended and the facts concerning them can be investigated by trained scientists, certain generali-ties begin to appear. Such criminals are almost invariably young unmarried males. Partly this is so because the male sex hormone lowers the threshold of stimulation for fight-ing, and partly it is because boys and girls receive different cultural treatment. These young male criminals are often unemployed and almost invariably have a history of broken or disordered homes. They may have been illegitimate chil-dren brought up by unwilling relatives, or children whose fathers were dead and whose stepfathers mistreated them. Many have lost both parents and been passed from one fos-ter home to another. In short, the great majority of such criminals come from disorganized families.

What does a male parent do in a well-organized fam-ily? In the first place, he provides an example of restrained and peaceable adult behavior and thus gives the child a model which he can follow and with whom he can identify himself. Second, he enforces peaceable behavior and thus starts the formation of useful habits, not only of peaceful living with peers and adults but also of respect and obe-dience for figures of socially accepted authority.

The reasons why any given individual becomes violent can be discovered only by a thorough investigation of that particular case. Besides the general absence of social con-trol, there are immediate factors which produce violence. In the case of fighting, one should always begin by looking at outside circumstances, for the physiology of fighting in-dicates that the primary stimulation comes from the outside rather than from a spontaneous inner need. There are two common sources of such external stimuli. One is the organization of a group for purposes of violence, as in many juvenile gangs and in the more highly organized forms of fighting seen in war. The other is direct emotional stimulation, and one of the best examples came to me many years ago in the case of a young boy who had been expelled from kindergarten for violent behavior. According to his teacher, he would begin each morning by attacking either her or his classmates for no reason. Investigation showed that the boy was coming to school on a bus with several older brothers who delighted in alleviating the tedium of the ride by teasing their little brother. As a result, he arrived at school seething with fury and attacked the nearest available object. Similarly, almost any case of destructive violence becomes understandable in terms of the past history and immediate provocation of the individual concerned. However, such facts are not ordinarily available to crime reporters, who are under pressure to turn out their stories at once rather than to wait out the days or even weeks which it may take to dig for these facts. And in any case, a mystery makes a better news story than a well-documented case history.

It is relatively easy to find a remedy for the behavior of a small boy who is just beginning a life of violence, but what is the cure for the person who has developed a strong habit of violent behavior over a period of years? This kind of person is often described as a psychopathic personality, as opposed to an individual who may have made one impulsive mistake or succumbed to unusual pressures. At present there is no conspicuously successful method for dealing with the psychopath. Psychiatrists agree that their chances of improvement are poor, and since they are highly dangerous, few people wish to work with them except under the conditions of physical restraint provided by prisons and detention centers. We can only conclude that prevention of violence is far more effective than its cure.

We must be concerned to prevent social disorganization, which has three main aspects: family disorganization, the disorganization produced by the normal transition from one's original home to the founding of a new family, and the occurrence of large disorganized populations in cities. (Social disorganization can also occur in rural areas, and studies by Alexander Leighton have shown that it has much the same symptoms and results: poverty, broken families, high crime rates and even high rates of mental illness. His results also give a laboratory demonstration of the improvement that results from improved organization.)

The remedy for the disorganization of city life is the restoration of social organization. Part of this is achieved by the creation of an honest and effective police force. Instead of each person observing his neighbor and looking out for his safety, we have a policeman standing on the corner and doing the job for everyone. There is no substitute for a well-trained and efficient police force.

More than this, in any city there are always well-known areas where violence is concentrated, and it usually turns out that these are areas of social disorganization of one sort or another. Neighborhoods in which large numbers of recent immigrants live, often crowded together and confined in ghettos where they cannot escape from one another, are an example. Other crime-ridden areas are the skid rows in which wandering men live without families.

Then there is the social disorganization associated with family life and not necessarily confined to any one area. Crimes are more likely to be committed by persons who have come from broken homes and neglectful parents, and in our society there is a regular developmental period of social disorganization when a person leaves his primary family and has not yet formed a new family group of his own.

The solutions to these problems of social disorganization are obvious but not easy. We need to develop honest and efficient law enforcement. We need to know our neighbors, troublesome as this is at times, so that we can cooperate with them when necessary. One answer is some sort of formal neighborhood organization for cities such as the block system which has been attempted in certain areas of Chicago.

We need to discourage broken homes and develop competent parents. Finally, we need to provide young adult males with useful, constructive and rewarding activities which will bring them back into the social structure. That is what the Peace Corps, and more especially the Job Corps, are attempting to do. This method for the control of violence was suggested by William James more than a generation ago. It is still as sound as it ever was and should produce widespread results when effectively and continuously used.

Such remedies will not completely control violence, nor is there any good prospect that it will ever be eliminated. They do act to *reduce* the rate of violence in proportion to the amount of effort expended. We need to remember that the problem of violence cannot be solved by one-shot emergency measures such as putting the police on extra duty for a week or setting up a Youth Corps for a few years and then letting it lapse. The price of a peaceful society is continuous effort.

QUESTIONS FOR DISCUSSION

1. *Why are scientists studying the behavior of animals to determine the causes of violent behavior in humans?*
2. *Did the studies show that wolves, by nature, are always slinking, treacherous animals?*

3. What were the means for controlling aggression in dogs?
4. How is peaceful behavior developed in a baboon society?
5. What is the major cause of outbreaks of destructive violence in animals?
6. Why can't we put the blame for irrational human behavior on man's animal nature?
7. What are some primitive methods of social control? On what do they depend? In what way does city life decrease the effect of these methods? How is this fact reflected in the incidence of crime in large cities?
8. Why are FBI statistics on crime often misleading?
9. What are the characteristics of the criminals who commit apparently purposeless violence?
10. What does a male parent do in a well-organized family?
11. What are two common sources of external stimuli which instigate fighting?
12. Why does Scott conclude that "prevention of violence is far more effective than its cure"?
13. What are the three main aspects of social disorganization?
14. What are the solutions that the author suggests for the problems of social disorganization?

Causes Of Violence

C. L. DANCEY

All the mystery and need for "research" about war and violence with studies instituted against the background of the assassination of national figures amazes us.

There really isn't all that much mystery about it.

Competent sociological studies have long since been made free from all the prejudices and pressures involved in the current Vietnam debates or from "crime" and "assassination" feelings.

It is so much easier to rant against inanimate hunks of metal than to face the unpleasant social facts about us humans—the fact that people who are NOT psychopaths kill other people, have been doing so since the dawn of history, and do so for such simple and straight forward motives as to remove opposition or acquire money.

In the undue modern emphasis on psychology, we study and apply everything that goes for the psychopath, and neglect the "normal" causes for "normal" people that have been functioning fatally for centuries.

C. L. Dancey, "Causes of Violence," *Peoria Journal Star*, June 30, 1968, p. A–6.

In war, revolution, group violence, and individual violence (Mafia or professional crook type as opposed to that of a psychopath or "crime of passion" situation) there is a long recognized PATTERN.

1. There is a group of associates who socially accept and justify violence for the purposes concerned.
2. There is a prospect of gaining something or some advantage by violence.
3. It is considered unlikely that it could be gained WITHOUT violence.
4. You can probably get away with it. The risks seem small.

This is the standard pattern. Do present activities and conditions depart from it? Or are the eternal elements present today in the violence that occurs?

Hell's bells! We have earnestly CREATED the classic conditions for violence!

In our zeal for good causes, plus political zeal for the votes of anybody who is unhappy, we've supplied such heated rationale as to supply the "justification" to almost everybody who doesn't get his way—and who does?

We have also provided the rewards, flippantly ("it's insured") to criminals, and by the "grease-the-squeaky-wheel" philosophy in politics and administration, public and private.

In many areas, what people want isn't THERE without violence in relation to their capabilities, and in others it isn't there because expectations are totally unreasonable thanks to the propaganda cited above. In too many cases, also, it isn't there AND IT SHOULD BE.

Simultaneously with these conditions, we launch on our greatest binge in history of a permissive philosophy ranging from don't-spank-the-baby to Supreme Court decisions crippling crime detection and "humanitarian" policies reducing punishments as well as the likelihood of punishment to criminals.

The students at Columbia expected "amnesty." They thought it a raw deal if they didn't get it. They were ENTITLED to break the law without punishment, attack the college without expulsion, and use the president's office for a toilet without disgrace.

Dr. Spock made it clear that he thought he could break the law, and the only result would be massive publicity but NOT JAIL!

Sirhan Sirhan proved to be completely knowledgable of his "rights" and the restrictions on police, and fully aware that the Supreme Court has been cancelling executions and freeing killers left and right—doubtless including the massive public speculation by "authorities" that Jack Ruby's shooting of Oswald was SO PUBLIC he could never be legally punished because no "fair trial" was POSSIBLE!

Police are all too familiar with juveniles, some of whom can't pass a fourth grade reading test, who know enough to jeer at them and holler: "You can't do anything to me! I'm a juvenile!"

(People don't have to be RIGHT in their assumptions. They only have to have the IMPRESSION the risks are small to become prone to violence and other illegal acts.)

People say the "causes" of violence should be removed.

That is right. All the causes to the degree possible.

The causes to be attacked include: (1) A social climate which seems to approve of UNOFFICIAL violence of many kinds; (2) The lack of other means of achieving LEGITIMATE objectives instead of by violence; (3) the prospects of violence paying any dividends; and (4) the expectation that violent action involves no REAL risk.

ALL OF THESE NEED TO BE CHANGED AS MUCH AS POSSIBLE.

The mystery is the sentimental refusal to face these long established facts, demonstrated historically and sociologically, and being demonstrated before our eyes, again—while we seem to prefer to pursue abstractions, excuses, and new studies.

Is it that those who were drum-majors in the creation of conditions for violence are too much involved to admit the facts of life? And that this involves too many of our political leaders, intellectual soothsayers, and "opinion makers?"

QUESTIONS FOR DISCUSSION

1. *What evidence does Dancey cite to support his notion that "people who are not psycopaths kill other people, have been doing so since the dawn of history, and do so for such simple and straight forward motives as to remove opposition or acquire money"?*

2. *What does the author mean by "the undue modern emphasis on psychology"?*

3. *What is the pattern for all forms of violence, according to Dancey?*

4. *According to the author, who is responsible for our "permissive philosophy"? What are some of the examples he mentions?*

5. *What are the causes of violence that Dancey believes should be attacked?*

The Crime of Punishment

KARL MENNINGER

Few words in our language arrest our attention as do "crime," "violence," "revenge," and "injustice." We abhor crime; we adore justice; we boast that we live by the rule of law. Violence and vengefulness we repudiate as unworthy of our civilization, and we assume this sentiment to be unanimous among all human beings.

Yet crime continues to be a national disgrace and a world-wide problem. It is threatening, alarming, wasteful, expensive, abundant, and apparently increasing! In actuality it is decreasing in frequency of occurrence, but it is certainly increasing in visibility and the reactions of the public to it.

Our system for controlling crime is ineffective, unjust, expensive. Prisons seem to operate with revolving doors— the same people going in and out and in and out. *Who cares?*

Our city jails and inhuman reformatories and wretched prisons are jammed. They are known to be un-

From *The Crime of Punishment*. New York: Viking Press. Copyright 1968 by Karl Menninger. Reprinted by permission of the author.

healthy, dangerous, immoral, indecent, crime-breeding dens
of iniquity. Not everyone has smelled them, as some of us
have. Not many have heard the groans and the curses. Not
everyone has seen the hate and despair in a thousand
blank, hollow faces. But, in a way, we all know how miser-
able prisons are. *We want them to be that way.* And they
are. *Who cares?*

Professional and big-time criminals prosper as never
before. Gambling syndicates flourish. White-collar crime
may even exceed all others, but goes undetected in the majority of cases. We are all being robbed and we know who
the robbers are. They live nearby. *Who cares?*

The public filches millions of dollars worth of food and
clothing from stores, towels and sheets from hotels, jewelry
and knick-knacks from shops. The public steals, and the
same public pays it back in higher prices. *Who cares?*

Time and time again somebody shouts about this state
of affairs, just as I am shouting now. The magazines shout.
The newspapers shout. The television and radio commentators shout (or at least they "deplore"). Psychologists, sociologists, leading jurists, wardens, and intelligent police
chiefs join the chorus. Governors and mayors and Congress-
men are sometimes heard. They shout that the situation is
bad, bad, bad, and getting worse. Some suggest that we
immediately replace obsolete procedures with scientific
methods. A few shout contrary sentiments. Do the clear
indications derived from scientific discovery for appropriate
changes continue to fall on deaf ears? Why is the public so
long-suffering, so apathetic and thereby so continuingly self-
destructive? How many Presidents (and other citizens) do
we have to lose before we do something?

The public behaves as a sick patient does when a
dreaded treatment is proposed for his ailment. We all know
how the aching tooth may suddenly quiet down in the den-
tist's office, or the abdominal pain disappear in the sur-

geon's examining room. Why should a sufferer seek relief
and shun it? Is it merely the fear of pain of the treatment?
Is it the fear of unknown complications? Is it distrust of the
doctor's ability? All of these, no doubt.

But, as Freud made so incontestably clear, the sufferer
is always somewhat deterred by a kind of subversive, internal opposition to the work of cure. He suffers on the one
hand from the pains of his affliction and yearns to get well.
But he suffers at the same time from traitorous impulses
that fight against the accomplishment of any change in
himself, even recovery! Like Hamlet, he wonders whether
it may be better after all to suffer the familiar pains and
aches associated with the old method than to face the complications of a new and strange, even though possibly better way of handling things.

The inescapable conclusion is that society secretly
wants crime, *needs* crime, and gains definite satisfactions
from the present mishandling of it! We condemn crime;
we punish offenders for it; but we need it. The crime and
punishment ritual is a part of our lives. We need crimes to
wonder at, to enjoy vicariously, to discuss and speculate
about and to publicly deplore. We need criminals to identify
ourselves with, to envy secretly, and to punish stoutly. They
do for us the forbidden, illegal things we *wish* to do and, like
scapegoats of old, they bear the burdens of our displaced
guilt and punishment—"the iniquities of us all."

We have to confess that there is something fascinating
for us all about violence. That most crime is not violent we
know but we forget, because crime is a breaking, a ruptur-
ing, a tearing—even when it is quietly done. To all of us
crime seems like violence.

The very word "violence" has a disturbing, menacing
quality. . . . In meaning it implies something dreaded,
powerful, destructive, or eruptive. It is something we abhor
—or do we? Its first effect is to startle, frighten—even to
horrify us. But we do not always run away from it. For vio-

lence also intrigues us. It is exciting. It is dramatic. Observing it and sometimes even participating in it gives us acute pleasure.

The newspapers constantly supply us with tidbits of violence going on in the world. They exploit its dramatic essence often to the neglect of conservative reporting of more extensive but less violent damage—the flood disaster in Florence, Italy, for example. Such words as crash, explosion, wreck, assault, raid, murder, avalanche, rape, and seizure evoke pictures of eruptive devastation from which we cannot turn away. The headlines often impute violence metaphorically even to peaceful activities. Relations are "ruptured," a tie is "broken," arbitration "collapses," a proposal is "killed."

Meanwhile on the television and movie screens there constantly appear for our amusement scenes of fighting, slugging, beating, torturing, clubbing, shooting, and the like which surpass in effect anything that the newspapers can describe. Much of this violence is portrayed dishonestly; the scenes are only semirealistic; they are "faked" and romanticized.

Pain cannot be photographed; grimaces indicate but do not convey its intensity. And wounds—unlike violence —are rarely shown. This phony quality of television violence in its mentally unhealthy aspect encourages irrationality by giving the impression to the observer that being beaten, kicked, cut, and stomped, while very unpleasant, are not very painful or serious. For after being slugged and beaten the hero rolls over, opens his eyes, hops up, rubs his cheek, grins, and staggers on. The *suffering* of violence is a part both the TV and movie producers *and* their audience tend to repress.

Although most of us *say* we deplore cruelty and destructiveness, we are partially deceiving ourselves. We disown violence, ascribing the love of it to other people. But the facts speak for themselves. We do love violence, all of us, and we all feel secretly guilty for it, which is another clue to public resistance to crime-control reform.

The great sin by which we all are tempted is the wish to hurt others, and this sin must be avoided if we are to live and let live. If our destructive energies can be mastered, directed, and sublimated, we can survive. If we can love, we can live. Our destructive energies, if they cannot be controlled, may destroy our best friends, as in the case of Alexander the Great, or they may destroy supposed "enemies" or innocent strangers. Worst of all—from the standpoint of the individual—they may destroy us.

Over the centuries of man's existence, many devices have been employed in the effort to control these innate suicidal and criminal propensities. The earliest of these undoubtedly depended upon fear—fear of the unknown, fear of magical retribution, fear of social retaliation. These external devices were replaced gradually with the law and all its machinery, religion and its rituals, and the conventions of the social order.

The routine of life formerly required every individual to direct much of his aggressive energy against the environment. There were trees to cut down, wild animals to fend off, heavy obstacles to remove, great burdens to lift. But the machine has gradually changed all of this. Today, the routine of life, for most people, requires no violence, no fighting, no killing, no life-risking, no sudden supreme exertion; occasionally, perhaps, a hard pull or a strong push, but no tearing, crushing, breaking, forcing.

And because violence no longer has legitimate and useful vents or purposes, it must *all* be controlled today. In earlier times its expression was often a virtue; today its control is the virtue. The control involves symbolic, vicarious expressions of our violence—violence modified; "sublimated," as Freud called it; "neutralized," as Hartmann described it. Civilized substitutes for direct violence are the objects of daily search by all of us. The common law and the Ten Commandments, traffic signals and property deeds, fences and front doors, sermons and concerts, Christmas trees and jazz bands—these and a thousand other things exist today to help in the control of violence.

My colleague, Brumo Bettelheim, thinks we do not properly educate our youth to deal with their violent urges. He reminds us that nothing fascinated our forefathers more. The *Iliad* is a poem of violence. Much of the Bible is a record of violence. One penal system and many methods of child-rearing express violence—"violence to suppress violence." And, he concludes [in the article "Violence: A Neglected Mode of Behavior"]: "We shall not be able to deal intelligently with violence unless we are first ready to see it as part of human nature, and then we shall come to realize the chances of discharging violent tendencies are now so severely curtailed that their regular and safe draining-off is not possible anymore."

Why aren't we all criminals? We all have the impulses; we all have the provocations. But becoming civilized, which is repeated ontologically in the process of social education, teaches us what we may do with impunity. What then evokes or permits the breakthrough? Why is it necessary for some to bribe their consciences and do what they do not approve of doing? Why does all sublimation sometimes fail and overt breakdown occur in the controlling and managing machinery of the personality? Why do we sometimes lose self-control? Why do we "go to pieces"? Why do we explode?

These questions point up a central problem in psychiatry. Why do some people do things they do not want to do? Or things we do not want them to do? Sometimes crimes are motivated by a desperate need to act, to do *something* to break out of a state of passivity, frustration, and helpless-

ness too long endured, like a child who shoots a parent or a
teacher after some apparently reasonable act. Granting the
universal presence of violence within us all, controlled by
will power, conscience, fear of punishment, and other devices, granting the tensions and the temptations that are
also common to us all, why do the mechanisms of self-
control fail so completely in some individuals? Is there not
some pre-existing defect, some moral or cerebral weakness,
some gross deficiency of common sense that lets some people stumble or kick or strike or explode, while the rest of
us just stagger or sway?

When a psychiatrist examines many prisoners, writes
[Seymour] Halleck [in *Psychiatry and the Dilemmas of
Crime*], he soon discovers how important in the genesis of
the criminal outbreak is the offender's previous *sense of
helplessness or hopelessness*. All of us suffer more or less
from infringement of our personal freedom. We fuss about
it all the time; we strive to correct it, extend it, and free
ourselves from various oppressive or retentive forces. We
do not want others to push us around, to control us, to domi-
nate us. We realize this is bound to happen to some extent
in an interlocking, interrelated society such as ours. No one
truly has complete freedom. But restriction irks us.

The offender feels this way, too. He does not want
to be pushed around, controlled, or dominated. And because
he often feels that he is thus oppressed (and actually is)
and because he does lack facility in improving his situation
without violence, he suffers more intensely from feelings of
helplessness.

Violence and crime are often attempts to escape from
madness; and there can be no doubt that some mental illness is a flight from the wish to do the violence or commit
the act. Is it hard for the reader to believe that suicides are
sometimes committed to forestall the committing of murder? There is no doubt of it. Nor is there any doubt that
murder is sometimes committed to avert suicide.

Strange as it may sound, many murderers do not realize whom they are killing, or, to put it another way, that they are killing the wrong people. To be sure, killing anybody is reprehensible enough, but the worst of it is that the person who the killer thinks should die (and he has reasons) is not the person he attacks. Sometimes the victim himself is partly responsible for the crime that is committed against him. It is this unconscious (perhaps sometimes conscious) participation in the crime by the victim that has long held up the very humanitarian and progressive-sounding program of giving compensation to victims. The public often judges the victim as well as the attacker.

Rape and other sexual offenses are acts of violence so repulsive to our sense of decency and order that it is easy to think of rapists in general as raging, oversexed, ruthless brutes (unless they are conquering heroes). Some rapists are. But most sex crimes are committed by undersexed rather than oversexed individuals, often undersized rather than oversized, and impelled less by lust than by a need for reassurance regarding an impaired masculinity. The unconscious fear of women goads some men with a compulsive urge to conquer, humiliate, hurt, or render powerless some available sample of womanhood. Men who are violently afraid of their repressed but nearly emergent homosexual desires, and men who are afraid of the humiliation of impotence, often try to overcome these fears by violent demonstrations.

The need to deny something in oneself is frequently an underlying motive for certain odd behavior—even up to and including crime. Bravado crimes, often done with particular brutality and ruthlessness, seem to prove *to the doer* that "I am no weakling! I am no sissy! I am no coward. I am no homosexual! I am a tough man who fears nothing." The Nazi storm troopers, many of them mere boys, were systematically trained to stifle all tender emotions and force themselves to be heartlessly brutal.

Man perennially seeks to recover the magic of his childhood days—the control of the mighty by the meek. The flick of an electric light switch, the response of an automobile throttle, the click of a camera, the touch of a match to a skyrocket—these are keys to a sudden and magical display of great power induced by the merest gesture. Is anyone already so blasé that he is no longer thrilled at the opening of a door specially for him by a magic-eye signal? Yet for a few pennies one can purchase a far more deadly piece of magic—a stored explosive and missile encased within a shell which can be ejected from a machine at the touch of a finger so swiftly that no eye can follow. A thousand yards away something falls dead—a rabbit, a deer, a beautiful mountain sheep, a sleeping child, or the President of the United States. Magic! Magnified, projected power. "Look what I can do. I am the greatest!"

It must have come to every thoughtful person, at one time or another, in looking at the revolvers on the policemen's hips, or the guns soldiers and hunters carry so proudly, that these are instruments made for the express purpose of delivering death to someone. The easy availability of these engines of destruction, even to children, mentally disturbed people, professional criminals, gangsters, and even high school girls is something to give one pause. The National Rifle Association and its allies have been able to kill scores of bills that have been introduced into Congress and state legislatures for corrective gun control since the death of President Kennedy. Americans still spend about $2 billion on guns each year.

Fifty years ago, Winston Churchill declared that the mood and temper of the public in regard to crime and criminals is one of the unfailing tests of the civilization of any country. Judged by this standard, how civilized are we?

The chairman of the President's National Crime Commission, Nicholas de B. Katzenbach, declared recently that organized crime flourishes in America because enough of the public wants its services, and most citizens are apathetic about its impact. It will continue uncurbed as long as Americans accept it as inevitable and, in some instances, desirable.

Are there steps that we can take which will reduce the aggressive stabs and self-destructive lurches of our less well-managing fellow men? Are there ways to prevent and control the grosser violations, other than the clumsy traditional maneuvers which we have inherited? These depend basically upon intimidation and slow-motion torture. We call it punishment, and justify it with our "feeling." We know it doesn't work.

Yes, there *are* better ways. There are steps that could be taken; some *are* taken. But we move too slowly. Much better use, it seems to me, could be made of the members of my profession and other behavioral scientists than having them deliver courtroom pronunciamentos. The consistent use of a diagnostic clinic would enable trained workers to lay what they can learn about an offender before the judge who would know best how to implement the recommendation.

This would no doubt lead to a transformation of prisons, if not to their total disappearance in their present form and function. Temporary and permanent detention will perhaps always be necessary for a few, especially the professionals, but this could be more effectively and economically performed with new types of "facility" (that strange, awkward word for institution).

I assume it to be a matter of common and general agreement that our object in all this is to protect the community from a repetition of the offense by the most economical method consonant with our other purposes. Our "other purposes" include the desire to prevent these offences from occurring, to reclaim offenders for social usefulness, if possible, and to detain them in protective custody, if reclamation is *not* possible. But how?

The treatment of human failure or dereliction by the infliction of pain is still used and believed in by many non-medical people. "Spare the rod and spoil the child" is still considered wise counsel by many.

Whipping is still used by many secondary schoolmasters in England, I am informed, to stimulate study, attention, and the love of learning. Whipping was long a traditional treatment for the "crime" of disobedience on the part of children, pupils, servants, apprentices, employees. And slaves were treated for centuries by flogging for such offences as weariness, confusion, stupidity, exhaustion, fear, grief, and even overcheerfulness. It was assumed and stoutly defended that these "treatments" cured conditions for which they were administered.

Meanwhile, scientific medicine was acquiring many new healing methods and devices. Doctors can now transplant organs and limbs; they can remove brain tumors and cure incipient cancers; they can halt pneumonia, meningitis, and other infections; they can correct deformities and repair breaks and tears and scars. But these wonderful achievements are accomplished on *willing* subjects, people who voluntarily ask for help by even heroic measures. And the reader will be wondering, no doubt, whether doctors can do anything with or for people who *do not want* to be treated at all, in any way! Can doctors cure willful aberrant behavior? Are we to believe that crime is a *disease* that can be reached by scientific measures? Isn't it merely "natural meanness" that makes all of us do wrong things at times even when we "know better"? And are not self-control, moral stamina, and will power the things needed? Surely there is no medical treatment for the lack of those!

Let me answer this carefully, for much misunderstanding accumulates here. I would say that according to the prevalent understanding of the words, crime is *not* a disease. Neither is it an illness, although I think it *should* be! It *should* be treated, and it could be; but it mostly isn't.

These enigmatic statements are simply explained. Diseases are undesired states of being which have been described and defined by doctors, usually given Greek or Latin appellations, and treated by long-established physical and pharmacological formulae. Illness, on the other hand, is best defined as a state of impaired functioning of such a nature that the public expects the sufferer to repair to the physician for help. The illness may prove to be a disease; more often it is only vague and nameless misery, but something which doctors, not lawyers, teachers, or preachers, are supposed to be able and willing to help.

When the community begins to look upon the expression of aggressive violence as the symptom of an illness or as indicative of illness, it will be because it believes doctors can do something to correct such a condition. At present, some better-informed individuals do believe and expect this. However angry at or sorry for the offender, they want him "treated" in an effective way so that he will cease to be a danger to them. And they know that the traditional punishment, "treatment-punishment," will not effect this.

What *will*? What effective treatment is there for such violence? It will surely have to begin with motivating or stimulating or arousing in a cornered individual the wish and hope and intention to change his methods of dealing with the realities of life. Can this be done by education, medication, counseling, training? I would answer *yes*. It can be done successfully in a majority of cases, if undertaken in time.

The present penal system and the existing legal philosophy do not stimulate or even expect such a change to take place in the criminal. Yet change is what medical science always aims for. The prisoner, like the doctor's other patients, should emerge from his treatment experience a different person, differently equipped, differently functioning, and headed in a different direction than when he began the treatment.

It is natural for the public to doubt that this can be accomplished with criminals. But remember that the public *used* to doubt that change could be effected in the mentally ill. No one a hundred years ago believed mental illness to be curable. Today *all* people know (or should know) that *mental illness is curable* in the great majority of instances and that the prospects and rapidity of cure are directly related to the availability and intensity of proper treatment.

The forms and techniques of psychiatric treatment used today number in the hundreds. No one patient requires or receives all forms, but each patient is studied with respect to his particular needs, his basic assets, his interests, and his special difficulties. A therapeutic team may embrace a dozen workers—as in a hospital setting—or it may narrow down to the doctor and the spouse. Clergymen, teachers, relatives, friends, and even fellow patients often participate informally but helpfully in the process of readaptation.

All of the participants in this effort to bring about a favorable change in the patient—i.e., in his vital balance and life program—are imbued with what we may call a *therapeutic attitude*. This is one in direct antithesis to attitudes of avoidance, ridicule, scorn, or punitiveness. Hostile feelings toward the subject, however justified by his unpleasant and even destructive behavior, are not in the curriculum of therapy or in the therapist. This does not mean that therapists approve of the offensive and obnoxious behavior of the patient; they distinctly disapprove of it. But they recognize it as symptomatic of continued imbalance and disorganization, which is what they are seeking to change. They distinguish between disapproval, penalty, price, and punishment.

Doctors charge fees; they impose certain "penalties" or prices, but they have long since put aside primitive attitudes of retaliation toward offensive patients. A patient may cough in the doctor's face or may vomit on the office rug; a patient may curse or scream or even struggle in the extremity of his pain. But these acts are not "punished." Doctors and nurses have no time or thought for inflicting unnecessary pain even upon patients who may be difficult, disagreeable, provocative, and even dangerous. It is their duty to care for them, to try to make them well, and to prevent them from doing themselves or others harm. This requires love, not hate. This is the deepest meaning of the therapeutic attitude. Every doctor knows this; every worker in a hospital or clinic knows it (or should).

There is another element in the therapeutic attitude. It is the quality of hopefulness. If no one believes that the patient can get well, if no one—not even the doctor—has any hope, there probably won't be any recovery. Hope is just as important as love in the therapeutic attitude.

"But you were talking about the mentally ill," readers may interject, "those poor, confused, bereft, frightened individuals who yearn for help from you doctors and nurses. Do you mean to imply that willfully perverse individuals, our criminals, can be similarly reached and rehabilitated? Do you really believe that effective treatment of the sort you visualize can be applied to people *who do not want any help*, who are so willfully vicious, so well aware of the wrongs they are doing, so lacking in penitence or even common decency that punishment seems to be the only thing left?"

Do I believe there is effective treatment for offenders, and that they *can* be changed? *Most certainly and definitely I do.* Not all cases, to be sure; there are also some physical afflictions which we cannot cure at the moment. Some provision has to be made for incurables—pending new knowledge—and these will include some offenders. But I believe the majority of them would prove to be curable. The willfulness and the viciousness of offenders are part of the thing for which they have to be treated. These must not thwart the therapeutic attitude.

It is simply not true that most of them are "fully aware" of what they are doing, nor is it true that they want no help from anyone, although some of them say so. Prisoners are individuals: some want treatment, some do not. Some don't know what treatment is. Many are utterly despairing and hopeless. Where treatment is made available in institutions, many prisoners seek it even with the full knowledge that doing so will not lessen their sentences. In some prisons, seeking treatment by prisoners is frowned upon by the officials.

Various forms of treatment are even now being tried in some progressive courts and prisons over the country— educational, social, industrial, religious, recreational, and psychological treatments. Socially acceptable behavior, new work-play opportunities, new identity and companion patterns all help toward community reacceptance. Some parole officers and some wardens have been extremely ingenious in developing these modalities of rehabilitation and reconstruction—more than I could list here even if I knew them all. But some are trying. The secret of success in all programs, however, is the replacement of the punitive attitude with a therapeutic attitude.

Offenders with propensities for impulsive and predatory aggression should not be permitted to live among us unrestrained by some kind of social control. *But the great majority of offenders, even "criminals," should never become prisoners if we want to "cure" them.*

There are now throughout the country many citizens' action groups and programs for the prevention and control of crime and delinquency. With such attitudes of inquiry and concern, the public could acquire information (and incentive) leading to a change of feeling about crime and criminals. It will discover how unjust is much so-called "justice," how baffled and frustrated many judges are by the ossified rigidity of old-fashioned, obsolete laws and state constitutions which effectively prevent the introduction of sensible procedures to replace useless, harmful ones.

I want to proclaim to the public that things are not what it wishes them to be, and will only become so if it will take an interest in the matter and assume some responsibility for its own self-protection.

Will the public listen?

If the public does become interested, it will realize that we must have more facts, more trial projects, more checked results. It will share the dismay of the President's Commission on finding that no one knows much about even the incidence of crime with any definiteness or statistical accuracy.

The average citizen finds it difficult to see how any research would in any way change his mind about a man who brutally murders his children. But just such inconceivably awful acts most dramatically point up the need for research. Why should—how can—a man become so dreadful as that in our culture? How is such a man made? Is it comprehensible that he can be born to become so depraved?

There are thousands of questions regarding crime and public protection which deserve scientific study. What makes some individuals maintain their interior equilibrium by one kind of disturbance of the social structure rather than by another kind, one that would have landed him in a hospital? Why do some individuals specialize in certain types of crime? Why do so many young people reared in areas of delinquency and poverty and bad example never become habitual delinquents? (Perhaps this is a more important question than why some of them do.)

The public has a fascination for violence, and clings tenaciously to its yen for vengeance, blind and deaf to the expense, futility, and dangerousness of the resulting penal system. But we are bound to hope that this will yield in time to the persistent, penetrating light of intelligence and accumulating scientific knowledge. The public will grow increasingly ashamed of its cry for retaliation, its persistent demand to punish. This is its crime, *our* crime against criminals—and, incidentally, our crime against ourselves. For before we can diminish our sufferings from the ill-controlled aggressive assaults of fellow citizens, we must renounce the philosophy of punishment, the obsolete, vengeful penal attitude. In its place we would seek a comprehensive constructive social attitude—therapeutic in some instances, restraining in some instances, but preventive in its total social impact.

In the last analysis this becomes a question of personal morals and values. No matter how glorified or how piously disguised, vengeance as a human motive must be personally repudiated by each and every one of us. This is the message of old religions and new psychiatries. Unless this message is heard, unless we, the people—the man on the street, the housewife in the home—can give up our delicious satisfactions in opportunities for vengeful retaliation on scapegoats, we cannot expect to preserve our peace, our public safety, or our mental health.

QUESTIONS FOR DISCUSSION

1. *Since this book is entitled* Violence, *why did the authors include this article about the punishment of criminals?*
2. *According to Menninger, why has the public done very little about crime, violence, revenge, and injustice?*
3. *What are some of the external devices that control our "innate suicidal and criminal propensities"?*
4. *What does Menninger mean by this statement: "Because violence no longer has legitimate and useful vents or purposes, it must* all *be controlled today"?*

5. *"Why do the mechanisms of self-control fail so completely in some individuals?"*

6. *What does Menninger mean when he says, "Violence and crime are often attempts to escape from madness"? What are some of the examples he cites?*

7. *What would Dancey, in the previous article, say about the Menninger article?*

8. *Why, according to the author, are people attracted to weapons?*

9. *What are the ways by which we can reduce the aggressiveness of our fellow men?*

10. *Does Menninger feel that aggressive violence is a symptom of an illness? Does the public look upon violence in this way?*

11. *If violence is to be treated effectively, what must be done first?*

12. *What does Menninger mean when he says, "The present penal system and the existing legal philosophy do not stimulate or even expect such a change [of violent behavior] to take place in the criminal"?*

13. *What are the elements of the "therapeutic attitude"?*

14. *What is the "secret of success" in all programs dealing with the violent?*

Why We Are Having A Wave of Violence

JAMES Q. WILSON

Whatever the deficiencies with respect to our knowledge of individual forms of violence, at least we know enough to be able to answer the question, "How much of this violence will occur next year, or over the next five years?" The answer, obviously, is "about the same as this year." However, with respect to collective violence—riots, disorderly demonstrations and the like—we cannot even say that. The best we can do—and what, indeed, many commentators are doing—is to predict widespread violence so that if *any* violence occurs the prediction will appear to have been "correct." Logically, of course, it will not be correct: it would be as if a meteorologist were to predict that it will rain every day and then, on the day it does rain, to say he has been proved right.

Most theories of collective violence have as their principal defect that they over-predict the phenomenon. Some say that Negroes riot because their lot is deplorable—they have nothing to lose but their burdens. But the lot of many

Negroes has always been deplorable; indeed, by most standards it is much less deplorable today than 20 years ago.

Others modify the theory by introducing the notion of relative deprivation, or the "revolution of rising expectations." But Negroes have experienced such deprivations and such expectations before—during World War I, World War II and the Korean War, when their incomes rose rapidly, migration to the big cities was heavy and an awareness of and contact with the advantages of white society were widespread. There were no major Negro riots then; the only major riots were begun by *whites* and aimed at Negroes (Chicago in 1919, Detroit in 1943). The only major *Negro* riot took place in Harlem in the depths of the Depression (1935), when presumably there was a "revolution of decreasing expectations."

A third theory is that the riots are caused by conspirators who have recently become organized. There may have been one or two riots that were clearly begun by conspiratorial leaders and there probably have been many attempts by such groups to cause riots, but in the major upheavals—Watts, Detroit, Newark—the activities of the conspirators did not begin in earnest until after the riot had begun from apparently spontaneous causes.

The central problem is not to predict violence, but to explain why violence has occurred during the last two or three years *but not before*. Some commentators, of course, argue that there has always been violence in this country—from the Draft Riots in the eighteen-sixties through the labor riots that began with the railroad strikes of 1877 and continued through the nineteen-thirties (15 men were killed in the Little Steel Strikes of 1937)—and that the Negro rioting today is no worse and perhaps no different from earlier forms of violence. It has even been suggested that violence is in some sense a "normal" and perhaps legitimate political strategy for oppressed groups.

Whether the present riots are any worse than earlier

disorders is beside the point; whether they are in some sense legitimate is not beside the point but outside the scope of this paper. What can be said is that they are different. The Draft Riots were popular reactions against a certain concrete public policy, the enforcement of which was resisted by Irishmen and others who were not willing to restrict themselves to "going limp." The violence attending the labor disputes (in 1934 alone, nearly 30 people were killed) was in almost every case the result of an effort by a union to persuade management to recognize it. When management responded by calling in the Pinkertons and the scabs, the workers reacted with violent protest.

Labor-management violence was in the nature of an internal war between two organized opponents struggling over a quite tangible stake. With the winning of union recognition, the incidence of such violence dropped off markedly, though isolated cases recur from time to time, especially in the South.* Even the anti-Irish riots of the eighteen-forties and fifties were directed at an "enemy" and resulted in the destruction of "enemy" property; in Philadelphia, two Catholic churches and two parochial schools were burned to the ground; in St. Louis 50 Irish homes were wrecked and looted; in New York a mob marched on City Hall to attack anybody who looked Irish.†

The Negro riots are not apparently aimed at a specific enemy, they do not arise over a specific *issue* (though they may be precipitated by an "incident") and they do not carry the war to the enemy's territory. While it is true that white-owned business establishments are burned and looted, the amount of property owned or occupied by Negroes that is destroyed is often much greater. The Detroit Fire Depart-

---

* Philip Taft, "Violence in American Labor Disputes," *Annals*, Vol. 364 (March, 1966), pp. 127–140.

† Arnold Forster, "Violence on the Fanatical Left and Right," *Annals, op. cit.*, p. 143.

ment listed 477 buildings destroyed or damaged by fire in the 1967 riot. Of these, 103 were single family and multi-family homes, 30 were apartment buildings and 38 were stores which contained dwelling units. The vast majority were inhabited by Negroes, and many were owned by Negroes. Only five liquor stores, two loan shops, four jewelry stores and one bank were burned, even though these establishments presumably represent "white business" and may be perceived as "white exploitation." Many other, more obvious symbols of white authority—churches, schools, newspaper circulation offices, police buildings—were scarcely touched. To compare these riots with earlier historical examples is like comparing assault to self-flagellation—such pleasure as the latter confers does not depend on the suffering it causes others.

When people destroy their own communities, even at high risk to themselves (43 persons died in Detroit, most from police and National Guard bullets), it is difficult to assert that the riot was an *instrumental* act—that is, an effort to achieve an objective. (The Draft Riots, the anti-Irish riots, the violence practiced by the Ku Klux Klan and the labor-management violence were all to some degree instrumental acts.) The Negro riots are in fact *expressive* acts—that is, actions which are either intrinsically satisfying ("play") or satisfying because they give expression to a state of mind.

Of course, for many people in all riots—whether instrumental or expressive—there are individual gratifications, such as the opportunity for looting, for settling old scores and the like. But these people operate, so to speak, under the cover of the riot and are not obviously the cause of it. To the extent riots are or can be organized, of course, the need to offer incentives to induce people to participate would make the encouragement of looting a prime objective for a riot leader—not only does it get people out on the street in large numbers and put them in an excited state of mind, it disperses and preoccupies police and military forces. There is little evidence yet, however, that it is the desire for loot that precipitates the riot or even plays a very important part in the early hours.

If we are to construct an explanation for what has occurred—and we may never have a testable explanation, for the requirements of experimental or statistical control necessary to test any riot hypothesis are not likely to exist— we must combine attention to the material conditions in which the Negro lives (which on the whole have been improving but are still poor) with the costs and benefits to him of expressing a desire for autonomy, manhood, self-respect and the capacity for independent action.

On the cost side, we note a significant reduction in the willingness of those who command the police to use them with maximum vigor in suppressing disorder. The attention given of late to real and imagined cases of "police brutality" has obscured the fact that, compared to the police response to labor violence even 30 years ago, most big-city police departments, especially in the North, have recently been less inclined, primarily for political reasons, to use instant and massive retaliatory tactics against any incipient disorder. It would appear that this is one reason the majority of serious riots have occurred in the North, not the South —in the latter region, political constraints on the police are less effective.

One need not deny that police-citizen contacts have often been the spark that triggered a riot, or that many departments have neglected or mismanaged their community relations program, to argue that the police, if they wanted to (that is, if they were willing to pay the price in lives and political support), could make the costs of rioting so high that either there would be no riots at all or there would be a massive convulsion equivalent to civil war.

On the benefits side, persons are coming of age who are several generations away from the rural South and who accordingly have lost their fear of white men without yet having had an opportunity to even scores. Young people are always rebellious; when young people grow up and discover that their elders are *also* rebellious, there is perhaps an urge for even more extreme actions. Just as the sons and daughters of New Deal liberals regard their parents as "square" for confining their demands for change to the rules imposed by the existing political system, so also the sons and daughters of Negroes who have demanded integration and equal opportunity may feel that such demands are not enough because they are based on an acceptance of the distribution of power within the existing social order.

Negro (and some white) leaders, aware of the drift toward violent sentiments, have attempted to take advantage of it by using the threat of violence as a way of increasing their bargaining power; the difficulty, of course, is that the responsible leaders have lacked the capacity either to start or stop a riot while the irresponsible ones have simply lacked the power to stop one.

Furthermore, the mass media—especially television— offer an opportunity for immediate expressive gratification that did not exist even 15 years ago. It is interesting to speculate on what the Know-Nothing violence might have been like if every American could watch in his living room the looting of a convent while it was happening and if every would-be looter could be summoned to the scene by immediate radio coverage of the event.

Finally, young people today, white and Negro, have become quite self-conscious, for reasons I obviously do not understand, about the social functions and therapeutic value of violence. A generation that was absorbed by Camus's intricate analysis of how in existential terms one might have justified the effort to assassinate the czar has given way to a generation some members of which are absorbed by Frantz Fanon's argument for violence: Violence, if practiced by the wretched and oppressed, may be intrinsically valuable as an assertion of self and a reversal of a previous act of violence—slavery—by which self has been denied and subjugation institutionalized.*

In short, the few things we know about the riots—that they develop out of a seemingly trivial incident, that they are more expressive than instrumental and that they have thus far occurred primarily in Northern cities or in the more "progressive" Southern cities (such as Atlanta or Nashville)—should lead us to be skeptical of arguments that the riots can be explained entirely or primarily on grounds of *material* deprivation, unresponsive local governments, inadequate poverty programs or the like. No doubt these factors play a part. After all, if the class characteristics of Negroes were identical to those of whites (measured by income, education, mobility and level of political organization), it is hard to imagine that there would be any riots, though there still might be a good deal of discontent. If there were no lower class, there would be fewer riots just as there would be fewer murders. But if class is a necessary explanation, it is not a sufficient one. To material (that is to say, to Marxian) explanations must be added explanations that take into account the role of *ideas* and the role of *force*.

It is hard to discuss such things without being misunderstood. To impute causal power to ideas or to the lack of force seems to imply the desirability of censoring ideas or imposing the most repressive kinds of force. That is not the implication I intend. To try to censor ideas is both wrong and futile; repressive force is neither available nor manageable. The argument here is analytic, not prescriptive, and is

* Aristide and Vera Zolberg, "The Americanization of Frantz Fanon," The Public Interest (Fall, 1967), pp. 49–63.

designed merely to suggest that we consider the possibility that ideas have consequences.

Theories of social change are often suspect in my eyes because they seem to lead automatically to the policy conclusion favored by their author: It is as if one decided what program one wanted adopted and then decided what "caused" an event in order to justify that remedial program. If one wants a "Marshall Plan" for Negroes, then economic want causes riots; if one wishes the political power of the "Establishment" weakened, then inadequate access and a lack of self-determination are the causes; if one wants Stokely Carmichael and Rap Brown put in jail, then conspirators are the cause. Since almost no one wants (at least publicly) ideas to be controlled, the causal power of ideas is rarely asserted; this theory gets fewer "votes" than it may deserve because it is not in anyone's interest to vote for it.

But if elsewhere ideas are readily conceded to have consequences—"nationalism," "self-determination," "the world community revolution"—might it not be possible that they have consequences here also? Only a fear of being thought illiberal may prevent us from considering that the probability of a riot is increased by demands for "Black Power," by a constant reiteration that white bigotry and racism are at the root of all the problems besetting the Negro, by the reaffirmation of the (untrue) assumption that most Negroes live wretched lives and that matters are going from bad to worse, by constantly predicting apocalyptic violence if "something isn't done" and by "discovering" the nontruth that all Negroes are alike in their hatred of "whitey" and their tacit or open approval of extreme solutions for their plight.*

If there is something in the climate of opinion, the mood of a generation or the drift of sentiments that contrib-

* Gary T. Marx, "Protest and Prejudice" (New York, 1967).

utes to Negro riots, there is no reason to suppose that only Negroes are affected by these currents. The special and urgent problem of the Negro may lead us to assume, without sufficient reflection, that the Negro case is not only special but unique. But it ought not be taken for granted that 20 million people are affected by ideas that have no effect on the other 180 million living in the same country.

More narrowly, are young Negroes involved in a radical discontinuity in American history or are they simply at the leading edge of a more general drift toward collective violence? Are we quite confident that there is no connection between Negroes burning down their communities and young whites storming the Pentagon, assaulting Cabinet officers and forcibly occupying university buildings? Or between these acts and the sharp rise in recruitment to the Ku Klux Klan and the emergence of the ominous White Knights and the Minutemen? And if there is a connection, is the entire phenomenon to be put down to "rising expectations" or "unresponsive government"?

I cannot say there is a connection, but I cannot accept without some persuasion the answer that the Negro is wholly a special case. Collective violence was once thought to be an inevitable aspect of the political life of any country, even this one. In 1947, in the second edition of his famous text on political parties, the late V. O. Key Jr. devoted a full chapter to the political role of force. By 1958, when the fourth edition appeared, that chapter had been reduced to a page and a half. And by 1961, when his book on public opinion appeared, there was a chapter on "conflict" but no mention of violent conflict.

Traditionally, one would expect violence whenever there were deep and irreconcilable differences of opinion on fundamental issues in a society where one party had no confidence in the capacity of the other party to govern. (The distrust between the Socialists and Conservatives in prewar Austria was, of course, a classic case; a postwar government was possible only on the basis of a coalition that permitted one party to check the other in the ministries as well as in Parliament—a form of "participatory democracy.") One would also expect violence when, though the nation is not deeply divided, established authority is unwilling to use force to make the costs of violence prohibitively great for any minority unwilling to resign itself to losing in a nonviolent struggle for power.

If the traditional understanding of violence were applied today, one would not expect it to subside once the "demands" of Negroes (or peace marchers, or whatever) were met. One reason is that the demands cannot be met—the competition for leadership among the (largely disorganized) dissident groups will inevitably generate ever more extreme demands faster than less extreme requests are fulfilled.

Another reason is that violent political conflict is only rarely over tangible resources which the government can allocate—it is typically over symbolic values which government either does not control (the sense of equality or human dignity or social acceptance) or does control but cannot redistribute without destroying itself (sending the Irish back to Ireland, abandoning military force as a tool of foreign policy). But primarily violence will not subside because it is the cleavage in opinion which gives rise to it, and concessions sufficient to induce one side to abandon violence (subject to the constraints cited above) might be concessions sufficient to induce the other side to resort to violence.

To cut through the vicious circle, governments historically have increased the application of force to the point that neither side found it rewarding to practice violence, thus inducing both sides to wait for long-term trends to soften or alter the cleavages of opinion. Such increases in force have often required a reduction in the degree to which the use of force was subject to democratic constraints. Parliamentary regimes have been replaced by presidential regimes; presidential regimes have been replaced by dictatorial regimes. Only when it is clear that *neither* side can gain through violent protest does the resort to such forms of protest cease. The case for dealing with the conditions under which Negroes (or poor whites) live is not, therefore, to be made on the grounds that such efforts will "stop riots"; it can be made only on the grounds that for other, and essentially moral, reasons changing those conditions is right and necessary.

Whether this analysis has any applicability to present-day America is difficult to say. One would first have to estimate the probability of white violence against Negroes (or hawk violence against doves) under various kinds of governmental concessions to Negroes (or doves), and no one is competent to make any confident predictions on these matters. What can be said is that long-term prosperity is no guarantee against political violence of some form. Prosperity cannot by itself eliminate the ideological sources of violence and indeed may weaken the institutional constraints on it so that the effects of the activities of even a few persons with violent intentions may be amplified by an increasingly larger multiplier and thus influence the action of ever larger numbers of persons.

This consequence of prosperity may arise through the dispersal of power and authority that tends to result from the entry of more and more persons into middle-class status and thus into the forms of participation in public life that are reserved for the middle class. Middle-class persons participate in voluntary associations and public affairs more than working-class persons (and certainly more than lower-class persons, who scarcely participate at all). The higher the level of participation, the larger the number and variety of voluntary associations (and social movements) and the more wills which must be concerted in the making of public policy.* "Participatory democracy" may be a slogan currently linked with the aspirations of the underprivileged, but in fact participatory democracy has all along been the political style (if not the slogan) of the American middle and upper-middle class. It will become a more widespread style as more persons enter into these classes.

Additionally, continued prosperity will increasingly free young people from the pinch of economic necessity (the need to get a job early in life), place more of them in colleges and universities—where, for better or worse, traditional values are questioned—and increase the number (if not the proportion) of those who find various kinds of personal and political nonconformity attractive.

With participation in greater variety and numbers, the possibility of any one or few organizations dominating the expression of some common interest (civil rights, peace, governmental reform) will be lessened and the competition among such groups will increase. The sensitivity of more and more persons to the substance of issues will reduce the capacity of government to act without regard to these views, and the high (but quite selective) visibility given to governmental acts by television will reduce the capacity of government to act at all in ways (e.g., the use of force or a display of indifference) once employed more readily because less visibly.

In short, marches, protests, sit-ins, demonstrations, mass meetings and other forms of direct collective action may become more rather than less common, though it is hard to predict what issues will prove sufficiently salient to generate such activities. How many will be violent no one can say, but it is not unreasonable to assume that if large numbers of people are brought together in public places be-

* Cf. Edward C. Banfield and James Q. Wilson, "City Politics" (Cambridge, 1963), esp. concluding chapter.

cause of issues about which they feel strongly, a certain though unknown proportion will—either because they seek violence ("confrontation politics") or because they feel provoked by the police or other opponents—take matters into their own hands.

Since people are most likely to feel strongly about symbolic or intangible issues, and since governments can only deal slowly (if at all) with such matters, the probability of at least disorder and possibly violence is likely to increase over time. The civil rights march on Washington in 1963 was orderly and well-led; early peace marches were of the same character. Recent peace marches were less orderly, and it seems unlikely any new civil rights march will be immune from the same forces leading to disorganization, spontaneity and violence.

But even this "prediction" must be hedged with qualifications. Other, as yet unforeseen, changes in sentiment and ideology may occur with the result that such tendencies toward collective assertion and violence may be redirected. Perhaps collective violence will undergo a transformation parallel to that affecting individual violence; just as murder gives way to suicide, child-beating to child "guidance" and rape to seduction and perversion with the middle-classifying of the poor, so also might political violence give way to civility and rhetoric.

The most that can be said for the argument sketched in this article is that one should not assume that these changes in character are themselves sufficient to change the manner in which politics is carried on. Profound institutional and organizational changes are likely to occur also, and these, by making the system more sensitive—even vulnerable—to the diminishing amount of violent instincts among individuals, will produce a net increase in violent *behavior* with no net increase in violent *attitudes*. If that occurs, the existence or threat of lower-class violence, which dominated the politics of the 19th century, may be replaced by the threat of middle-class violence during the 21st.

QUESTIONS FOR DISCUSSION

1. *According to Wilson, what is the principal defect in the theories of collective violence?*

2. *How does the author react to the following theories about why Negroes riot? 1. Their lot is deplorable. 2. They are experiencing a "revolution of rising expectations."*

3. *What does Wilson say about the theory that riots are caused by conspirators who have recently been organized?*

4. *According to the author, how do the Negro riots differ from previous periods of violence in our history?*

5. *What is one reason why the majority of serious riots have occurred in the North, not the South?*

6. *Why are the young particularly inclined to violence?*

7. *How has the mass media affected violence?*

8. *According to the author, how do young people feel about the social functions and therapeutic value of violence?*

9. *What are the few things, according to Wilson, that we know about riots?*

10. Traditionally, *where or under what conditions would one expect violence?*

11. *Why does Wilson believe that we should not expect violence to subside once the "demands" of Negroes are met?*

12. *When, historically, do groups cease to resort to violent protest?*

13. *Why does Wilson believe that "long-term prosperity is no guarantee against political violence of some form"?*

14. *Will "participatory democracy" reduce violence?*

15. *Does Wilson feel that middle-class violence may be the major threat in the twenty-first century?*

The Ways of Violence

ERNEST W. RANLY

Now that the making of homemade bombs has become a popular indoor sport, people are asking "where have all the flowers gone." How has the simplistic nonviolence of the flower children evolved into the fire-bombing crazies of today? Most answers simply recount the sequence of historical events. Beginning with the sit-ins and the freedom riders of the early 60's, through the slow disenchantment of the leaders of SNCC and the early Berkeley protests against the Vietnam war, leading to the bloody bath of the 1968 Democratic Convention in Chicago, the general direction of all civil demonstrations has been from nonviolence to violence.

Discussions on violence and nonviolence are, however, difficult and confusing. Precise definitions and clear moral evaluations are hard to come by. Gandhi himself spoke of "the violence of nonviolence." So my aim here is not to present a swift survey of the protest movement of the past decade, but to classify and define six distinct groups of people in respect to their relation to violence and nonviolence. My goal is clarification and understanding.

1. First of all there is Mr. Straight Citizen, who never consciously breaks a law and never violates the personal or property rights of his neighbor. He believes the laws of the land are generally fair and just, and that all necessary social and political change can be brought about through normal legal, political processes. Mr. Straight Citizen may have no personal *credo* about nonviolence. He probably uses corporal punishment on his own children, believes in the right of physical self-defense and supports the foreign wars of his country. Mr. Straight Citizen considers himself a "law-abiding citizen" and somehow feels that he is opposed to all violence and that something should be done about the "prevention of violence."

2. Secondly, there is Miss Simple Protester (like the heroine of *I Am Curious: Yellow.*) Miss Simple Protester sees racial discrimination, class distinctions, economic inequalities and a number of civil, social problems. She feels that the normal political processes are adequate for social reform, but she thinks the public needs education and the political machinery needs prodding. Her forms of protest are very carefully planned and always perfectly legal. She checks the areas where free assembly is allowed, acquires the proper parade permits and makes sure that no banners are destructive of public morals. There is no force here, no threat of violence, no threat even of economic boycott. The demonstrations have as their goal to influence public opinion to the extent that due legal processes will be undertaken to remedy the particular evils under attack.

The Straight Citizens of America appreciate free speech and free assembly and the history of women suffrage and labor strikes; they must allow the Simple Protesters to

stage their demonstrations. As long as no laws are broken
and the rights of others are in no way curtailed, Mr.
Straight Citizen cannot really forbid his own daughter to
become a Miss Simple Protester. These were the activities
of the early Civil Rights Movement. But this is as far as
non-violence dare go!

3. The third personality is the Rev. Passive Resistance.
Fired with moral and religious indignation over man's injustice toward his fellow-man, the person of passive resistance
aggressively initiates all possible legal alternatives to bring
about civil reform. Rev. Passive Resistance organizes and
supports legal strikes, economic boycotts and "sick-ins." He
will organize citizen committees to bring pressure to bear
upon school boards, city councils, labor unions and state-
federal legislatures.

The single most effective and dramatic weapon of Rev.
Passive Resistance is the dramatic weapon of deliberate and
cautious civil disobedience. He will disobey those laws he
feels with warm and reasoned conviction are unjust laws,
laws opposed to the common good, laws opposed to the
rights and dignity of man. At this point he becomes Rev.
Civil Disobedience, breaking a civil statutory (non-crimi-
nal) law, but a non-moral law, which in no direct way in-
jures the person or the property of another person. In the
best tradition of Gandhi, he willingly faces arrest, jail, trial
and all the due process of law, as befits one who breaks a
civil law.

Meanwhile, his acts of civil disobedience initiate legal
and political action in two directions. Either a legal action
will challenge the constitutionality of the law itself, or new
legislation is enacted to remedy and reform the situation. It
is evident that Rev. Passive Resistance fully trusts the actual authority and the effectiveness of government, law and
society. He has some particular, very severe criticism, but he
feels that this can be reformed within the system itself. He

sincerely and publicly declares himself non-violent. Mr.
Straight Citizen is quite disturbed, for he sees only an infringement of law and order; but Rev. Civil Disobedience
calmly stands his ground. He in no way seeks to injure his
antagonist; he "breaks an unjust law openly, lovingly," as
Dr. Martin Luther King, Jr. stated it. He inflicts no physical
injury upon others, nor damages the property of others. He
breaks only those laws or those applications and interpretations of laws he sincerely considers to be unjust.

4. The fourth man is Mr. Active Resistance. A man
turns from passive to active resistance when he recognizes
that the evils he wishes to eradicate are so deeply imbedded
in society and government that civil reform through a few
court decisions and a few new laws are wholly inadequate.
Staughton Lynd, writing from jail, states in the booklet
Delivered Into Resistance: "Resistance attacks evils which
cannot be remedied by a single administrative decision or a
particular new law. Its targets are deep-seated ills, such as
racism, or this country's imperialist foreign policy. . . . Without yet seeking to overthrow the government, resisters de-
clare their determination to overthrow a given policy or
complex institutions by refusing to obey them or to permit
them to function."

The line between passive and active resistance is precisely the line between liberalism and radicalism. William
Kunster is a case in point. For almost a decade he was a
"liberal" lawyer, slowly working out his civil rights cases
within the tradition of the American courts. After Chicago,
1968, he became radical. He now holds that reform and
reconstruction of legal and political institutions must come
about more rapidly and more directly.

The tactics of active resistance are two-fold. Mr.
Active Resistance will engage actively in Gandhi's strategy
of non-cooperation. He will "refuse to obey" those laws or
those policies that directly continue or support areas of

social-political life he considers evil. He will burn his draft card and be imprisoned before serving in military service. Or once inducted, he will obstruct military procedures from within. At other times, he blocks entrances to offices, sits down in doorways and engages in any number of obstructionist tactics. Moreover, he will actively plot to disrupt those policies and institutions he considers evil. He will burn files of selective service offices, destroy the private property of companies manufacturing lethal products.

Mr. Active Resistance, as we shall see, is not a revolutionary and, in his special meaning of the word, he insists that he is completely non-violent. He is not a revolutionary, because, for all his biting criticism of the establishment, he does not seek to overthrow the government. As Staughton Lynd goes on to say: "The resister does not rely on the electoral process or the courts to bring about the change he seeks, but he leaves open the possibility that these conventional institutions can adapt themselves to change effected by more direct means."

While the actions of Mr. Active Resistance are disruptive and destructive to a degree, they are completely open and largely symbolic. They are meant to be publicly shocking, in order to draw dramatic attention to the evils under attack. Each action, therefore, is immediately related in fact and in the public imagination to the so-called evils in the social-political body. Mr. Active Resistance offers himself as a classic martyr to his cause. He will draw attention to his act, undergo public arrest and use every private and public opportunity to speak out against the social evils he deplores.

In *The History of Violence in America*, a report to the National Commission on the Causes and Prevention of Violence, the editors, Hugh Davis Graham and Ted Robert Gurr, narrowly define violence in their introduction "as behavior designed to inflict injury to people or damage to property." If all "damage to property" is violence, then many acts of Mr. Active Resistance are "violent." But he strongly insists he is not violent. He refuses to injure his antagonist. He carefully avoids all physical harm to persons. His actions are directed against only those policies or those programs by the government or by private corporations that are considered to be the chief perpetrators and the major symbols of evil.

Mr. Active Resistance declares, in the words of the nine arrested at Catonsville, Maryland, for the burning of selective service files: "We believe some property has no right to exist. Hitler's gas ovens, Stalin's concentration camps, atomic-bacteriological-chemical weaponry, files of conscription and slum properties are examples having no right to existence."

According to the principle made popular by so many student protesters, "people are more important than property," the destruction of private property may at times be necessary in order to stop and restrain many more corrosive types of social violence. The property destroyed, however, is governmental or corporate, not the private, personal property of individuals, such as someone's home. In all his actions, Mr. Active Resistance declares himself very much in the tradition of non-violence. He speaks of warm, personal values and peacefully accepts arrest and imprisonment.

5. The fifth man is the Militant. The Militant makes his presence known very aggressively by his dress, word and stance. His stance is one of impatience, anger and readiness to strike. Some of our militants come through the ranks, from simple protest to passive resistance to active resistance; others come right off the streets and out of the jails. The Militant is less reflective; he tends to be all talk, all action. At different times he will cooperate with all the

lower levels of the so-called Movement, but he will always add his own style. Intrinsic to the Militant's style and rhetoric is his active threat of violence.

The Militant has no theoretical objection to the use of active violence as part of his strategy and tactics. In fact, he makes the threat of violence an integral part of his position. There is open and eager talk of violence; there is active, immediate preparation for violence; arms are stacked, personnel are trained. The Militant insists, however, that he will not *initiate* violence. For him, therefore, the threat of violence is a means of deterrence to avoid and stop future violence—an extension, as it were, of every man's right to self-defense. The nations of the world build up their military strength for the same reasons. Each nation claims to be peaceful, yet feels that military preparations are a necessary means to maintain peace. It is a moot question whether stockpiling of deterrent weapons necessarily involves a hypothetical intention to resort to the use of such arms. Can one actively threaten violence and still insist he is non-violent, that he really does not intend to use these weapons?

The Militant, nevertheless, is not yet an out-and-out revolutionary. There is an openness, an honesty, a frankness about the Militant that is refreshing and healthy. He has a sense of personal responsibility about his own need for self-determination. He seeks not so much to overthrow the establishment, as to "do his own thing" without interference from the establishment. What he thinks he speaks out very publicly; his plans and strategies are published in his own underground papers. He is an easy subject for the mass media.

6. The sixth and last man is the Revolutionary who seeks to destroy the existing establishment. He may be an out-and-out anarchist, seeking the total abolition of authority, government and laws. Or he may be some social-political visionary who feels that the destruction of the old

order will automatically issue in a new and better order. Or he may want to destroy precisely in order to replace things with a new structure, a new system, new laws and new authority. The Revolutionary enters upon the scene only after there has been a long and notable break in communication and trust between the established authorities and discontented segments of the population. A number of sporadic, spontaneous outbursts of burning, looting and rioting are early signs of revolutionary fever. The second stage is the planned, deliberate attacks upon the police and the military. This is followed by waves of terrorism, and, finally, the fourth stage, of fully deliberate, planned, total revolution.

One characteristic of the Revolutionary, in contrast to the other five types, is that he is elusive, furtive, secretive about his activity. He avoids public talk and public arrest. He strikes and runs. A second characteristic is that open and deliberate violence is intrinsic to his strategy and to his activity. At the first stage, that of burning and looting, there may be no direct personal attack or bodily injury to persons, but there is no theoretical objection to personal violence. At each of the next steps in revolution, direct violence is explicitly called for.

The violence of terrorism is particularly unnerving, for terrorism involves the indiscriminate bombing and mining of public places, the killing of the innocent as well as of so-called combatants, in a deliberate effort to terrorize the people and to undermine the loyalty of the government's subjects. In most revolutions, terrorist tactics are matched by counter-terrorism on the other side until, finally, clear battle lines are drawn up and the revolution takes on the style of a traditional war, with opposing armies and governments. In Mao Tse-tung's guerrilla theory and tactics this last stage may never fully emerge. Some Committee or Front is organized among the revolutionaries, and it becomes the spokesman and the arbitrator for the revolution.

But the entire "war" (usually a war of liberation carried on by the indigent natives against some "foreign" or "colonizing" government) will be little more than minor military skirmishes in the form of terrorist raids and guerrilla ambushes.

From the time of John Locke and the American Revolution, a theory that justifies violent revolution has been universally accepted by political theorists and practical statesmen. While anarchical revolution seems to have little theoretical moral justification, a "positive" revolution is justified by the same conditions required for a just war. According to this theory, therefore, if the social-political situation is irredeemably bad, if all other avenues of reform have failed, if there is reasonable, practical hope for a real improvement of conditions, then revolution, with due proportionate violence inherent in it, is morally and humanly justified.

These six categories represent six distinct attitudes towards violence and nonviolence. What is sorely needed today is understanding on all sides. Those outside the Movement must carefully note and sympathetically understand the rather technical meaning of "nonviolence" for Gandhi, Martin Luther King, Jr., and their followers. All groups, except the actual revolutionaries, publicly and sincerely profess a type of nonviolence. There are, however, carefully distinguished degrees of violence in nonviolence.

On the other hand, those inside the Movement should become more reflective and critical about the meaning and the effects of their words and actions. Postures, words and actions have necessary consequences. Those in both passive and active resistance movements, in spite of their original sincere dedication to nonviolence, tend to overstate their position or to over-react to political and juridical repression. As a result, they suddenly find themselves in positions where violence seems to be the only alternative. One hesitates to admit that any historical necessity can drive the nonviolent to violence. But then, those dedicated to the principles of nonviolence must never allow themselves to act or react on grounds outside their own principles.

QUESTIONS FOR DISCUSSION

1. *How can those who are advocating some degree of violence and those who are not benefit from reading this essay?*
2. *Explain how Mr. Straight Citizen differs from Miss Simple Protester.*
3. *What is the chief difference between Miss Simple Protester and the Rev. Passive Resistance?*
4. *What separates Rev. Passive Resistance from Mr. Active Resistance?*
5. *Is there really a difference between Mr. Active Resistance and the Militant?*
6. *What distinguishes the Militant from the Revolutionary?*
7. *In which category do you fit?*
8. *Which category is most responsible for violence in our society?*

Violence: the View from the Ghetto

HARLAN HAHN

It has become almost commonplace, in some quarters, to refer to America as a "sick society." Although a number of symptoms may be cited to support this diagnosis, perhaps the most discussed indication of a general malaise is the prevalence of violence. Rising crime rates, the assassination of public leaders, urban riots, and the continuing scourge of war seem to suggest the strains of modern life that could result in a massive social conflagration.

Violence, however, can be viewed in several ways. In particular, civil disorders that have erupted in the black ghettos of many cities may reflect an understandable reaction to centuries of deprivation and frustration. As the Kerner Commission[1] concluded, perhaps the basic cause of the disturbances was not the antisocial tendencies of the rioters, but the pervasive effects of "white racism." The riots, therefore, may be symptomatic of a deeper social malady that could pose an even more dangerous threat than the outbreak of ghetto violence.

Harlan Hahn, "Violence: The View from the Ghetto," *Mental Hygiene*, October 1969, pp. 509–512.

An informed approach to the issues raised by urban riots will require increased knowledge of both the causes of disorders and the distribution of sentiments about violence among groups that are susceptible to rioting. One of the most accurate methods of assessing social patterns and conditions is provided by public opinion surveys. Although the technique cannot replace detailed psychiatric and personality evaluations, this appraisal may be of great value to professional and voluntary workers in mental health who must deal effectively with the problems that they encounter in the community.

Since the riots of 1967 indicated that the greatest propensity for violence may be found in urban ghettos, this study will compare the attitudes and behavior reported by ghetto residents in two separate surveys. The first survey was of a modified quota sample of 270 black residents of the Twelfth Street area of Detroit conducted by the author shortly after the riots in 1967. The second survey, of a random probability sample of 2,814 black respondents in 15 cities, sponsored by the Kerner Commission and conducted by Campbell and Schuman[2] in 1968, found that "the Negro mass is far less revolutionary in its outlook than its more militant spokesmen" and that the "changes they have in mind are essentially conservative in nature." Although both the questions and procedures used in the surveys were generally comparable, there was a basic difference between the two investigations. Only five of the cities studied by Campbell and Schuman had experienced a major disturbance, whereas all of the respondents in the Detroit research had been personally affected by a serious riot. This major distinction between the studies seemed to yield sharply contrasting results.

In assessing the probable outcome of riots, for example, black citizens who had experienced a major disorder were much more optimistic about the prospects for social progress than those who lived in relatively untroubled communities. Only a third of those questioned in the Campbell-Schuman study felt that the disturbances had "helped the cause of Negro rights," and at least one-fourth believed that their main effect would be harmful. By contrast, 62 per cent of the residents in Detroit predicted that the riot would "help what most civil rights groups were trying to accomplish."

The tendency of respondents in the Campbell-Schuman study to emphasize the negative consequences of violence was also reflected in their sentiments about black militancy: only 9 per cent agreed with the statement "Negroes should have nothing to do with whites if they can help it." On the other hand, when Detroit residents were asked whether they "should integrate with whites" or "try to get along without whites," support for black separatism was expressed by 22 per cent of the respondents.

Persons who had undergone a major riot were more likely to support the need for violence than the mass of black Americans who had not been involved in civil disorders. In reply to a direct inquiry about "the best way for Negroes to gain their rights," only 15 per cent of those in the Campbell-Schuman survey asserted that they would "be ready to use violence." A similar question in the Detroit survey, which asked persons to assess the fastest way "for Negroes to get what they want," revealed that twice as many respondents—32 per cent—chose violence rather than peaceful or non-violent protests.

Since violence may often be triggered by a provocative incident rather than by an explicit plan, both surveys included questions about hypothetical events that could foment rioting. In the Campbell-Schuman study, when respondents were asked what they would do about a situation involving a "white storekeeper in a Negro neighborhood" who "refuses to hire any Negro clerks," 73 per cent suggested formally sanctioned methods of protest such as boycotts, petitions, appeals to public agencies, and non-violent demonstrations.

As the Kerner Commission noted, however, most of the major riots in U. S. cities have been sparked by an encounter with the police. In the Detroit survey, residents of the Twelfth Street area were asked how they would react to "a policeman beating up someone from the neighborhood." More than 27 per cent said they would engage in the potentially riot-precipitating activity of "going to other people for help," and 10 per cent stated that they would "wait around to see what happens." Only 44 per cent reported that they would respond in the socially approved manner of lodging a complaint with a city agency.

The results of the two surveys were also sharply divided in their estimates of riot participation. The Campbell-Schuman survey posed the question: "If a disturbance like the one in Detroit or Newark . . . broke out here, do you think you would join in, or would you try to stop it, or would you stay away from it?" Only 8 per cent stated that they would join the riot. Although the Detroit survey did not include a comparable question on self-reported rioting, several other measures disclosed that actual participation in the disturbances may have been more extensive than had been estimated. More than 60 per cent of the residents of the Twelfth Street ghetto reported that, during the riot, they "got out to see what was happening." In addition, 58 per cent estimated that one in ten or more of their neighbors were involved in the violence; and one-third reported participation at more than 25 per cent. In addition to their optimism about the effects of civil disorders, greater militancy, and increased support for violence, black residents of a riot-torn neighborhood gave higher estimates of riot participation than those who lived elsewhere.

Why were there important discrepancies in the findings of the two studies? As Campbell and Schuman commented, "The word 'protest' is a key one." Although many people viewed the disorders as a protest against economic and social conditions, those who had experienced violence were inclined to attribute other objectives to the rioting. In fact, the Detroit respondents were somewhat less likely to perceive the riots as a means of protest than ghetto residents in other cities.

The Detroit survey revealed that the rioting was motivated by many factors, including a wish for vengeance and a desire for the consumer goods associated with middle-class life. But the responses obtained in the Twelfth Street area were also distinguished by a prevalence of demands for fundamental social and political changes.

The tendency to see the riots as a form of protest, or an attempt to obtain recognition and assistance from white authorities, seemed to be associated with a degree of confidence in public officials. In the Campbell-Schuman study, 47 per cent of the respondents felt that their local mayor was "trying as hard as he could" to solve the problems of the city. Furthermore, 39 per cent said the federal government was seriously trying to solve urban problems, and one-third ascribed the same intentions to state governments.

On the other hand, members of the Detroit community, who had been involved in the riots, expressed little respect for political leaders or government programs. More than 36 per cent were critical of the way Mayor Jerome Cavanaugh had handled the disturbances, and 22 per cent sought to remove him from office. Seventy-eight per cent of the Detroit respondents believed that, before the riots, the government was merely trying "to keep things quiet"; only 18 per cent thought that government leaders "really were interested in solving the problems that the Negro faces in this city." Their faith in the efficacy of violence, however, was reflected in growing optimism as a result of the disorders. After the riot, the proportion that believed the government would really try to solve problems increased by nearly one-half.

Black respondents in the Campbell-Schuman survey, who viewed the riots as an effort to secure reforms without basically restructuring the political system, supported present policies to aid the ghettos. For example, 75 per cent evaluated the federal antipoverty program in favorable terms. By contrast, in the Detroit survey, 41 per cent disapproved of the way the antipoverty program was being handled, only 36 per cent approved, and 23 per cent were undecided.

Dissatisfaction with existing political programs, public officials, and government objectives in the Twelfth Street neighborhood, however, did not necessarily imply a desire to retreat from social or political movements. On the contrary, the violence seemed to inspire a stronger sense of community and a hope for increased participation in the development of public policy. Forty-six per cent of the area residents stated flatly that people in the neighborhood would have "more power" after the riot, and 61 per cent predicted that they would receive "more attention from city officials." In addition, 73 per cent believed that they would have "more to say about what should be done in this neighborhood." The people who had lived through a major riot sought—and expected—an increased opportunity for political participation and an expanded public role in the solution of local problems.

The differences in the attitudes and behavior of residents in an area that had undergone violence and others living elsewhere seemed to reflect distinct social or political objectives. Black citizens outside a neighborhood that had exploded in riots tended to perceive the violence as a method of securing a response rather than as a conflict with white authorities. On the other hand, those who had experienced a major disturbance appeared to view it as part of a rebellion or a direct confrontation.

The evidence also suggests that violence may occur in areas where it has erupted previously. Specific local problems that were not present in most communities may have played a critical role in sparking the disturbances.

Perhaps the most important implication of the comparison of the two surveys, however, is that the mood of black Americans should not be misjudged by neglecting the sentiments of special segments of the population. Many black Americans may have essentially conservative objectives; but other—and perhaps equally important—groups seem to express radical goals and expectations. The results of the Detroit survey indicated that the riots were not stimulated solely by destructive or antisocial behavior. Instead, the disorders appeared to represent a direct effort to obtain basic changes in existing social and political arrangements.

The violence in the ghettos does not seem to indicate a unique ailment, but it may reflect a general malady that has prevented social philosophies and institutions from adapting to new demands and aspirations. The future health of the society may depend on the ability of public programs to accommodate to the needs of particular groups in the population.

The sentiments voiced by residents of the Twelfth Street area would seem to imply more extensive social changes than most leaders have been willing to consider. An awareness of the special problems of a ghetto could be the first step toward solving them. But this task will require the support of many voluntary groups as well as public officials. The maintenance of a nation relatively free from violence and other disorders may require more of this society than it has previously been asked to provide.

REFERENCES

1. Report of the National Advisory Commission on Civil Disorders, Washington, D.C., Government Printing Office, 1968.

2. Campbell, A., and Schuman, H.: Racial Attitudes in Fifteen Cities. In: Supplemental Studies for the National Advisory Commission on Civil Disorders. Washington, D.C., Government Printing Office, 1968.

QUESTIONS FOR DISCUSSION

1. *Hahn says violence can be viewed in several ways, and suggests that it "may be symptomatic of a deeper social malady." What does he mean?*
2. *According to the author, studies show that "persons who had undergone a major riot were more likely to support the need for violence than the mass of black Americans who had not been involved in civil disorders." With what facts does he illustrate this statement?*
3. *According to the two surveys cited by the author, what are the chief reasons motivating the rioting?*
4. *According to Hahn, "Violence seemed to inspire a stronger sense of community and a hope for increased participation in the development of public policy." Why does he say that?*
5. *What do the following two statements mean? "Black citizens outside a neighborhood that had exploded in riots tended to perceive the violence as a method of securing a response rather than as a conflict with white authorities. On the other hand, those who had experienced a major disturbance appeared to view it as part of a rebellion or a direct confrontation."*

3

The Enculturation
of Violence

*"Just think, sugar, as the moral fiber of this once proud land
breaks down amid riots, strikes, and the on-going sexual revolution, we'll see it all here in living color."*

[Cartoon by Henry R. Martin. Copyright 1968 by Saturday Review,
Inc.]

VIOLENCE IS ONE OF THE BASIC AMBIVALENCES IN OUR society. We use it and sometimes even like it. Other times, we tiptoe around it, hoping it will go away. But it doesn't, for violence is a necessary part of American life. While some tendency toward violence may be hereditary, its functions and uses are certainly acquired. We learn it shortly after birth, and practice it until death.

The authors in this section explore various points of view about the learned nature of violence. We spend much of our leisure time viewing and enjoying violence as a form of entertainment. Our children gleefully follow it every Saturday morning as they watch the antics of Underdog and Dick Dastardly. Even beloved children's rhymes are not free of violence: consider the actions of the farmer's wife who cut off the tails of the Three Blind Mice. There are violent aspects included in "Little Red Riding Hood," the tale of the "Old Woman Who Lived in a Shoe," and so many other nursery favorites. Was Du Maurier's *The Birds* foreshadowed in part by the maid's losing her nose to four-and-twenty blackbirds? Have you seen a detective story or read a western? Violence is a basic element of both. As adults we are exposed to violence in the evening news summary, presented at the very hour when psychologists tell us we should be relaxing and enjoying our families in pleasant conversation. We never seem to consider its psychological impact on our nervous systems and the violence it does to our digestive tracts.

Implied violence seems inherent in most sports activities from football and hockey to boxing, wrestling, and ladies' roller-skating. Violence of itself is not even considered socially unacceptable. After all, if every school eliminated its "fight song" (that thinly veiled encouragement to deal violently with an opponent), how would the cheerleaders raise the spirits of the team?[1]

At certain times, we have learned, violence is good. We accept the hero's "good" violence as he bashes the "bad" guys who had previously roughed him up. In some instances, violence has been an expression of community action against some evil. John Jay, the unfortunate treaty-maker of our early years, was hanged and burned in effigy. Since then, numerous other Americans—coaches, university officials, civic leaders—have shared his fate. In many instances, communities actually hanged miscreants without trial to halt horse-stealing or some other undesired neighborhood enterprise. Our history drips with "the dark and bloody ground," "Bleeding Kansas," and "Bloody Williamson." Some of our present violence may be tied to our perennial nativism. Recent bumper stickers have declared, "*America—Love it or Leave it!*" and "*World Opinion Be Damned—America First!*" and other ethnocentric slogans.

Defiance in the face of any adversary—that's what we learn. "Don't take nothin' offa nobody!" is common parental advice. The whole issue is which *adversary* will *win*. One American-built automobile, according to its commercials, "fights back" against foreign import compacts. The soap opera actor declares, "If that little snip ever comes near my grandson, I'll. . . ."

One major sport of Americans is making the other fellow uncomfortable. "Putting him down" is not new with the present generation, although they sometimes think they invented the tactic. Cutting remarks were the long suit for W. C. Fields and Mae West—perhaps that is why they are so "camp" and popular among the young of today. Some of our national holidays, in addition to their original mean-

---

[1] The ancient satiric cheer of Knox College is subtle:
"Retard them, retard them!
Make them relinquish the ball!"

ings, are remembered in our folklore as anniversaries of notable acts of violence: the massacre of St. Valentine's Day and the severe riot between police and steel strikers on Memorial Day.

As outlets for our frustrations, we often resort to milder forms of violence, usually in sports and similar activities. Occasionally, less socially acceptable actions relax us. A little excitement in a barroom brawl will relieve the routine of some dull job. Even the smashing of a bothersome fly may be a beneficial outlet for violence.

Who has not chuckled at the misery of the hapless, falling clown, or felt humor in the cream pie thrown into the face of the comic? It is healthy to be able to laugh at our own shortcomings. Have you noticed the cartoons in this book? Using humor to release our tensions and uncertainties about violence—one of the basic problems of our society—may be useful to our understanding it. Of course, if we do not come to understand it, we may die laughing.

'So you heard another shot. It's nothing to get panicky about!'

[Bill Sanders in the *Milwaukee Journal*]

We're Teaching Our Children that Violence Is Fun

Eve Merriam

When something becomes part of everyday life, we no longer notice it. By now, make-believe weapons for children are part of the daily scene, ranging all the way from bomber models to gun-shaped teething rings. On Christmas and birthdays, doting grandparents give toddlers the latest mock-up missile. This year, toy grenades are popular.

Also available in variety stores, dime stores and department stores are toy bazookas, rifles, machine guns and pistols. "Pull the trigger," say the ads, "loud bang is followed by whining noise of bullet. Wisp of smoke curls from the end of the barrel." Or, "Load it with caps! Single shot or rapid fire—real live action—loads, fires and ejects shells!" All part of the everyday scene. . . .

Here, too, are newsstands proffering their accustomed children's wares: smoking guns and snarling faces peering from ever-new installments of Rawhide Kid, Two-Gun Kid, Space War, X Men, Metal Men, Superman, Superboy, super violence. . . . Comic books have been in existence since

Eve Merriam, "We're Teaching Our Children That Violence Is Fun," *Ladies Home Journal*, October 1964. Reprinted by permission of the author.

1937; it is estimated that 90 percent of all children between the ages of seven and 14 read them. Part of the everyday scene.

And here, day in and day out, movie houses hawk the standard marquee messages: "Suspense shocker" . . . "sexy, sexy" . . . "brute of a man with the instincts of an animal" . . . "the bullet wasn't made that could stop him" . . . "why did the thing want to devour women?" . . . "vividly depicts ax murders." A movie week like any other.

And, blaring endlessly, a television week like any other. Except for occasional pauses for national-conscience identification, business goes on as usual: the bullets whine in the Westerns, the police sirens shriek in the Easterns. To what dramatic purpose? Rarely is the brutality vital to the plot. The shooting scenes are thrown in for shock effect, to keep the viewer "entertained."

A report to the Federal Communications Commission states that between the ages of five and 14 the average American child witnesses the violent destruction of 13,000 human beings on television. If that figure seems exaggerated, consider that children spend more time watching television than on any other activity outside of sleep and school. Consider also what is available on "the children's hour," that period between four and nine P.M. when young people do most of their watching.

After a survey of one week's programming by four commercial channels in a major U.S. city, Stanford University published these findings: "The picture of the adult world presented on the children's hour is heavy in physical violence, light in intellectual interchange, and deeply concerned with crime."

In a five-day period, Monday through Friday, programs showed a stabbing in the back, four attempted suicides (three successful), four people falling or pushed over cliffs, two cars rolling over cliffs, two attempts to run cars over persons on the sidewalk, a raving psychotic loose in a flying airliner, two mob scenes (in one of which the mob hangs the wrong man), a horse grinding a man under its hooves, 12 murders, 16 major gunfights, 21 persons shot (apparently not fatally), 21 other violent incidents with guns (ranging from near-misses to shooting up a town), 37 hand-to-hand fights, an attempted murder with a pitchfork, two stranglings, a fight in the water, a woman being gagged and tied to a bed, and a great deal of miscellaneous violence, including a hired killer stalking his prey, two robberies, a pickpocket working, a woman killed by falling from a train, a tidal wave and a guillotining.

Scheduling for the 1964–65 season indicates that a high proportion of "action-adventure shows" is continuing, along with new private-eye and public mayhem features. And as television goes, so goes the rest of the entertainment scene. Movie battles are bigger and bloodier than ever, comic books and toys tie in with the goriest spectacles. It's all offered in the name of leisuretime "fun."

Combat, for instance, is a weekly hour-long show based on World War II. Broadcast during an early-evening hour, it has millions of child viewers. In addition, 30 kinds of "play" items are licensed for sale by the show. A child can be in a state of total combat from morning until night. He can wear an official *Combat* uniform and helmet . . . wind a *Combat* watch . . . read a *Combat* comic book . . . play a *Combat* board game . . . carry a *Combat* field medical kit complete with bandages and stretcher . . . throw a rubber *Combat* grenade (10 points for knocking out infantry, 100 for a tank) . . . and he can sport several different kinds of official *Combat* guns.

In some societies children are taught the violence of hatred and prejudice, and the violence of war. But does any other society teach its children that violence is a form of entertainment? What will happen to a generation raised upon such an idea? We do not know, because today's children are the first guinea pigs.

Our nation's crime rate is high compared with most other countries' and has been rising steadily. The rate of juvenile crime has been rising even more sharply. What baffles authorities is the increasing number of youthful crimes committed for no obvious reason—not for revenge, not for greed, not for any cause that can be uncovered. These crimes are just for "kicks": slashing the tires of a car, beating up an old man on a dark street, and one of the newest teen-age "games"—the mock-up, where a couple of pals pretend to shoot or drag off a third, and what fun when the police come running!

Violence as a gimmick, as a toy, as a show. Why not? Isn't that the fashion? If you're too young or timid for active play, you can always tell a sick joke about a cripple or send some friend a "drop dead" greeting card. These acts of violence, big and little, are part of the everyday scene. And dominating the scene is the box in the living room in 91 percent of the total households in the continental United States, so that our nation's children can simply press a button and tune in.

We tend to think of children's television as a special category: cartoon programs, games, animal stories, folk songs. In fact, these programs take up little network time and little of the child's life. What they are watching, from babyhood up, are the adult programs. For every 100 sets tuned to *Gunsmoke* and *The Untouchables*, for instance, there are 40 child viewers.

We have not seemed to care much, at least not until now. The Bureau of Applied Social Research of Columbia University last year conducted an extensive study of family viewing habits. It was found that parents object most to violent programs; this element was mentioned overwhelmingly as the chief irritant. Yet only 5 percent of the families interviewed could recall trying to regulate their children's viewing. Parents who did exercise control merely limited the *amount* of television viewing per week, or the times it could be watched—after homework, for instance. The actual content of programs was ignored. Apparently, most of us are using television as a baby-sitter, and not bothering to ask for references. We do not reflect that this particular sitter may be a wicked influence.

Over a three year period a special U.S. Senate subcommittee has been investigating crime-sex-and-violence television programming for its possible role in juvenile delinquency. Sen. Thomas Dodd of Connecticut, chairman of the committee said:

"Glued to the TV set from the time they can walk, our children are getting an intensive training in all phases of crime from the ever-increasing array of Westerns and crime-detective programs available to them. The past decade has seen TV come of age. However, the same decade has witnessed the violence content in programs skyrocket and delinquency in real life grow almost two hundred percent."

Further hearings were held last summer. Testimony already gathered provides insight into the attitudes of those who sell violence as entertainment. Here, for instance, is what the president of the Television Writers Guild of the West Coast told the committee:

"Nobody ever sends you a memo saying 'Kill.' I feel that violence happens because . . . a producer feels he has an obligation to top the violence of the show opposite him."

Consider the paternalistic advice from a producer of *The Untouchables* to a member of his staff: "On page 31 of this script, I wish we could come up with a different device than running the man down with a car, as we have done this now in three different shows. I like the idea of the sadism, but I hope we can come up with another approach to it."

The vice president of the Television Writers Guild added a postscript out of his own experience: "I wrote one show recently that did not have a heavy gun in it or a weapon of any sort and it was well received by the studio. Regretfully, this show is now off the air."

But still on the air are syndicated installments of programs like *The Untouchables*. The Senate committee hearings revealed a script reader's comments to the studio producing the series:

"This (installment) is loaded with action. Many exciting scenes. Opens right up on a lot of action—running gunfight between two cars of mobsters who crash, then continue the fight in the streets. Three killed, six injured—three killed are innocent bystanders."

We often hear the timeworn argument that the games children make up for themselves are far more frightening than anything that could pass the self-imposed codes of the comic books, publishers, movie makers, television authorities and toy manufacturers' council. Today's entertainment, the violence vendors say, is a pale reflection of children's naturally wild state.

Look at what parents and educators urge upon children (the argument continues), with no fear about their junior psyches being damaged. Punch and Judy is full of vicious beatings, and fairy tales are really horror stories.

Unfortunately, such parallels are not reassuring: for today's vicarious violence is both pervasive and *realistic*. Witches and dragons do not exist; getaway cars, bank robbers, and switchblades do.

Because the medium is relatively new, studies of the effects of indiscriminate and prolonged television viewing on today's children are still being evaluated. However, many studies have been completed describing the effects of radio, comic books and movies portraying violent scenes. The consensus is that reactions among children vary from mild anxiety to nightmares; from pulling the covers over their heads, to bed-wetting and to insisting on getting into bed with parents for protection. Yet radio offers no scary pictures, only sound effects; in comic books the pictures do not move; and at the movies there is an adult alongside, or at least an extended period of "coming to" in the lobby and the street on the way home.

Reactions to a threatening scene on television are likely to be more intense; the child is already at home.

The violent entertainment forms affect children in other ways. If they are not becoming actively delinquent— our "good" middle-class children, yours and mine—they are becoming passively jaded. As a kind of self-protection, they develop thick skins to avoid being upset by the gougings, smashings and stompings they see on TV. As the voice of reason is shown to be a swift uppercut to the chin, child viewers cannot afford to get involved, for if they did, their emotions would be shredded. So they keep "cool," distantly unaffected. Boredom sets in, and the whole cycle starts over again. Bring on another show with even more bone-crushing and teeth-smashing so the viewers will react. The dramas reach new peaks of intensity; occasionally the continuity acceptance editor at the network has had to admonish: "On page 40, scene 85—delete the way Johnny kills Mrs. Zagano. As described it is not acceptable. . . . Delete the screams and gurgles. There's a commercial coming up." And further on, "Try to cut down on the killings please."

Please. Of another script, the network editor comments: "Violent death, pages 3, 19, 53, 61, 63, 64, 65. On page 4, scene 14, don't overdo the violence here—slapping woman, rabbit punch, etc. Page 53, scene 135—I don't see how we can do this scene acceptably. It's too gruesome a killing; a woman does it—the man is laughing—it's the end of an act before a commercial and we've got too much violent death in the show as it is. Please kill him another way. Even off camera it's too awful. This is a good show and I hope we can fix it for acceptance."

A good show. Sit back and watch the show as the world of entertainment crosses over to the real world. Newspapers tell how a youthful Midwest gang has modeled itself upon its favorite TV program. "We are untouchable," yells the 17-year-old leader when the gang is picked up after an attempted killing, "you can't do anything to us!"

And the real world crosses over to the entertainment world. A definition of true-life delinquency could just as easily apply to many of the amoral private-eye and Western heroes playing on movie and television screens.

Dr. Lewis Yablonsky, youth worker and sociologist, says that "one of the violent gang leader's vital functions for gang membership is to serve as a symbol of idealized violence."

The leader of a violent gang called The Bombers, for instance, demanded that new members, as part of their initiation, go out and beat up somebody, any somebody, some anybody. That behavior is recognized as socially delinquent. Yet here is socially acceptable behavior in the form of a character outlined for the hero of a projected "action-adventure" series on a leading network:

"Curiosity is the keynote to Barton's character, curiosity to the point of danger and death . . . He doesn't always find out, he may almost get killed, somebody always gets badly hurt, but the audience gets a hell of a ride. Despite his many protests that he is only interested in research, it is obvious that he is fascinated with the amount of punishment and pressure the human body can sustain. The fact that it is quite often his own body that takes the punishment makes the razor's edge that much more fascinating."

Following a consultation with a high executive at the network, it was decided, in the interests of gaining a wider audience, to add a generous dose of sadism to the basic masochism.

"As our protagonist is . . . in a hazardous occupation, the inclusion of sex and violence is not only desirable but can be accomplished correctly and organically. . . . We look forward to a successful season."

A psychiatrist, Dr. Eugene David Glynn, raises some pointed questions about these sex-and-violence programs that children see. Doctor Glynn asks:

"How high can excitement be raised? What will be the result of such constant stimulation? It is too soon to know what children so massively exposed to sex on television will consider exciting and sex-stimulating as adults. Will reality live up to the fantasies this generation has been nursed on?

"These children are in a peculiar position; experience is exhausted in advance. There is little they have not seen or done or lived through, and yet this is secondhand experience. When the experience itself comes, it is watered-down, for it has already been half lived, but never truly felt."

Where is the dividing line between the real world and the fantasy world? The problem, if it is any consolation, is not exclusively American. A group of schoolteachers in Tokyo is currently forming an anti-TV-violence committee. A poem in a Russian magazine deplores the fact that too many parents permit their children to watch unsuitable programs. In England authorities filter out the most offensive material, such as the too-raw scenes in wild Westerns coming from America. Programs deemed unsuitable for child audiences may not be shown until after nine P.M. Yet the British are by no means blameless; in Canada there are complaints that one of the worst programs children get to see is *The Saint*, a private-eye series originating in Britain.

However, in many countries around the world the most violent TV programs, films, comic books and toys are referred to simply as "American style." Can that style be changed, can nonviolent values be substituted?

Some parents think so. Believing that education against violence should start as early as possible, they are refusing to buy their children toy weapons of any kind. Others are taking to heart the opinion of Sen. Abraham Ribicoff of Connecticut:

"If a child is permitted to sit like a vegetable, pursuing moronic murders and ceaseless crimes, he suffers, and his parents do too, in the end. Parents must learn to say, 'No, you may not listen to or look at that' as well as 'Yes' or just shrug and say 'OK.'

"Parents must take positive steps to improve the tele-viewing habits of their children and themselves. And the television industry must fulfill its obligation to its viewers. It has produced programs of real significance. It has reported public affairs with insight and imagination. It can use its resources if it only has the will to do so."

There are many forms that protest can take, short of parents' picket lines around the studios. As an individual you can express your disapproval by writing to the sponsor, in care of the station or network, to your Congressman and to the Federal Communications Commission in Washington.

You can also express your sentiments through group action. The PTA, for instance, has several regional groups that evaluate television programs. If your local PTA doesn't belong to such a group, write for information to: National Congress of Parents and Teachers, 700 North Rush Street, Chicago 11, Ill.

The American Association of University Women, 2401 Virginia Avenue N.W., Washington 7, D.C., also evaluates the content of mass media. There are organizations devoted exclusively to broadcasting. The oldest (established in 1949) is the National Association for Better Radio and Television, 882 Victoria Avenue, Los Angeles 5, Calif.

N.A.F.B.R.A.T. publishes a quarterly newsletter, an annual survey of children's programs, and occasional pamphlets. Its president, Mrs. Clara S. Logan, often testifies at Congressional hearings.

Another national organization is The American Council for Better Broadcasts, 423 North Pinckney Street, Madison 3, Wis., Dr. Leslie Spence, executive director. Founded in 1953, A.C.B.B. monitors programs and submits its rating reports to sponsors' networks, Congressional committees and Government agencies. Like N.A.F.B.R.A.T., it publishes a news bulletin (*Better Broadcasts*, issued five times a year), an annual look-listen report, and other material.

Above all, it is important to form a personal watch society; for all of us to sit down with our children and watch what they are seeing, to check on the programs at regular intervals, and to issue our own home license as to what may or may not be seen.

Such a schedule may be demanding but at present we have no alternative; we cannot afford to leave our children unguarded in the care of the television baby-sitter. Not, at least, until the baby-sitter comes forward with more reliable references.

QUESTIONS FOR DISCUSSION

1. *What areas of violence does the author discuss?*
2. *Since this article was written, has the level of violence on television lowered?*
3. *What kinds of youthful crime have increased and are of particular concern to the author?*
4. *What did the Columbia University research indicate about parental control of TV viewing habits?*
5. *According to research, how does violence on the radio, in comic books, or in movies affect children? How are their reactions to TV violence different?*
6. *What does the author mean when she says that children are becoming "passively jaded" to violence?*
7. *What does Dr. Glynn mean when he says that for children who watch violence on TV, "experience is exhausted in advance"?*

The Need to Control Aggression in Young Children

BENJAMIN SPOCK

Is it good or bad for boys to play with toy weapons? For many years I emphasized its harmlessness. When a thoughtful mother expressed doubt about letting her son have guns and other warlike toys—because she didn't want to encourage him in the slightest degree to become delinquent or militaristic—I would explain how little connection there was between these toys and the development of an aggressive personality. I used to say that in the course of growing up, a child has a natural tendency to bring his aggressiveness more and more under control, provided his parents encourage this. When a child is one to two years old, for instance, and angry with another child, he may bite his playmate without hesitation; but by the age of three or four he has learned that crude aggression is not right. However, he likes to pretend to shoot a pretend Indian. He may pretend to shoot his mother or father, but he grins to reassure them that his gun and his hostility aren't to be taken seriously.

In the six-to-12-year-old period boys will play an earnest game of war, but it has lots of rules that limit aggression. There may be arguments and roughhousing, but real fights are relatively infrequent. At this age a boy doesn't shoot at his mother or father, even in fun. It's not that his parents have become stricter; his own conscience has. He says, "Step on a crack, break your mother's back," and tries to avoid stepping on the sidewalk cracks—which means that even the thought of wishing harm to his parents now makes him uncomfortable. In adolescence, aggressive feelings become much stronger, but the well-brought-up boy sublimates them into athletics and other competitive activities, or into kidding his pals.

In other words, I explained to parents, playing at war was a natural step in the disciplining of the aggression of young boys (few girls play war); most clergymen and pacifists probably played the same games. An idealistic mother doesn't really need to worry about producing a scoundrel. The aggressive juvenile delinquent was not distorted in personality by being allowed to play bandit at five or ten years of age. He was neglected and abused in his first couple of years, when his character was beginning to take shape; he was doomed before he had any toys worthy of the name.

But nowadays I'd give a mother much more encouragement in her inclination to guide her son away from violence. A number of occurrences have convinced me of the importance of this.

One of the first things that made me change my mind —several years ago—was an observation made by an experienced nursery-school teacher. She told me that her children were crudely bopping each other much more than previously, without provocation. When she remonstrated with them, they protested indignantly: "But that's what the Three Stooges do." ("The Three Stooges" was a children's TV program full of violence and buffoonery that recently had been introduced and immediately had become very popular.) This attitude did not signify a serious undermining of character. But it certainly showed me that watching violence can lower a child's standards of behavior.

What further shocked me into reconsidering my point of view was the assassination of President Kennedy and the fact that some school children cheered about this. (I didn't so much blame the children as I blamed the kind of American parent who will say about a president they dislike, "I'd shoot him if I got the chance!")

These incidents made me think of other evidences that Americans have often been tolerant of harshness, lawlessness and violence. We were ruthless in dealing with the Indians. In some frontier areas we slipped into the tradition of vigilante justice. We were hard on the later waves of immigrants. At times we've denied justice to groups with different religious or political views. We have high crime rates. We have a shameful history of racist lynchings and murders, as well as of regular abuse and humiliation of black people. In recent years there apparently has been a rise in the frequency with which infants and small children have been taken to hospitals with bruises, fractures, internal hemorrhages and fractured skulls caused by gross parental brutality. Is it a coincidence that a great proportion of our adult as well as our child population also is endlessly fascinated with dramas of Western violence and brutal crime stories in movies and on television?

Of course, some of the phenomena I have described are characteristic of only a small percentage of the population. Even the others that apply to a majority of people don't necessarily mean that we Americans, on the average, have more aggressiveness in us than the people of most other nations. I think, rather, that the aggressiveness we have is less controlled from childhood on.

To me, it seems very clear that in order to have a more stable and civilized national life we should bring up the next generation of Americans with a greater respect for law and for other people's rights and sensibilities than in the past. There are many ways in which we could and should teach these attitudes. One simple way is to show our young children our own disapproval of lawlessness and violence in television programs and in play.

I also believe that the survival of the world now depends on a much greater awareness of the need to avoid war and actively to seek peaceful agreements. There are enough nuclear arms to utterly destroy all civilization. One international incident in which belligerence or brinkmanship was carried a small step too far could escalate into annihilation within a few hours. This terrifying situation demands a much greater stability and self-restraint on the part of national leaders and populations than they have ever shown in the past. We owe it to our children to prepare them, very deliberately, for this awesome responsibility. I see little evidence that this is being done now.

When we let people grow up feeling that cruelty is all right provided they know it is make-believe, or provided they sufficiently disapprove of certain individuals or groups, or provided the cruelty is in the service of their country (whether the country is right or wrong), we make it easier for them to go berserk on provocation.

But can we imagine actually depriving American boys of their pistols or of watching their favorite Western or crime programs? I think we should consider it—at least to a partial degree.

I believe that parents should stop children's war play or any other kind of play firmly when it degenerates into deliberate cruelty or meanness. (By this I don't mean they should interfere in every little quarrel or tussle.)

If I had a three- or four-year-old son who asked me to buy him a pistol, I'd tell him—with a friendly smile, not a scowl—that I didn't want to give him a gun for even pretend shooting because there is too much meanness and killing in the world; that we must all learn how to get along in a friendly way together. I'd ask him if he didn't want some other present instead.

If I saw him, soon afterward, using a stick for a pistol in order to join a gang that was merrily going "bang-bang" at one another, I wouldn't rush out to remind him of my views. I'd let him have the fun of participating as long as there was no cruelty. If his uncle gave him a pistol or a soldier's helmet for his birthday, I myself wouldn't have the nerve to take it away from him. If when he was seven or eight he decided he wanted to spend his own money for battle equipment, I wouldn't forbid him to. I'd remind him that I don't want to buy war toys or give them as presents, but that from now on he will be playing away from home more and more and making more of his own decisions; he can make this decision for himself.

I wouldn't give this talk in such a disapproving manner that he wouldn't dare decide against my policy. I would feel I'd made my point and that he had been inwardly influenced by my viewpoint as much as I could influence him. Even if he should buy weapons then, he would be likely to end up— in adolescence and adulthood—as thoughtful about the problems of peace as if I'd prohibited his buying them, perhaps more so.

One reason I keep backing away from a flat prohibition is that it would have its heaviest effect on the individuals who need it least. If all the parents in America became convinced and agreed on a toy-weapons ban on the first of next month, this would be ideal from my point of view. But this isn't going to happen for a long time, unless one bomb goes off by accident and shocks the world into a banning of all weapons, real and make-believe. A small percentage of parents—those most thoughtful and conscientious—will be the first ones who will want to dissuade their sons from war toys; but their sons will be most likely to be the sensitive, responsible children anyway. So I think it's carrying the issue unnecessarily far, for those of us who are particularly concerned about peace and kindliness, to insist that our young sons demonstrate a total commitment to our cause while all their friends are pistol toters. (It might be practical in a neighborhood where a majority of parents had the same conviction.) The main ideal is that children should grow up with a fond attitude toward all humanity. That will come about, basically, if this is the general atmosphere of our families. It will be strengthened by the attitudes we specifically teach toward nations and groups. The elimination of war play would have some additional influence, but not as much as the two previous factors.

I feel less inclined to compromise on brutality on television and in movies. Although children have their own fantasies of violence, the sight of a real human face apparently being smashed by a fist has a lot more impact on children than what they imagine when they are making up their own stories. I believe that parents should flatly forbid programs that go in for violence. I don't think they are good for adults either.

Young children can only partly distinguish between dramas and reality. Parents can explain, "It isn't right for people to hurt each other or kill each other and I don't want you to watch them do it." If a child cheats and watches such a program in secret, he'll know very well that his parents disapprove, and this will protect him, to a degree, from the coarsening effect of the scenes.

QUESTIONS FOR DISCUSSION

1. *On what grounds in previous years did Dr. Spock emphasize the harmlessness of children playing with toy guns?*
2. *What occurrences convinced the author that mothers should guide their sons away from violence?*

3. *How would Dr. Spock control children's interest in buying toy guns?*
4. *How does the author's attitude toward violence on TV differ from his attitude toward toy guns?*

Are the Movies Teaching Us To Be Violent?

FREDRIC WERTHAM

If I should meet an unruly youngster in a dark alley, I prefer it to be one who has not seen "Bonnie and Clyde." For concrete clinical studies have shown me that a lot of violence is learned behavior. Currently, film violence is grossly overdone. We have learned to transplant hearts, but we teach heartlessness. More and more youths get the idea that violence is not only acceptable but enjoyable.

It seems barbaric to let children go freely to any movies that are produced. Adults may have the right to production, but children have a right to protection. There is a social necessity for a law that would bar children under 14, unless accompanied by a parent, from admission to movies with a surfeit of brutality, violence, murder, torture, cruelty and sadism. Such movies should be labeled as being in a category which, because of high violence content, is not suitable for young children. (It is misleading to link the representation of unsadistic sex with the display of brutal violence as if they were comparable.)

Adults' rights would not be affected by such a law. Any parent would be perfectly free to show his 11-year-old son a girl's bathtub filled with blood, with the murder victim's arm sticking out ("The Tingler"); he can show him endless murders in a big city ("The St. Valentine's Day Massacre") or teach him how to shoot men point-blank in the head ("Rough Night in Jericho"); he can try to give him his first sexual stimulation and a genuinely sadistic mixture of sex and violence ("The Penthouse"). But the boy will not be able to go alone and his parent will be informed that the film belongs to a category considered unsuitable for children. This would help parents.

The problem of violence in movies is really the problem of violence itself. Can anybody who heard what Senator Edward Kennedy said in the Cathedral still doubt what havoc our violence wreaks in people's lives? One little step forward would be to end the risk of presenting the constant lure of violence to the immature.

QUESTIONS FOR DISCUSSION

1. *What does Wertham mean when he says, "A lot of violence is learned behavior"?*
2. *What is the author's one suggestion for reducing violence in this country?*

'Censorship Is No Answer'

Marya Mannes

It is now apparently obligatory for all "adult" films to show a naked man and woman in bed, pre-, during, and post-coitus. They are usually handsome and naturally wrapped up in each other.

The few remaining niceties are sometimes preserved by judicious cutting and the convention of sheets. Otherwise little or nothing is left to the imagination.

Should it be? Is this compulsory scene pornographic or just graphic? Is it prurient or is it merely honest? Is it art—or simply realism?

Having observed approximately two or three such scenes a week during months of reviewing films, I would suggest that the pertinent question remains: Is it necessary? Apart from titillation, does the rendition of the sexual act on the screen tell us anything we didn't know before? Does it enlarge our consciousness?

I would be inclined to say: Very seldom. A woman's hand on a man's arm can tell as much. What they say to each other, how they speak to each other, can tell most. But

From the *New York Times,* June 30, 1968, p. 13. © 1968 by The New York Times Company. Reprinted by permission.

these need the words of a sensitive writer and the subtleties of a superior actor. They need also the imagination of an audience not bludgeoned by the illiteracy of the obvious.

The new freedom, marvelous in many ways, including its recognition of the human body as an object of beauty, has erased taboos that were often more the product of hypocrisy than of natural restraint.

But the verbal and visual license now widely indulged (in the name of art) for commercial ends, is another matter. So, in the name of truth, is the concentration on psychotic brutality for profitable shock.

Censorship, since it feeds the appetite it hopes to quell, is no answer. Audience revulsion might be. In time, familiarity with the public act of sex may breed not only contempt but tedium, and too much blood turn the stomach.

A recognition of this by the good film-makers may be the only alternative to curbs which the worst ones could bring upon the medium—to our common loss.

QUESTIONS FOR DISCUSSION

1. *What does the author feel is the best way to curb the use of sex in films?*

'When Emmett Till Was Slain'

Claude Brown, Jr.

During the past few months, many have expressed surprise, alarm, shock, astonishment bordering on disbelief, over acts of violence perpetrated against Americans of international renown. It is true that Martin Luther King Jr. and Senator Robert F. Kennedy were both humanitarians who successfully sought to make significant contributions to mankind. It is also conceivable that the most momentous contribution of both men was rendered unintentionally—their premature and brutal deaths that awakened the nation to its true nature, extreme violence.

I experienced a profound grief at the losses of Dr. King and Senator Kennedy, neither of whom I knew personally. Presumably, numerous people all over the world shared this emotion. But I was also bereaved in 1955 when 14-year-old Emmett Till was bestially slain in Mississippi. And in 1963 and 1965 when Medgar Evers and John F. Kennedy and Malcolm X were slain. This grief, needless to say, was not shared by millions all over the world. The surprise that has been the reaction of many in this country is not shared by me. I've never doubted for one moment in my entire life that Americans are capable of extreme violence.

Another reaction, which should have been expected, was the hue and cry raised about violence in the movies and on television. At times such as this, apparently, there arises an overwhelming need to attribute blame to someone or something. In modern America, television and movies provide convenient and perhaps culpable scapegoats. When "nice people" of any society begin searching frantically for a sacrificial lamb, it is time for all but the lions of society to run for cover or risk being forcibly covered in wool and served up on a skewer to a fictitious god who is manipulated by the "nice people"—the powers that be.

It is conceivable that if television and movies had not been invented, those heathens who believe that a sacrifice will quell the wrath of all gods would be headhunting among authors and even attempting to ban the Bible, because it tells of rape, incest, massacres, theft and hate. I would caution the "nice people," who presently have the lamb (in mass communications media) by the throat, to still their knives and reflect for a moment upon the question: do movies and television cater to us, or we to them? In all probability, having considered the question, reason would compel one to conclude that television, radio, and the movie scripts the American public sees and hears have been meticulously prepared to meet the demands of the "nice people" in America—this excludes all ethnic minorities and poor people. Perhaps the hue and cry have arisen as a tactic whereby one who feels guilty seeks to divert the attention of the crowd before anyone observes the blood on his hands.

Let's face it, it is not television or the movies that has produced so much violence in America. Americans are the cause of violence—their hypocrisy and violent nature.

QUESTIONS FOR DISCUSSION

1. *Does the author believe that we would have less violence if we did not have TV and the movies?*
2. *According to Brown, why are people criticizing TV and the movies for violence in this country?*
3. *What has produced so much violence in America, according to the author?*

The Violent
Bugs Bunny et al.

JOHN F. McDERMOTT

Today's parents who are worried about the violence on children's television programs might rest a little easier if they would look back for a moment. Our parents went through the same bit a generation ago when we seemed to be completely beguiled by comic books. And most of us turned out to be solid citizens. Our parents were also subjected to the same conflicting advice and theories. Fortunately, in the span of a generation we have learned a number of things about ourselves and our reactions to violence that may clarify some of the conflicts in our thinking about the subject.

TV violence is said to corrupt morals and encourage violent behavior in children. It is also said to provide a vicarious outlet for aggressive feelings, something fervently to be desired. No wonder parents are confused.

The fact is that it can do either or both depending on the circumstances. Aggressive and violent thoughts *do* exist in the mind of the child. Television *does* influence these thoughts and the way they are expressed. It also provides an experience that is the basis for much of children's play, especially group play. Youngsters often turn the TV experience into action. Emotionally healthy children keep the actual violence at an imaginary level, however, when they are playing out the story.

We have seen instances where a youngster who is not allowed to watch a certain program that all his schoolmates follow is turned into a "social isolate" because he is unable to talk about or engage in play based on the program. Many parents who dislike certain programs still let their youngsters watch them for just this reason.

Many of us tend to let our adult prejudices and perceptions cloud our thinking on TV violence. It is more important to examine the differing perceptions that young children and adults have of the same experience than it is to argue whether certain television programs are good or bad for children. Too frequently, we make judgments concerning our children and television because a program has upset *us*. Adults have become much more sensitive about children and television because of the tragic events of the recent past—assassinations, riots, war. They puzzle us and deeply trouble us. What many parents do not realize is that these events are just as upsetting for young children as they are for us, possibly more so, because they are on live television showing real adults losing control of themselves.

Most parents do not actually watch their children's programs. They overhear or glimpse fragments. TV thus offers a convenient scapegoat when we need to find a reason why our little angels are fighting or acting up. We may also need to fight against our own secret enjoyment of violence and our guilty conscience over it. After all, the deluge of Western shoot-'em-ups in the fifties was mostly watched by adults. Batman and Superman are old friends of ours from childhood and their revivals were initially enjoyed immensely by adult audiences. They, of course, did not make us killers. But we have no difficulty in deciding that the new television mythology and folklore—for example, the outer-space programs—should be condemned. Yet these third-rate modern-day fairy tales are only technologically advanced versions of the old-fashioned tales of giants and witches who devoured and destroyed people themselves— without benefit of scientific gadgets.

The problem has been that we tend to judge TV from our own standpoint, rather than the child's. Sit down some-time and watch television with your pre-school child. Observe him, after he has gotten over the shock of your interest, and ask him to explain the television program to you. You may notice that the dialogue on many of the programs is way over his head, more oriented toward adult minds. He may ignore the actual story, and instead focus on the pictorial action upon which he superimposes his own experience and interpretations. When several children watch the same program, they often see parts of the story differently and argue about who is right about what is going on. Often a youngster sees mainly what appeals to him at his particular developmental stage. Thus some may act withdrawn and hypnotized while others are restless or per-haps even acting up during the same episode.

If you have been pleased because of the newspaper reports that parental pressure has forced changes in the Saturday morning viewing for young children, then I suggest that you watch the "improvements." The Saturday morning programs are indeed slowly changing from programs developed around the semi-human space monsters repugnant to adults. But these bizarre animals and people, atomic guns and radioactive destructive devices usually appealed more to older children anyway. Pre-schoolers preferred the simpler themes of cartoons. Now the familiar animal cartoons are back. They are considered healthy, perhaps because the figures don't look so much like us, so that we adults can relax and enjoy them. The form of aggression has changed, perhaps, but hardly the amount. Bugs Bunny is still the model of a lazy, irresponsible, selfish individual who outwits and frustrates the serious purposes of the adult world. The action enters on a repetitive chase. Bugs and his adversaries, alternately destroy and are destroyed by each other, but bounce back quickly. They are inevitably flattened and squashed into paper-thin images, burned, shot, stabbed, blown up, drowned, and have their bodies distorted and changed in a variety of ways. A favorite is falling from or being exploded to great heights. We laugh and tolerate this because it is all in fun, impulsive and not carefully planned, and, of course, it's "only animals." Yet animals are much closer to people in the minds of children. They often secretly represent their own inner experiences. Children's stories have utilized animals for generations because of this.

So Bugs Bunny has fooled the adults once again. Violence has not disappeared or even been reduced; it has simply become more acceptable to us. Adults object less to "unrealistic" forms of violence like the kind of body changes that the Bugs Bunny characters go through (always quickly restored to their original shape) as these seem to us to have no possibility of fulfillment. We can laugh at them. It is only when characters and their forms of violence begin to resemble human form and behavior that we are bothered. The behavior and motives of cartoon animals, however, are much closer to the inner life of the child. In fact, when small children see animals facing experiences that resemble too closely their own experiences it can be extremely upsetting even though there may be less actual violence displayed. In fact, such programs are usually considered "good, wholesome" shows. Lassie, a program generally approved of by parents of small children, is on just before bedtime. Animals and human family members are very much involved with each other in this program and routinely experience series of injuries or near-injuries. If a particular episode is divided into two parts, part one may end with Lassie about to be killed. Parents may then wonder why their youngster can't sleep that night. They may not realize that he has been left at bedtime like Lassie, alone and in terrible danger with no solution for another week.

On one psychiatric ward the hardened delinquent adolescent boys would not watch Lassie. We members of the staff assumed that it was because it was a "baby" program until the boys corrected us and told us that it was too "scary" for them. On the same ward, the girls become intrigued with an afternoon soap opera called "Dark Shadows." Each afternoon they were spellbound by this program with its plots and counterplots, threats of intrigue, death by poisoning or at the fangs of vampires. After an active debate among the staff of the effect of this program on the girls, it was decided to study their reactions during and after watching it before deciding whether or not to forbid the program. However, before any direct evidence of adverse effect on the children or their behavior was found, the staff turned off the program and terminated the study, because the program was so repellent to them.

While some programs may prevent resolution of very young children's fears of injury and death by making them too real, others, with all their violence which is done, redone, and then undone, not only may be less disturbing but also may help them outgrow their fears. For instance, the themes of cartoon violence fit more with the pre-school child's understanding, both intellectual and emotional, of death, which is quite different from our understanding. At that age the youngster has a heightened fear of being hurt, hence his enjoyment of the repetitive themes in cartoons which help him laugh at this fear. He sees death as reversible and this, too, fits in with the cartoon theme. When he is 7 or 8 years old he will lose some interest in these programs because his concepts change and approach ours more closely. He begins to view death as final—and something from which he is not immune. We see small youngsters playing and toying with death every day in their games. The angry small child who says, "I wish you were dead," really means, "I wish you would go away because you bother me and I can't cope with you in actuality." This sharp difference in the conception of death between adults and children is very much evident these days when children play with toy guns. They are surprised when adults say, "Don't ever point your gun at me or anyone else." The youngster knows that the gun play was not real, only pretend, and is startled when adults take seriously his magical power as if he and his gun have real potential for killing.

Superman and Batman, with their daily diet of violence, always occurring at the same point in the program and in the same way, illustrated with fireworks and labels, "Zap, Pow," etc., can become so predictable and routine to children that after a while they become boring. Television westerns with the barroom brawl and showdown on the main street are also so easily anticipated as to be routine. On the other hand, a television "special" or "good" children's movie, classics such as Snow White or Hansel and Gretel, can be terrifying to the same child because he is not used to that form and expression of the violence. Perhaps we should be more concerned that the daily diet of violence may produce children who are immune, callous and indifferent rather than children who want to emulate it.

There are other themes within these programs that may appeal to some children more than we suspect. The fact that Bugs Bunny outwits adult-like figures may provide his real appeal for children. Superman, Batman, and their newer version, Spiderman, all have two identities: one that is very harmless, almost foolish, and "childlike," in the real world. The other, unknown to the outside world, is one of limitless power, strength, scientific intelligence and tricks. Children like to imagine what it would be like to have the ability to unleash this secret power whenever necessary. It helps them deny the helpless position they often find themselves in. Other themes commonly encountered are children rescuing adults in trouble, little people versus big people, protection of one's own group from unknown outside dangers of "other worlds," etc. The violence may be incidental to these themes in importance, although we are likely to react to the violence as it is more obvious to the casual viewer—i.e., the adult, as opposed to the child who is absorbed in other aspects of the story.

If you take the time to watch your children's programs for a few days, you may find yourself becoming more annoyed at the commercials than at the programs. The seductive commercials about food just before a youngster's dinner time are inevitably more attractive than the dinner awaiting him. Commercials are supposed to be "true," and to be believed. The TV programs they surround are "pretend." Yet the commercials advertise shoes that will "run faster and jump farther" than their competitors and cereals that will bestow "superpower." A TV child who refuses to drink his milk at mealtime finds it magically transformed into a candy bar which is supposed to be its exact equivalent nutritionally. His mother marvels at this and suggests that this candy bar substitute for his milk thereafter.

Children remember, repeat and sing these commercials for days and weeks. They are much more firmly imprinted on their minds than the content of the program. Compare the amount of excitement and activity children show during the commercials to that during the actual program itself. They are likely to be much more active during the commercials, shouting insistently that their parents get them something that is advertised.

Naturally the child's own life experience will shape the way in which he is influenced by a television show. If violent or bizarre programs are interwoven into a good mixture of life events and experience, and thus do not become a "life" in themselves, they will be less influential than for the child in whom they assume special significance. The most important people in children's lives are their parents, not television actors. Children who see or experience aggressively violent behavior in their own parents are most likely to be aggressive in their own relationships.

Children will also identify with TV characters to the extent that their parents are unavailable. When a mother uses TV as a babysitter and leaves her 2 year old in front of the set for most of the day, the child may very likely find television actors to be the only models to imitate in his vacuum-life.

Youngsters from families in which violence is commonly experienced will see television violence as representing the world as it really is rather than as a fantasy world that is detached from their own experience. The youngster who has been deprived of and isolated from a variety of stimulating and satisfying experiences may view the violent world of television as representing the way things really are on the "outside." All this accords with the report this month of the National Commission on the Causes and Prevention of Violence, which found that TV violence encourages violence, particularly among children of poor, disorganized families.

Furthermore, a certain type of show may produce very different reactions in children from different socio-economic levels. The child from a disadvantaged lower class family may have much greater violent feelings aroused in him by a pleasant "family type" show with warm, close relationships in a spacious happy home in a middle class neighborhood than he would from a program involving outer space monsters killing each other. And for him, Bruce Wayne, alias Batman, is no amusing pedantic fop; he is "whitey," with too much of everything in life.

Parents have the responsibility to know what their children are watching and to balance their day, to keep the children interested in other things. Parents' interest in the television programs their children watch and their "censorship" of these reflect the level of their own interest in their children. For most children, individual judgments must be made as to whether a particular program allows aggressive feelings to remain in and perhaps be drained off in fantasy, or whether it only builds up excitement without providing discharge and thus it spills over into his behavior.

But certain youngsters must be even more carefully considered. TV may indeed suggest patterns of behavior as outlets for anger in youngsters who are already angry with others. A few children seem to fuse with characters on television and actually "become" those characters, unable to pull themselves out of the shoes of the character when the program is over. Thus, for some children with their own problems of behavior, certain programs must be limited: just as a diabetic child may not eat sweets while others may, some children have a deficient mechanism for handling television's violent ingredients which other youngsters can manage without difficulty.

It is wise for the parents to reexamine their children's TV diet but to examine it with *them* and observe their reactions. Television specials which can be anticipated for several days and for which interest, curiosity and excitement can be built up, are often good vehicles for this interaction between parents and child. A parent who talks to his youngster about such a special will see that his interest, curiosity, and excitement action over this "special event" is responsible for most of the emotion he shows, regardless of how exciting or disappointing the show might turn out to be.

QUESTIONS FOR DISCUSSION

1. *What are the two apparently contrasting theories about the effect of TV violence on children?*

2. According to McDermott, what is the difference between the effect of TV violence on emotionally healthy children and its effect on emotionally unhealthy children?

3. What does the author mean when he says, "Too frequently, we make judgments concerning our children and television because a program has upset us"?

4. According to the author, what happens when we observe children watching a violent program on TV?

5. In what way have the new children's programs come to seem less violent? In reality are they less violent?

6. What does the following statement mean? "It is only when characters and their forms of violence begin to resemble human form and behavior that we are bothered. The behavior and motives of cartoon animals, however, are much closer to the inner life of the child."

7. Why does McDermott feel that some violent TV programs may help certain aged children outgrow their fears of injury and death?

8. What does the author mean when he says, "Perhaps we should be more concerned that the daily diet of violence may produce children who are immune, callous and indifferent rather than children who want to emulate it"?

9. Why do children enjoy shows that have characters who have limitless power?

10. What danger does the author see in the advertisements on children's TV programs?

11. What problems can develop when a child sees too much violence on TV?

12. How do reactions of children from different socio-economic levels differ toward the same program?

13. What does the author suggest to parents about their children's viewing violence?

The Church and Civil Disobedience

JAMES GROPPI

[Photo by Frank Lodge/Image.]

James Groppi, "The Church and Civil Disobedience," *Motive*,
February 1969, pp. 42–47.

The church's record on civil disobedience is blemished. Our skirts aren't clean and our admonitions are terribly inconsistent. The church laments those who advocate civil disobedience in the name of the church and in the context of the gospel, yet seldom wavers in offering tribute to saints like Joan of Arc.

It's impossible for the church not to be involved, one way or another. At times, it just sits back, as it did when it sanctioned the rape of the African continent. The established churches allowed the black man in his country to be subjected to slavery, and was slow to raise its voice in opposition. Religious silence helped Hitler in his rise to power. Even when the church is silent, it speaks.

How do churchmen have the gall to talk about civil disobedience when they are so silent, so supportive of the system? How does the church justify its presence in a state like Mississippi where ninety-seven percent of the vote in the last presidential election was white though forty percent of the population is black?

Many of us who have publicly protested the church's double standard of ethics, who have used nonviolent tactics for demonstrating our concern for humanity, have mostly met only hostility or suspicion. As we have marched and picketed and gone to jail, the same question gets repeated: "Why do you violate 'just' laws?" I remember one priest in particular. For thirteen years, he was in a parish which included a plant which employs 5,000 workers—99½% Anglo-Americans. The plant had a terrific record of discrimination. But the priest never said a word. Finally, we asked him after he had asked us about violating laws, "What about the law of God?"

Now in the black community of Milwaukee and at St. Boniface's Parish, we aren't talking about means and ends any longer. We agree completely with the Bishop of Panama who said: "When we talk about the use of violence in the struggle for equality, we're not talking so much about morality as we are talking about tactics." So if you want to discuss violence as a tactic—that's another question. But I'll have nothing to do with a discussion of the morality of violence. I've read just a little too much, seen a little too much.

And I don't like to talk about tactics without talking about specific issues, specific objectives, and effective means for obtaining ends. I still believe in the picket line, the demonstration. But its use has to be judged in accordance with an objective. If you are talking about the church and a justification for revolution, I say fine. Let's start talking. But every time the church remains silent about the injustices that are in society, she is guilty. And to talk about justifying little actions such as blocking school buses and violating a Mayor's proclamation is just sheer hypocrisy.

VIOLENCE

[Photo by
Frank Lodge/Image.]

Violence is many things.

It's watching little black children go to bed at night wondering whether or not the rats will come through the wall and bite them. It's sitting in the house for two weeks with overcoats on and wrapped in blankets trying to keep warm.

Violence is watching the kids across the street walk out of the house without any shoes on.

It's knowing they're wondering whether they'll get a next meal.

COURTS

[Photo by Frank Lodge/Image.]

I went to court. The two D.A.'s were both white. The judge was white. There were eleven white jurors, and one black man who had a habit of nodding his head. I knew where I stood.

And this is how a black man feels.

The same judge who gave me a six months stay of sentence, two years probation and a $500 fine, had previously sentenced a landlord who owns 16 slum houses. One house had 27 building code violations; another had 34. That same judge gave the landlord a stay of sentence and fined him $1 each on 12 of the properties.

The average fine paid in Milwaukee on building code violations is $35, including court costs. Draft protestors were recently placed under $25,000 bond. But two white men recently went before the same judge and were released on $2,500 bond. They had ridden through the black community, stuck a .22 rifle out of the window, and killed a black woman. A black Vietnam veteran was arrested as a suspect in a burglary—$25,000 bond. Two clansmen bombed the Milwaukee NAACP office and were out on $2,500 bond.

This is the kind of judicial system we live under. This is the one the black man sees.

The Poor Pay More

I was sitting on the rectory steps. Some of the brothers and sisters came from Third Street carrying clothing, furniture, and a few small items. "Hi, Father Groppi. Black Power!" they called, pointing to their loot. I said, "Be careful. Don't get caught."

That surprises you. But maybe you don't know much about gyp merchants. You go in a store and there are no prices on the merchandise. Or old stuff is sold for new. Or they sell you a $3 pair of shoes for $25.

Go read *The Poor Pay More*. The author sent a white man into a Harlem store to buy a TV set. The charge was $129. A Puerto Rican woman who followed paid $139. The black woman who came next paid $200.

[Photo by Frank Lodge/Image.]

That's stealing. And there's no difference between that kind of thievery and the man who busts the window and grabs the loot. Maybe he figures he's got it coming. He's probably paid for it five times over already.

Robbery? I call it restitution.

Fair Housing

We marched for fair housing. They asked, "Why are you working on a fair housing bill? Do black people want to live with white people?" I said, "I don't know." We'll never know until white people's intransigent attitude toward integration, and toward equality, is changed.

But the black man needs territorial expansion. If all the white people want to move to the suburbs, fine. But we want to live in fine communities too.

We marched twice on the south side in Milwaukee and nearly got killed by whites. I asked for the protection of the National Guard, but the Mayor said he couldn't call them out. "Good hard-working people live out there," he said.

I don't know how good they were, but they were certainly hard-working. They hit us with everything they could throw. They called us black bastards. And then violence broke out on the north side. The Mayor called out the National Guard and put the entire city under a curfew . . . and issued a proclamation. He didn't want us to demonstrate, he didn't want us to march, he didn't want us to use civil disobedience. He said it led to violence.

What are we supposed to do? Submit to this kind of system?

QUESTIONS FOR DISCUSSION

1. *According to Groppi, how has the church reacted to civil disobedience?*
2. *Why have the editors placed this article in this particular section—"The Enculturation of Violence"?*
3. *How does Groppi account for the violence of the black man? Does the priest condemn violence?*
4. *In what way does Groppi's evidence or support for his ideas differ from that used by the other authors in this section? Is Groppi's reasoning as valid as that of the other authors?*

4

Planned and Unplanned Violence

"*I meant get out* there *and fight!*"

[Cartoon by Virgil Partch. Reproduced by special permission of *Playboy* magazine; copyright © 1968 by *Playboy*.]

VIOLENCE IS OFTEN PLANNED AND JUST AS OFTEN unplanned. It can be a calculated strategy or a spontaneous outburst of either a rational or a deranged mind. Violence, then, may be a cause as well as an effect.

The defective, the deranged human being unable to control himself, is responsible for a significant amount of the violence in our lives—he is "born to raise hell." We might well ask how much his behavior has intensified the atmosphere of hate and spurred the national mind to undertake violence. We believe that men like Lee Harvey Oswald and Richard Speck have done wrong, yet we have done little as a society to study and care for them. Study of their cases indicates that they frequently provided warnings of their sickness before they committed murder, yet little had been done to cure them. Rosenthal, Rifkin, and Martin offer findings and suggestions in this section that give insight into these people and the problems they contribute to our society.

Unplanned violence may also be the result of exhaustion or fatigue, or an inability to act in any other way. How often in the midst of social confrontation are social inhibitions reduced to a level where violence is impulsively used in an attempt to terminate the matter?

Much of today's organized violence—civil rights protests, the college sit-ins, strikes, and welfare demonstrations —is supposedly the product of the rational, healthy mind. These forms of violence are still within the framework of Western thought, which has emphasized reason for at least three hundred years. Many of the protesters are articulate, intelligent, and fairly well-educated. However, when the young reject reason as a tool for settling differences or resolving disputes, violence occurs. Too often, young revolutionaries turn to violence, not as a last resort, but as an early, even initial, resort. They take a violent, direct approach to the perceived problem.

Americans do not have a passive approach to life or its problems. Violence may be one key to their vigor. Violence *is* immediate. It is sudden. In using it, many ignore the preconditions for the successful implementation of violence suggested by Richard Hofstadter in "The Future of American Violence" (reprinted in Part One). Wheeler in this section sets up some more propositions for your consideration. Sometimes the rules don't fit the game being played. In the Populist era, a lady orator frequently demanded that the farmers of Kansas and the midwest "Raise less corn and more hell!" Have we arrived at another watershed moment in our national development when orators are again urging a new set of rules, with a new referee?

"*I certainly think violence has its place. What I object to is
<u>senseless</u> violence.*"

[Drawing by Mischa Richter; © 1968 The New Yorker Magazine,
Inc.]

Violence Is Predictable

ALAN ROSENTHAL

Is violence a medical problem? Is there a type of person who is violence-prone—for organic, not psychiatric, reasons—and whose aggressive tendencies can be treated by physicians? If organic causes are identified, could they be prevented, heading off potential violent behavior?

A growing number of scientists are responding to these questions with a qualified "yes." These investigators believe that a large number of individuals suffer from a tendency to commit violent acts because they have a disorder which short-circuits their emotional control.

Frank R. Ervin, M.D., a leading researcher in this field, contends that the brain abnormalities may take a variety of forms, but the aggressive behavior fits a common pattern.

"We call the syndrome episodic dyscontrol," says Doctor Ervin, who heads a psychiatry research laboratory at Massachusetts General Hospital, Boston. "The person with this abnormality may go to extremes of behavior in response

Alan Rosenthal, "Violence is Predictable," *Today's Health*, November 1970. Published by permission of the author and *Today's Health*, published by the American Medical Association.

to a relatively small stimulus. If another driver annoys him in traffic, he may try to ram the other car or drive him off the road. A minor disagreement may cause him to lose control, and he winds up beating his wife or children or fighting at work."

Much of the violence that plagues our society falls into this category. The majority of crimes in the United States go unreported, according to the National Crime Commission. Most family squabbles, wife-beating, and fights never make the police blotters. The President's Commission on Law Enforcement pointed out that violence is far more often an act among friends than strangers. In two-thirds of all murders and aggravated assaults, the victim and offender know each other.

Until recently, such factors as the criminal's family life and environment were considered the chief underlying causes of his actions. But, in the past several years, the scientific community has begun to give serious study to the theory that personal violence may have a biologic base. Research with animals and humans is revealing that aggression, rage, and other emotional extremes correspond with strong electrochemical activity in the brain. Genetic disorders, poorly developed central nervous systems, glandular secretions, brain diseases, and severe head injuries have been linked to aggressive actions.

Psychiatrist Ervin points out that many different factors—chromosomal abnormalities, maternal malnutrition, poor infant care, serious diseases, traumatic head injuries—can affect the development and functioning of the brain, resulting in episodic dyscontrol. And the incidence of this syndrome may be substantial.

"There are an estimated 10 million Americans with gross brain disorders—epilepsy, mental retardation, serious illnesses," Doctor Ervin points out. "There are probably another 10 million neglected, unrecognized cases of minor brain disorders resulting from traumas or infections.

"Now I'm not saying all these 20 million people are violence-prone. But they are a reservoir of individuals with impaired central nervous systems, with impaired resources to cope with various kinds of stress."

These individuals may be major contributors to crimes of violence.

Dr. Marvin Ziporyn, a Chicago psychiatrist, has concluded that Richard Speck (convicted murderer of eight student nurses) suffered brain damage from severe illnesses and injuries in infancy and childhood. The senseless shooting spree of Charles Whitman (the "Texas Tower sniper" who shot 44 persons, killing 14) was believed to have been triggered by a small brain tumor.

Emotionally impaired persons also might play a significant role in traffic accidents, Doctor Ervin believes, since most of the individuals he has studied admit using the automobile as a mechanism of assault.

Doctor Ervin's conclusion that brain abnormalities may spark violent actions grew from his research with epileptic patients. Working with Dr. Vernon Mark, director of neurosurgical service at Boston City Hospital, and Dr. William Sweet, chief of neurosurgery at Massachusetts General, he studied the fits of destruction and rage exhibited by patients with temporal lobe epilepsy (a disease that affects the limbic structures of the brain—those linked to a person's emotions and instincts).

The investigators found that the violent attacks corresponded with an erratic pattern of electrical activity in the brain, as recorded by electroencephalograph (EEG). They discovered that electrical stimulation, through surgically implanted electrodes, of certain points in the limbic system could trigger violent behavior; stimulation of other points could "turn off" an attack once it had started.

"Next we probed the question of whether there are individuals who exhibit the same symptoms of violent episodes as the epileptics, but who do not have epilepsy," relates Doctor Ervin, a specialist in brain functions. "Our research indicates that the same kind of activity does occur in persons with episodic dyscontrol as goes on in the epileptic."

This observation leads to the most exciting aspect of his theory: "If this is true, then the condition is diagnosable; it's potentially treatable; and it's certainly preventable. It becomes a practical medical and educational problem that can be approached in an orderly way."

This optimistic outlook stems from the Boston researchers' experience in controlling the syndrome in some patients and in detecting many of the causes.

They are studying individuals who consult doctors because of chronic behavior problems. In the past two years, they have worked with more than 200 so-called self-referred patients.

"These people are concerned about their inability to control their actions," Doctor Ervin explains. "They find their own behavior puzzling, frightening, depressing. They are asking for help."

More than half of the patients report owning a weapon and using it at least once. Eight admit committing murder. Most say they use a car as a dangerous weapon.

"Of the entire group, more than 25 percent show clear evidence—by EEG or other neurological testing—of brain disease," Doctor Ervin reports.

"I think that episodic dyscontrol is primarily a male problem," he adds. "In our study, men outnumber women by a ratio of five or 10 to one. One reason it's a man's syndrome may be that the behavior is much less tolerated in a male than a female. When a woman runs amuck, smashes dishes, that sort of thing, her husband doesn't get anxious and call the cops. But if he does the same thing, she *is* liable to call the cops.

"So women may experience the same impulsive feelings, but they are liable to handle them in ways other than overt aggression."

Serious wife-beating was the most common manifestation of loss of control among men studied at Massachusetts General.

"One individual had hospitalized his wife three times in two years," the psychiatrist recalls. "Once her spleen was ruptured after he kicked and beat her; another time she suffered fractured ribs and a broken arm. He was in despair about his behavior, so he sought medical help. It turned out he had a clear limbic brain disease."

Almost all the violent persons were dangerous drivers; when they got angry while behind the wheel, they frightened even themselves.

One man, who was referred to Doctor Ervin by a neurologist, exhibited a variety of symptoms: "He was afraid of losing emotional control while driving a car in the city; he beat his wife regularly. On a visit to his parents' home, he got into an argument about which television channel to watch. This sparked a violent reaction in which he destroyed every piece of furniture in the living room and hurled most of it out the front window." (This patient is now being treated with medication to help him control his behavior.)

Through detailed medical histories, the Boston researchers found that loss-of-control episodes often could be traced to childhood. In many cases, a clear change in personality occurred after a head injury, a bout with measles, or a prolonged high fever in eary years. Brain damage might be tracked back even further—to some problem in infancy or in the fetal stage.

"The majority of what we call brain damage may result from poor prenatal care, a difficult delivery, inadequate post-natal care, and infant malnutrition," Doctor Ervin states. "The brain is a very sensitive little computer, especially early in life. Factors such as lack of oxygen, low blood sugar, or traumas may mean that the baby's brain doesn't have a chance to get well organized, doesn't develop properly.

"If there were good nutritional and medical care for all pregnant women and for all babies up to 12 months of age, what's considered brain disease could be knocked down to perhaps one-tenth of what it is today."

Early causes of the dyscontrol syndrome suggest that violent behavior may show up in childhood. There are warning signs that could alert parents that youngsters may be violence-prone. But they are difficult to spot, since many of the activities are shrugged off to the boys-will-be-boys category. Normal youngsters do most of the same things. With the brain-damaged, it's primarily a matter of degree.

"We find that violence-prone persons have a childhood history of hyperactive behavior, multiple fire-setting, prolonged enuresis (bed wetting), cruelty to animals—destructive activities generally out-of-keeping with their peers," Doctor Ervin relates.

Parents should be able to spot many of these signals. And they should heed the reports of teachers who view the child and his behavior in the pespective of his classmates. The youngster may repeatedly get into fights in school, smash windows, or display other actions indicating loss of emotional control.

If such behavior is recognized, the child should be examined by his physician or a specialist to determine whether a brain disorder might be involved.

In a violence-prone adult, the syndrome is most likely to be spotted by immediate family members. Of course, episodes of aggression will be obvious. In addition, members of his household might detect a set of symptoms which lead up to overt acts of dyscontrol.

For example, the individual may complain of "feeling funny" when he wakes up in the morning; he may experience a strange sensation on one side of the head, feel irritable or tense, "see flashing lights." There may be subtle changes in behavior, small differences in attitude, activity, or speech. Then, perhaps a few minutes or hours later, a minor occurence sets off a violent episode.

The individual himself, as well as his family and co-workers, may learn to recognize these warning periods before the storm.

If an impending outburst is detected, the person should not proceed with activities which might trigger violence. He should not drive a car. He should avoid family squabbles. Perhaps he shouldn't even go to work that day.

Some of the Massachusetts General patients phone a psychiatrist or come to the hospital when they feel an attack coming on.

The research project has pointed up several other caveats for the violence-prone individual.

"Unfortunately, when this type of person notices his rising tension and other warning signs, he frequently tries to medicate himself with alcohol," Doctor Ervin notes. "This doesn't work. In fact, alcohol makes things worse. It probably affects the limbic system, exacerbating the dyscontrol episodes."

Amphetamine drugs ("pep pills") also should be shunned by anyone with this emotional problem.

"It's likely that intense, acute amphetamine intoxication or chronic use can produce a kind of paranoid behavior disorder, contributing to certain kinds of violence," the psychiatrist believes. "If dosage is prolonged and high enough, it may actually produce brain damage."

What should a violence-prone individual do?

Primarily, the possibility that the behavior problem might stem from organic causes should be recognized. Then, specialized medical attention should be sought. Psychiatrists and neurologists, like those at the Stanley Cobb Research Laboratories for Psychiatric Research, where Doctor Ervin is director, are trained to diagnose the dyscontrol syndrome and to initiate appropriate treatment.

"First we obtain a careful medical history and conduct a complete neurological examination," the psychiatrist says. "We take an EEG, do a careful study of the visual and auditory systems, perhaps x-ray the skull."

If brain abnormalities are believed to be a cause of violent actions, physicians may choose from three main treatment routes—medication, surgery, or psychotherapy. In some instances, two methods may be utilized in combination.

Tranquilizers and/or anticonvulsant drugs have been effective with many patients. Usually, the psychiatrist supplements this with discussion sessions with the individual and his family. The patient and those around him, particularly his spouse, must learn to spot the signs of impending violent episodes and to realize the importance of taking the medication regularly.

"If the problem is associated with identifiable gross brain disease, a tumor or lesion, then surgical treatment of the underlying disease is indicated," Doctor Ervin says. The offending portion of the brain is removed, allowing the central nervous system to function normally.

Doctor Ervin cites the case of one man, referred to Massachusetts General by a psychiatrist who recognized the pattern of aggressive behavior. Medication was tried first, but the patient did not respond. Finally, doctors detected scar tissue from an injury that occurred nearly 20 years earlier. The damaged portion of the limbic system was destroyed by surgery. It has now been more than three years since the operation, and the man has had no recurrences of assaultive behavior.

The third possible treatment method, which is still in the experimental stage, is a special type of psychological conditioning process in which the individual learns to mentally control the workings of his body or brain.

Through stimulus and reward (or punishment) techniques, medical researchers have demonstrated that animals can be "taught" to increase or decrease such functions as heart rate, blood pressure, and brain activity. Most pertinent are experiments at Rockefeller University, New York, in which cats were taught—through electric stimulation—to modify both the level and behavioral activity of their brain waves.

"It should be possible to teach a well-motivated patient to change undesirable responses to more desirable ones," says Neal Miller, Ph.D., of Rockefeller's research laboratories. "It is even conceivable that, in some cases, responses reflected in abnormal EEG activity can be modified by learning."

Doctor Ervin is intrigued by this possibility of teaching a violence-prone individual to control his own brain functions through conditioning, but so far, the technique has not been attempted on any patients with episodic dyscontrol.

Some observers suggest a fourth potential method of therapy. Since work with epileptics and animals shows that violent activity can be almost literally turned on and off by electrical stimulation of the brain, it is conceivable that this technique could be used to control patients with severe abnormalities.

This is not considered feasible by Doctor Ervin. Electrodes would have to be implanted at specific points deep within the brain. This is a major surgical procedure, performed only in rare, serious cases.

Even if this were accomplished, the individual would have to be taught to feel an attack coming on and to initiate electrical impulses at precisely the right moment. In addition, some sort of portable electronic mechanism would have to be carried by the person at all times to provide the impulses.

"In all, it's not very realistic," Doctor Ervin feels. "The complexities boggle the mind."

The work going on at Massachusetts General, plus that being conducted at several other research centers in the United States, Europe, and Japan, may represent a substantial step toward understanding the problem of personal violence. But it marks only the initial stage in efforts to control and treat these individuals.

A growing number of scientists now recognize that violent behavior often has a biologic base and may respond to treatment. But to actually help large numbers of people who have the problem, physicians and social workers must be alert to the syndrome and aware of its symptoms. Family members must help spot these aggressive individuals and see that they seek treatment. Society should pay special attention to those who repeatedly get into trouble with the law.

"The best single indicator to whether a person is going to commit a violent act is whether or not he has before," says Doctor Ervin. "Most people convicted of a crime of violence have a previous conviction for a violent crime. Nearly 60 percent of our self-referred patients had been arrested for some such violent behavior.

"So we should look at why a person is up before the judge. He may be severely mentally retarded; he may be epileptic; he may have brain disease or damage; he may simply never have learned any better in the subculture he lives in. Each of those situations requires a different rehabilitative approach.

"Our organic theory does not account for all violent crimes, and neither does strict emphasis on environmental factors. Undoubtedly the two influences overlap."

In addition to education and social awareness, there must be further research into the basic biologic mechanisms and refinement of research techniques, the psychiatrist says.

"More direct tests of limbic functions must be developed," he notes. "Maybe we can utilize computer analyses of EEG activity or neuroendocrine assays [measurement of amounts of hormones—especially sex hormones—circulating in the body]. Perhaps a set of psychological tests can be designed to diagnose the syndrome. We are moving along those three routes now."

The next step is more orderly investigations of the various modes of treatment, using control subjects who do not receive therapy, then subjecting the results to modern analysis procedures.

"We also need to develop facilities to house these individuals for diagnosis and treatment," Doctor Ervin points out. "Currently we do not have adequate facilities that are both medically sophisticated and tolerant of patients with behavioral abnormalities.

"Overall, we need the kind of prevention which recognizes that most brain damage is avoidable. Then we must provide proper medical care, proper prenatal treatment, and proper nutrition."

With such professional attention, and a modification of society's view toward these disorders, a substantial portion of the personal violence problem may be brought under control.

QUESTIONS FOR DISCUSSION

1. *Is violence a medical problem?*
2. *What is a symptom of episodic dyscontrol?*
3. *How much violence in our country is caused by episodic dyscontrol?*
4. *What disorders have been linked to aggressive actions?*
5. *What factors can affect the development and functioning of the brain?*
6. *What people does the author cite as examples of emotionally impaired persons?*
7. *What is significant if epilepsy and episodic dyscontrol have the same cause?*
8. *Why is episodic dyscontrol less tolerated in men than women?*
9. *Do most people suffering from episodic dyscontrol have histories of failure to control themselves?*
10. *How may a pregnant mother's diet affect the behavior of her child?*

11. *What are some of the signs of episodic dyscontrol in children?*

12. *What activities should be shunned by adults with emotional problems?*

13. *What are the three main treatments for brain abnormalities?*

14. *What is a fourth potential method of therapy?*

15. *What is the best single indicator of whether or not a person is going to commit a violent act?*

16. *What areas are ripe for future research, according to Dr. Ervin?*

Violence in Human Behavior

ALFRED H. RIFKIN

The role of violence in human behavior was discussed in the program sponsored by the Academy of Psychoanalysis and by the Committee on Science in the Promotion of Human Welfare at the AAAS Philadelphia meeting on 28 and 29 December 1962. The papers ranged from studies of animal behavior to psychoanalytic interpretations and studies of the use and control of violent behavior in various cultures. The outstanding feature of this symposium was the affirmation implicit in all the presentations and discussions that the behavioral sciences can indeed contribute to the control of the ultimate violence which hangs over us, that behavioral scientists must bring their several and collective skills to bear on the problem, and that behavioral scientists have a real responsibility to the community to make known what they *have* learned.

In his keynote address David McK. Rioch (Walter Reed Army Research Center) pointed out that the symposium would consider different aspects of violence from dif-

"Violence in Human Behavior," Rifkin, A., *Science*, Vol. 140, pp. 904–906, 24 May 1963. Copyright 1963 by the American Association for the Advancement of Science.

ferent points of view with the aim of better understanding human aggressive behavior and its socially organized expression in warfare. In such an endeavor it is necessary to keep in mind the setting, objectives, and limitations of each study, and to exercise great caution in translating concepts from one level of investigation to another. Rioch reviewed briefly such diverse contributions as Von Clausewitz's treatise on war, Marshall's reports on the experiences of combat troops, Clark's studies of the northern grasshopper mouse, and various experimental studies of the areas of the brain involved in aggressive behavior in animals. His overall conclusion was that there is no occult force which pushes people to violence; rather, violence is a pattern which may be reasonably used, or it may be resorted to in situations of uncertainty and social disorganization.

"Ceremonial" battles were depicted in color films of combat between male marine iguanas in the Galapagos Islands (Irenäus Eibl-Eibesfeldt, Max Planck Institut). These battles are "ceremonial" in the sense that they follow a specific pattern of display, threat, and combat, but rarely result in actual damage to either combatant. Certain behaviors trigger or stop the combat. Many species exhibit such "ceremonials" which differ from the aggressive action taken against other species. This differential aggression toward con-specifics appears to be a biological mechanism designed to "space" animals within their range and at the same time to protect the species against self-annihilation. The analogue in man may be represented by submissive posture or crying which may evoke pity or inhibit an aggressor. In the modern scene, however, a bullet or a nuclear missile can kill a con-specific before he has any opportunity to appeal to any possibly inborn inhibitions in the aggressor.

John B. Calhoun (Institute for Advanced Study of Behavioral Sciences) studied rat behavior as a function of the relation of each individual to its neighbor in its life space. The significant experimental variable was the size of the group, which in turn determines the social velocity or social temperature. There is an optimal size as well as a maximum tolerable size for the groups. Beyond this size individual and group behavior break down. The most striking products of breakdown were the "predator rats" which terrorized their group.

A series of ingenious experiments on the induction and expression of hostility in human subjects was revealed by Leonard Berkowitz (University of Wisconsin). The investigations were directed to the role of previous learned responses, the expectations of the subjects, the degree of specificity or generalization of hostile reactions, and the catharsis of hostility. The results suggested that (i) aggression is elicited and cued by stimuli which have particular meaning; (ii) an internal state, usually labeled anger, is necessary but not sufficient for the production of aggression; (iii) anticipation of an opportunity increases hostile activity; and (iv) expression of hostility (under the conditions of the experiment) did not have any cathartic effect and inability or lack of opportunity to express hostility did not intensify the hostility.

Anger was described as a basic emotion with a creative potential in the face of an actual anticipated threat (Bella S. Van Bark, New York City). The relatively healthy individual often knows the sources of his anger directly and is willing to become involved in the threatening situation and to expose himself to the possibility of struggle and conflict. In neurotics such sources are outside the realm of their awareness, the sense of identity is precarious, and the willingness to become involved is lessened. Suppression, regression, and alienation from self are substituted for inner controls. This creates an explosive potential which may find expression in outbursts of intense emotion and seemingly unrelated acts of violence.

Harold Lief (Tulane University) regards aggression as a term used too loosely. It should be restricted to behavior motivated by the wish to injure, remove, or destroy a threatening object. [Violence is an end point on a continuum of behaviors with similar motivation. At least three types of violence may be discerned: the type driven by rage; a detached type in which the significant aspect is the violent act rather than the subject of the attack; and a detached type in which destruction of the object is the significant aspect and the violence is an instrument required for the attainment of the goal.] Man in the 20th century is familiar with these in the form of the movie gangster, the Western gunman, the violent gang member, a genocide, and nuclear war. Increasing dehumanization in society leads to an increase in detached violence; dissociation from man's basic emotions is the greatest danger to man's survival. There is obviously an urgent need for societal controls which will prevent detached, dehumanized violence from being carried out, but the institutions to accomplish this must be created. There is need for a long-term and revolutionary new approach to education in which the realities of emotional life are taught to children from the nursery on and which is designed to bring our cave man emotions into appropriate resonance with our technical genius.

The thesis was advanced by Joost A. M. Meerloo (New York) that an even greater danger than nuclear war arises from within man himself in the form of smoldering fears, contagious panics, primitive needs for cruel violence, and raging suicidal destructiveness. Confronted with inner and outer threats that appear insoluble, man reads with rage and fury that mask a deeper wish for surrender. Hyper-charged emotional words such as aggression, violence, first-strike, and preventive war reflect the primitive process of thinking as it takes place in the unconscious. The thought of nuclear destruction causes the dangerous return of wishes for infantile omnipotence. The assumption that fear of atomic destruction will frighten the nations into planning for a constructive peace is an unrealistic fantasy.

The either-or approaches, world government or dying together, Red or dead, are primitive vacillations which reveal
the inner paradox. Fortunately there are more constructive
forces active in man. History has seen many lasting periods
of peaceful coexistence. Peace is derived from a word
meaning pact, a mutual agreement between forces in equilibrium. This idea of peace opposes the utopian illusion of
perfect human harmony and the millenium in favor of a
balance of growing mutual control. The passive inner acceptance of the dilemma of surrender versus glorious suicide is the greatest danger. Our great hope lies in the fact
that potential enemies, who are psychologically not different
from us, must ask themselves similar questions.

In his paper on "A psychoanalytic suggestion for the
prevention of nuclear disaster," Sandor Rado (New York)
said he touched on but a tiny fraction of the problems posed
by the nuclear threat. It is clear that a vast plan is needed
for global adaptation to the atomic threat. Such a plan
would require contributions from the many sciences, would
extend over a long period, and would be composed of all
the rational elements that can be assembled. But the problem of survival, now no longer the problem of survival of
individuals or small groups but of the survival of all, cannot
wait. What can be added to the rational schemes that have
yet to be created? Strong emotional forces! Peoples all over
the world rely on spiritual and emotional forces to achieve
security. Self-reliance is augmented by the hope that parental figures will help. These parental figures cannot be called
upon in the present issue; they have already been invoked
to aid the contending groups against each other. A symbol
that is uniquely suited for the present purpose is the human
infant. Every infant is an offspring of the human species, a
continuation of the life of his parents, a carrier of our hopes
for the future, an inspiration of present efforts for the benefit of generations to come. Said Rado: "I believe mankind
is ready for an emotional, cultural and not religious cult of

the infant that would be based on no illusions of any kind, no deceit of any kind. The emotional security of survival, global survival, would then be complemented by the economic security to be achieved by nuclear technology."

One approach to organized violence was developed after a study of conflict between members of related lineage and clan groups in Central Somalia (David H. Marlowe, Walter Reed Army Research Center). Among these people disputes are perceived in absolute, all-or-none, win or lose terms, and armed force is still the ultimate and preferred mode of achieving a solution. But individuals and groups do not fight at random, nor is violence directly in proportion to the gravity of the interests involved. Instead, conflict is controlled through the invocation of kinship, contracts, alliances, and myriad other legal and traditional mechanisms built into the social system. These mechanisms determine whether and to what extent and toward whom violence is permissible, obligatory, or interdicted. The distinctions are built into the very language. If an outsider assaults a clan member the act is referred to as "war," the spot where it occurred as the "place where war stands." If the assailant was of the same clan the event is assault; if within the clan and of the same blood lineage, the term of reference is invariably "accident." Suitable rationalizations support the perception of the event in the terms required by the system. Where violence is sanctioned, the system also sets limits upon it, and establishes the criteria for acceptable compromise.

Lewis A. Coser (Brandeis University), speaking on social control of violence, pointed out that outbreaks of violence, such as homicide, do not vary at random, but are socially patterned. The rates vary in the United States in terms of ethnic and class membership, region, and so forth. Lower position in the status hierarchy of American society and the frustrations which such lower position brings lead to higher homicide rates. Hence negroes have higher homicide rates than whites, the depressed Southern regions have higher rates than the developed Northern regions, and lower class rates are higher than upper class rates. Not only is aggressive acting out in general, and the rate of homicide in particular, connected with the relative deprivation of various status categories, but there are differences in the built-in barriers within the various groups. In moments of particular stress the lower status person experiences a lower degree of internalized restraint against the acting out of violence. Data on differential homicide rates in the United States were compared to data on the participation in riots, revolutions and the like, both here and abroad, and it was found that the patterns are broadly similar. In both cases, the "underdogs" participate much more widely in violence than the "topdogs." These findings substantiate the view that rates of violence, far from resulting from biological impulse or idiosyncratic propensities, can be explained in terms of the position of people within the social structure of a given society.

It was proposed by Anthony Leeds (Pan-American Union) that war must be approached as if it were merely another social phenomenon, to be understood with the same armamentarium of concepts, the same weaponry of analysis, the same strategy of socio-cultural explanations as any other social phenomenon, and without a priori value positions however much the analyst may personally derogate war. Viewed in this way, war has functions in the social order which include consolidation and redistribution of internal power; consolidation of trends already present in a society, such as industrialization, administrative centralization, or militarism; the establishment of institutions of community coordination and control over the populace with removal of effective opposition; technological innovations; the revitalization of existing norms and values, and the resolution or intensification of old social conflicts. If decisions are made to cope with nuclear war in the assumption that war in general and a qualitatively new kind of war, nuclear war, is undesirable and to be eradicated, then this range of functions must be transferred to other social institutions. These institutions must be multi-functional so as to have a high likelihood of persistence. Such institutions include the family, the state, and the church.

Margaret Mead (New York City) called attention to a basic biological characteristic which man shares with most other animals, the protection of females and the young by the male. In no known human group has this responsibility disappeared. Man's cognitive and imaginative abilities, not shared by other animals, enable 100 million people who never see each other to define themselves as con-specifics, or, on the other hand, enables two adjacent tribes to define each other as prey and predator and spend their time killing each other off. The basic biological ability of humans to live in small groups and protect each other can be extended through the knowledge that all men are in fact interdependent in the modern world scene. All human cultures attempt to ritualize and stylize destructiveness in ways that are reminiscent of the iguanas or stags. This is done through symbolic processes, understanding of which is the daily work of psychoanalysts, who can illuminate why the processes succeed with some individuals and fail in others. The concept that all men are, after all, con-specifics is relatively new. It can be the basis for Rado's suggestion of the human infant as a symbol that as one species all men will take responsibility for all the children of that species.

Several possible models of what a disarmed world might look like were described by Arthur I. Waskow (Peace Research Institute). This, he said, is not only a necessary exercise of scholarship, but a practical political one, of importance in making disarmament more likely. Even a government that wants disarmament and believes that problems of inspection and enforcement have been solved will not take such a step if it has no idea how its conflicts with other states and how the hostilities of its own citizens will be handled. One possible model is a "world under law," with controls vested in a world government, with an appropriate parliament, executive and peace police. The difficulty with this model is that existing conflicts between states are too intense and there is not sufficient agreement on the bases for the legal codes to be followed. Another model is that of "disarmed disorder," in which each nation could attempt to advance its interests and defend its ideology so long as it did not use violence. The main objection here is that nations would not stay disarmed very long. The dilemma is between placing so much emphasis on preserving order that no nation agrees to disarm, and having so little machinery to maintain order that the world cannot be kept disarmed. The dilemma might be resolved by a "world state" which would have a monopoly of legitimate violence, but not the physical power or legal authority to change the social systems of any country. Substitutes for war would have to be invented. Research in this direction can be undertaken at once, and is urgently needed.

Jules H. Masserman (Northwestern University Medical School), in a final critique and integration, concluded that the speakers at this program had shown that aggression is not to be regarded as a mythical, absolute quantity, which must be channeled, directed, turned on or off, discharged or accumulated. It is, rather, a panchrestic term, which does not have the same operational connotation to any two persons or to the same person in two successive transactions. Then, referring to Rado's proposal to adopt the human infant as a universal symbol of peace, Masserman offered a concrete alternative. He suggested that we send to Russia, as soon as possible, large numbers of students, and invite the Russians to reciprocate, in order to broaden mutual education and promote a new and advantageous understanding.

Masserman said, "Perhaps, in this way we can help awaken the world out of its current nightmare of violence into a happier day of welfare through sanity."

QUESTIONS FOR DISCUSSION

1. *What was the outstanding feature of this meeting?*
2. *According to Rioch's study, is there an "occult force which pushes people to violence"?*
3. *What factor affects how rats behave in a group?*
4. *According to Harold Lief, what are the three types of violence?*
5. *What did Meerloo say in his paper about violence?*
6. *According to Coser's work, are outbreaks of violence random? Can rates of violence be explained in terms of the position of people within the social structure of a given society?*
7. *What function does war serve in a society, according to Leeds?*

The Criminal Mentality

JOHN BARTLOW MARTIN

Somewhere in the United States tonight, the chances are a young man is planning to kill several people. He would be in his early 20s, mild-mannered, polite and rather studious. He would likely be married but not satisfactorily. He might be attending college, though on a basis both accelerated and irregular. Once in recent years, he would have spent time in apparently aimless wandering; friends will recall later that, yes, now they remembered he once disappeared for a while. They will also remember that he was "the quiet type," didn't say much; and one, a neighbor who knew him when he was a child, will remember that he did odd things and that there was something vaguely "unhappy" or even "unhealthy" about his home life with his parents. But his mother will tell reporters he was a "perfect" son; his pastor will recall that he sang in the choir; and a grammar school teacher, that he was a "model student." A psychiatrist he visited voluntarily a few years ago will find in his records routine notes: "loveless childhood," "severe anxiety and tension," "low affect,"

John Bartlow Martin, "The Criminal Mentality," originally appeared in *Playboy* magazine (December 1967); Copyright © 1967 by HMH Publishing Co., Inc.

"seems flat," "relates poorly to authority figures," "feels inadequate," "paranoid trends." The records will show that what appeared to precipitate his visit to the psychiatrist was trouble with his wife, and that the psychiatrist urged him to return next week at the same time—but he never did.

The people he is planning to kill tomorrow mean nothing to him. Chances are he doesn't even know them yet. But he knows dimly they will be women. Tonight he will stay up all night, making preparations. Tomorrow, after it is all over and he is being led away manacled from the bodies, surrounded by newspapermen and television photographers, he will smile and say, no, he isn't sorry he did it and, no, he had no particular reason to do it except that he wanted to become famous.

It would perhaps not be good public policy to pursue further this sketch of a mythical murderer. Several recent mass murderers have said they were "inspired" to horror by the publicity given a previous mass murderer. Psychiatrists know that such publicity can never be more than a trigger mechanism, releasing a homicidal drive already deep-set.

In recent months, a Minnesota farmer shot and killed his wife and set a fire in which his four children burned to death; a 21-year-old high school dropout shot and killed a family of nine in Canada; a sniper high on the tower of the University of Texas in Austin killed 13 people and wounded 31; a man entered an apartment in Chicago and strangled eight student nurses; another man shot five people to death in New Haven, Connecticut; and still another invaded a beauty parlor in Mesa, Arizona, forced five women and two children to lie down on the floor and shot them methodically.

Such shocking, spectacular and seemingly senseless crimes make us wonder whether "a criminal mentality," or "killer instinct," exists and what can be done to protect ourselves from its work. This article explores those questions and related ones.

It may be well to dispose at once of the notion that man is a peaceable animal, though this should hardly be necessary if one remembers Auschwitz. As Konrad Lorenz has shown, of all the carnivores, only two lack built-in inhibitions against killing members of their own species—rats and men.

All human societies distinguish between killing members of one's own group and killing outsiders. The latter is called "warfare"; the former, "murder." Since man does not feel inhibited against killing his own kind, he has enacted laws against it. We punish murder. Nonetheless, we feel fairly comfortable with murder for profit, or revenge, or jealousy, or some other "rational" motive that we can understand. What shocks us is a murder "without reason." What shocks and bewilders and frightens us most of all is mass murder "without reason."

Some mass murders are completely rational. In the 1890s, Dr. H. H. Holmes lured more than 20 ladies to his murder castle in Chicago, mulcted most of them, married some and dispatched all. People were shocked but not bewildered; greed they could understand. In 1948, two young men were paroled from the state "reformatory" in Ohio, embarked on a series of stick-ups, killed a tavern owner, remembered that a reformatory guard had treated them ill, went to seek him out, entered the home of his superior instead, took this man and his wife and daughter to a cornfield, shot them dead and, during the ensuing manhunt, killed two other people who happened to impede their flight. The state killed both, but with understanding: Robbery, revenge and flight are comprehensible.

But the emotions aroused by the Austin sniper or the Arizona beauty-parlor killer or the nurses' strangler are different. They differ even from the emotions aroused by Howard Unruh, who in 1949 slaughtered 13 people in Camden, New Jersey; for Unruh was psychotic—the diagnosis was schizophrenia—and people can accept the idea that lunatics kill. (Actually, they seldom do: They cannot often organize and direct their energies toward so sustained an undertaking as murder, especially mass murder.) What bothers people about the noninsane unmotivated murderer is that he simply cannot be explained. His activities do not yield to rational analysis. Spectacular inexplicable crime simply calls public attention to a fact that experts must confront every day: We simply do not know much about the roots of criminality.

Day in, day out, judges must assess criminal responsibility; wardens must keep, and may try to "rehabilitate," those adjudged dangerous to society; parole boards must decide when it is safe to loose a prisoner on society. These are sometimes life-and-death decisions. And they must involve the roots of crime. Yet knowledge and theory on this subject are a treacherous swamp.

Through this swamp flow three main streams of thought. One is the theory that criminality is biologically conditioned, or even inherited. An Italian physician, Cesare Lombroso, in 1876 postulated the born criminal. Lombroso said he had established by anthropological measurements that the physical and psychological characteristics of criminals differed strikingly from those of noncriminals. But soon a British study exploded them and, as psychoanalysis arose, Lombroso became almost a joke. In 1939, however, Earnest Hooton, an American anthropologist, after studying 15,000 criminals, published his view that criminals are biologically inferior to noncriminals. Dr. William H. Sheldon, after studying several hundred delinquent young men, concluded that there is a necessary relationship between body type—physique—and temperament; his work is an attempt to ground psychiatry in biology. He found three kinds of delinquents—people who get into trouble because of mental or medical insufficiency (e.g., feeble-mindedness), because of psychotic or neurotic difficulties or because of none of these and for no other apparent reason. This last, Sheldon termed the component of "primary criminality." In most cases, all three components were intermingled. In a considerable number of the boys, Sheldon discerned the component of "primary criminality." He thought that he had seen in his series of criminals the same thing Lombroso and Hooton had seen—true qualitative differences in personalities that, because of inadequate techniques, eluded them. Sheldon suggested that further biological studies may show that "delinquency may reside in the cellular morphogenotype." He maintained that the parents of his delinquents were themselves delinquent and in "very much the same way" and to about the same degree that their boys were.

Earlier, a German psychiatrist had reported that of the *identical* twins of 13 convicts, 10 had also served prison terms—but that of the *nonidentical* twins of 17 convicts, only 2 had. He concluded that criminality was biologically determined and hereditary. Dr. Franz Kallmann has advanced the view that schizophrenia is hereditary. He has reported that the mathematical probability of suffering schizophrenia is only .85 percent in the general population, but is 16.4 percent among the children of one schizophrenic parent; it is 14 percent for a *nonidentical* twin of a person who has schizophrenia, but it is 85.8 percent for the *identical* twin of a schizophrenic.

Psychiatry has always been split between those who attribute mental disorder to physical causes and those who insist it is of purely emotional origin.

Most psychiatrists do not consider the case for heredity proved (but it has never been disproved, either). Until a few years ago, the work of Hooton, Sheldon and Kallman was largely ignored. Then, when doctors discovered the

effects of certain tranquilizing drugs, such as chlorproma-
zine (Thorazine) and reserpine (Serpasil), on mental
patients, the whole biological school of thought gained sudden ascendancy. Too sudden, perhaps—false hopes were
sometimes raised, and the drugs have not proved to be cure-
alls for mental illness. Nevertheless, interest in the drugs
stimulated interest in biological research, especially bio-
chemistry. To date, this work has produced no final answer
on the "cause" of mental illness—indeed, it is unlikely to do
so, since a single cause for so complex and varied a phenomenon is unlikely. But it has focused the interest of
laboratory men on human behavior.

The second broad school of thought about the roots of
criminality is sociological. As everybody knows, children
who grow up in slums, badly treated at home and poorly
educated at school, surrounded by teenage delinquency, are
likely to end up in prison. Studies have documented it, from
such great sociological works of the 1920s and 1930s at the
University of Chicago as *The Gold Coast and the Slum, The
Gang* and *Delinquency Areas*, down to the HARYOU work
of the 1960s. They show that certain areas of the city favor
criminal behavior—slums in the older parts of the city
where housing is bad, schools are crowded, poverty is great,
family and community life disorganized, recreational facilities few, and a tradition of delinquent behavior is passed on
from one generation to another, as is the tradition of eating
with a spoon. Other studies showed, too, that "white-collar
crime"—embezzlement, tax evasion, and so on—increased
as urbanization increased, removing the brake of neighborhood disapproval.

But the sociologists could not explain everything, as
they themselves said. What of the slum boy who grows up
straight? What of the suburban boy enjoying all the outward "advantages" who goes wrong? The sociologists called
attention to many important problems of our cities, problems that are today made screamingly acute by the Negro

revolution. But in the end, they concluded that of all the factors involved in criminality, the most important was the subtle emotional relationship among members of the family. And this is far closer to psychiatry than to sociology.

The third theory of the roots of crime is the psychiatric view: that crime is the product of psychic deficiency or disorder. Like the psychoses, the neuroses and the use of alcohol and drugs, crime is merely one way of solving problems, of resolving conflicts. The "sick" personality is the factor that predisposes a man to crime; the social environment triggers the explosion. (Sociologists would put it the other way around.) The difficulty with the psychiatric theory is that mental hospitals are full of psychotics who committed no crimes; while prisons are full of people who could not be called either psychotic or neurotic—and the free world is full of people who have suffered severe psychic traumas and yet have never committed felonies nor been declared insane.

Eleanor and Sheldon Glueck have attempted to synthesize the three views, matching 500 delinquent boys with 500 nondelinquent boys and studying them with Dr. William Sheldon's body-typing, psychology's Rorschach testing of personality structure and the techniques of sociology. They have found that although both groups of boys came from under-privileged neighborhoods, the delinquents' individual homes were markedly inferior to the nondelinquents' and so were their relations with their families; and they differed significantly from the nondelinquents in both body type and personality structure. The Gluecks concluded that delinquency results from the interplay of biological, psychological and cultural factors.

Hardly anyone today questions that the sociological and psychiatric views of criminality have validity, and some believe the biological view may be valid, too. None alone seems sufficient, for some criminals exhibit traits that support one theory but not the others, some exhibit two or all three and a few exhibit, at least as far as we can discern, none.

The members of this last group, the group that shows no discernible pathology—the seemingly "normal" boy who may have grown up in an "average" home and shows no biological predisposition to crime, the boy who kills for no apparent reason—are usually labeled "psychopathic personality." The psychopathic personality has been called "the wastebasket of psychiatry," into which are dumped all men who are not psychotic, not neurotic, not mentally deficient —yet there is something very wrong with them. Sometimes they are called sociopaths. They seem to be warriors, at war with the world; and upon occasion, some sort of psychic storm seems to overtake them and they kill "senselessly." The psychopath is not "insane." He knows who he is and where he is and what time it is. He dwells in our world, not the fantasy world of psychosis. He may be of above-average intelligence. But his emotions are out of kilter: his moral development, his "character," is deficient. He "knows" the consequences of criminal acts, but is unable to "feel" them. He never learns by experience. He never feels remorse or shame. He is never sorry he killed. He is the stranger among us. He rejects society and any obligation to it. He has never learned to wait. He lacks brakes. He is unpredictable. He is cold, remote; he cannot be reached by the chaplain's exhortations or the jailer's blows or the psychiatrist's ministrations. He is a wanderer; earlier in American history, he went West (and today he often dwells in the fringe jungles of our civilization). He is impulsive, immature and unstable. He commits the daring, dangerous crimes—bank robbery, assault, rape, cop killing. He is the mob's hired killer. He commits the "senseless" crimes. One man called him a "rebel without a cause."

We do not know what produces him. Perhaps he does not exist; perhaps "psychopathic personality" is only a term we have invented for those who fit no other class, for those who baffle us utterly. He may be the "born criminal" that Lombroso saw, the "biological inferior" that Hooton saw, the "primary criminal" that Sheldon saw, the teenage gang leader that the sociologists saw, the "defective superego" that the psychiatrists saw, the classic failure at resolving the Oedipal triangle that the psychoanalysts saw, the ratlike, animalistic aggressor without inhibition that the anthropologists saw, the "plain ornery cuss" that frontiersmen knew—or the "mad-dog killer" of tomorrow's headlines. And he may be only an imaginary beast we conjure up in the darkness of our ignorance.

All this is of far more than theoretical importance. To put the matter somewhat extremely, if Sheldon is right, if criminality resides in the cellular morphogenotype, then the solution is sterilization; if the sociologists are right, then we must totally rebuild our cities; if the psychiatrists are right, we must put a psychiatrist in every kindergarten. Stating the matter thus extremely suggests the importance of theory to public policy. Public policy for the protection of society—what should it be? Ideally, it would await the answers of science. But it cannot; crime occurs; what should we do? And inextricably entwined with the protection of society is, in a free society, the protection of individual freedom.

It is no exaggeration to say that the administration of criminal justice is the best measure of any society. So measured, our society seems superior to, say, China's or Cuba's, though it exhibits serious flaws. Despite high-court strictures, too many police still hold suspects illegally and extract confessions by force. Too often the adversary system makes trials contests by trickery, not searches for truth. Overzealous prosecutors withhold important evidence; overzealous defense lawyers coach witnesses and even subvert jurors. Only recently have state courts been obliged to provide counsel in noncapital cases. Occasionally, the innocent are convicted; more often, we hope, the guilty go free. Eyewitnesses make mistaken identifications. Innocent men with previous criminal records are in great danger. The press influences juries. Political pressures and private prejudices sway judges. Inequitable sentences are common —a man can be sentenced to a long term of years for stealing cows in a rural area but given probation for robbery in the city. A man can spend his life on skid row, in and out of jail almost constantly, and never see a lawyer: Criminal justice simply doesn't operate here. Almost no adulterers, fornicators, drunken drivers and people who bet on the numbers are prosecuted, and probably only about 30 percent of those who commit major felonies. More poor men than rich men go to prison. So do, proportionately, more Negroes than white men. Almost no rich men are executed. One prosecutor who obtained 13 death penalties recalls that only four actually were executed and all four of those were Negroes.

But progress occurs. Increasingly, the courts protect the rights of the accused, despite ignorant outcries of "coddling criminals." The law moves slowly, but it moves, and one has the impression it is improving the quality of justice in this country.

One question the judge must decide is the limit of criminal responsibility. After 1843, the M'Naghten Rule applied—a man was responsible for his acts if he possessed the ability to know their nature and quality and to distinguish right from wrong. In 1954, the District of Columbia Circuit Court of Appeals in Washington, D. C., set forth instead the Durham Rule—a man is not criminally liable if his act was "the product of mental disease or defect." Last year, Congress repealed the Durham Rule, but the President vetoed the bill; the courts are still deciding cases in this shadowland, while eminent lawyers and jurists are seeking new formulas. Meanwhile, in trial courts, the shameful contest between opposing "expert" witnesses continues. The man accused of killing eight nurses in Chicago in July 1966 was adjudged fit to stand trial—and convicted. On the other hand, Howard Unruh, the Camden killer of 1949, was adjudged insane. Sometimes the decision on who goes to prison and who goes to a mental hospital seems almost capricious.

In the past, if a man was found not responsible because of mental illness, he was consigned to a mental hospital until he recovered his sanity and could stand trial. But a few months ago, a man who had been found not guilty by reason of insanity sued for release from St. Elizabeths Hospital in Washington, claiming he had received no psychiatric treatment there; and the appellate court remanded the case: "The purpose of involuntary hospitalization is treatment, not punishment. . . . Absent treatment, the hospital is 'transformed . . . into a penitentiary where one could be held indefinitely for no convicted offense . . . .' The patient's right to treatment is clear." By thus asserting the "right to treatment," the court also spotlighted the facts that even such good public mental hospitals as St. Elizabeths are woefully unable to afford their patients treatment and, further, that the present state of both our understanding of mental disease and methods to treat it are woefully faulty.

Once a man is adjudged responsible and guilty and sent to prison, society, in the person of the warden, guards and, in more enlightened jurisdictions, social workers and psychologists and even psychiatrists, undertakes the task of "rehabilitating" him—reshaping him so he can someday safely be set free. This effort is, almost without exception, a farce. How can they rehabilitate a man in prison unless they know what drove him there in the first place? Teaching a convict to weld fenders may keep him out of mischief while he is in prison, but it has little to do with what made him a criminal and is unlikely to change him and so prevent him from repeating his crime after he is released. Teaching a boy to read, encouraging his relatives to visit him and write to him, providing a chaplain and a counselor are all very well; but if his cellmate is an experienced bank robber, he is more likely to heed that elder's wisdom than the counselor's or the teacher's or the chaplain's. Keeping a bank robber busy in a prison industry may keep him out of trouble in prison; it is not likely to persuade him to mend his ways. Putting a man out on an honor farm or conservation camp may convince him it is better to stay than to run away; it is not likely to make him a law-abiding citizen. Providing a counselor to help him with his prison-made problems, such as a faithless wife, may help him sleep better in his cell; it has nothing to do with rehabilitation. For it was not illiteracy, or "poor work habits," or indifferent relatives, or any of the rest that brought him to prison in the first place; it was something else, we know not what. And until we do know, rehabilitation inside prison is a myth. Indeed, prison, far from protecting society, is society's enemy. It does not fit men for freedom. It prisonizes men, makes them wholly unfit for life in the complicated free world. It teaches far more young men to hate than to repent, teaches them criminal techniques, not lawful vocations. The fact is that most "rehabilitation" programs are designed to ease the warden's lot—and no wonder, for big prisons are so crowded, so heterogeneous and so filled with the world's misfits and failures and warriors that simply keeping the place running without riot is all but impossible. Busy, reasonably contented convicts are less likely to mutiny than idle malcontents. But this has nothing to do with rehabilitation. The busiest, most contented convict in the prison may be the most dangerous to release; he has learned to live in prison, which means he is unfit to live outside it. Only a hardcore few dangerous criminals need maximum-security imprisonment to protect society—but thousands upon thousands of other miscreants get it. Nearly all are worsened by it. Some boys could safely be released after the first night in the prison reception cell. On the other hand, some armed robbers ought to be locked up forever; they are warriors and they will continue their war on the world whenever able. Some murderers—situational murderers—could safely be set free the day after their arrest. One such was called the Spaghetti Man. He and his family had been on relief a long time. They had no job, no money, and they had nothing to eat but spaghetti. Finally his luck turned. He got a job as a laborer. He brought home a ten-dollar advance on his wages and told his wife to go out the next day and buy the biggest sirloin steak she could find. That night, he came home and found her drunk, wearing a new hat and swaying back and forth in front of the stove. What was she cooking? Spaghetti. He knocked her downstairs and her neck was broken. He was uselessly sentenced to 1 to 14 years.

Increasingly enlightened thought holds that punishment should fit the criminal, not the crime. Since punishment alone seems not to have successfully protected society, it is now generally believed that not punishment but treatment should be the goal. But in the present state of knowledge, this seems almost an idle dream.

Meanwhile, 98 percent of the men sent to prison someday return to free society. Most return worse than they left. And about one half of them commit new crimes. It is surprising that the record is not worse.

The true interest of society lies not in apprehending, dealing justly with and imprisoning criminals after they have committed crimes but in identifying them before they commit them. Sometimes this is possible. Warning signs may appear early in a boy's life—he may hide things senselessly, develop odd eating habits, throw his mother's perfume down the sink, become afraid to walk on grass, seem polite but remote and strange, fall behind in his studies, set fire to his parents' bedroom, break furniture and, growing older, molest a child and ransack a neighbor's house without stealing anything. A few years ago, a boy in New Jersey did just this. No criminal charges were filed, but his worried parents took him voluntarily to New Jersey's famed new diagnostic center. A doctor there, after studying him for a month as a voluntary paying patient, got the "diagnostic impression" of schizophrenia but did not consider him sick enough to recommend commitment to a mental hospital. He said later that if the boy had been sent to him by juvenile court, he would have recommended either putting him in an institution or sending him home under supervision. But he had come as a voluntary patient; so when his 30 days ended, he went home—New Jersey had no legal hold on him. Five years later, he strangled a high school girl.

Few parents of criminals go to so much trouble to try to help their boy before it happens. Few institutions are as good as New Jersey's diagnostic center. What can we expect from less conscientious parents and worse state institutions?

Thumbing through prison files, one finds with dreary monotony a terrible if less bizarre story repeated—drunken father and absent mother and truant child, rebellious boy and petty pilfering and juvenile court, runaway boy and disciplinary school, car theft and probation, carrying concealed weapons and broken probation and reformatory, parole and broken parole and reformatory, release and armed robbery and penitentiary—and so on, sometimes to the electric chair.

All too often, patients tell private psychiatrists they intend to kill somebody—and do. There were private warnings in the lives of both the Austin sniper and the assassin of President Kennedy. People ask, Why wasn't something done? Why doesn't a diagnostic center or a juvenile court, discovering warning signals early in a boy's life, isolate him immediately from society? The answer is that the patient's —and the boy's—rights are involved. Courts and psychiatrists have no legal right to lock up somebody because they think that someday he might kill. Not every wayward boy turns out to be a murderer. And anyway, we simply cannot put a psychiatrist in every kindergarten—there are fewer than 20,000 psychiatrists in the United States and most are in private practice. And even that is no sure answer, as our New Jersey case indicates.

Nevertheless, those two cases—the slum boy and the strange New Jersey boy—do suggest three lines of action.

The slum boy might have a chance if the slum were eliminated. Although slums do not "cause" crime, the high crime rate there—and the high percentage of Negroes in prisons, not because Negroes are "more criminal" but because they are more disadvantaged—argues powerfully that we must spend the billions necessary to alter fundamentally the character of our disintegrating cities.

Second, the chance of identifying troubled youngsters early argues powerfully for spending more public money to train psychiatrists and school guidance directors, establishing juvenile diagnostic centers and putting our minds to work on how to protect society against incipient criminality without infringing on the rights of the youngsters.

Third, prison reform is essential. It is not too much to say that the prison system as it exists should be abolished. It does not reform the criminal. It fails to protect society. When we know how to prevent crime or rehabilitate criminals, we will not put them into prison to do it. We can abolish prisons. Meanwhile, we ought to stop making men worse in prisons. Various steps can be taken, including these: Build a wide variety of prison farms and camps, medium-security institutions and facilities for the criminally insane, to permit classification and segregation of inmates; raze such gigantic maximum-security institutions as the Michigan State Penitentiary at Jackson, or at least break them up into small units; put under Civil Service and raise the salaries of guards, parole and probation supervisors and prison classification experts; increase the supply of psychiatric advice to parole and classification boards; let about half the inmates out of all maximum-security prisons; and enforce ironclad security measures on dangerous men.

But, in the long run, what is needed is more research into the causes of criminality. Research is going forward at several private institutions, but not enough of it. At present, no Federal research program on crime exists. One would be costly, but so is crime.

It seems likely that all such programs—rebuilding the cities, reorganizing the prison system, training personnel and staffing schools and diagnostic centers, and research—may have to await resolution of the Vietnam war. But perhaps even before money becomes available, forward planning could start and would probably be more fruitful than further Congressional debate on the "gun law." The ultimate emphasis should be on a program of research bearing directly on the roots of criminality. For until we know far more than we know now, there is not much we can do to protect ourselves. What we don't know can kill us.

QUESTIONS FOR DISCUSSION

1. *What two carnivores lack built-in inhibitions against killing members of their own species?*
2. *How do human societies distinguish between killing members of one's own group and killing outsiders?*
3. *Why do some murders disturb us while others don't?*
4. *What are the three schools of thought concerning the roots of criminality?*
5. *Which factor involved in criminality did the sociologists conclude was the most important?*
6. *How, according to the Gluecks, does delinquency occur?*
7. *Why is knowing the theories of criminality important to public policy?*
8. *Has the rehabilitation of prisoners been successful in this country?*

9. *What does Martin mean by the following?* "*Indeed, prison, far from protecting society, is society's enemy. It does not fit men for freedom.*"
10. *In what area are we perhaps doing even less work?*
11. *What are the four suggestions offered by the author to reduce crime in the United States?*

A Moral Equivalent for Riots

HARVEY WHEELER

About a year ago Malcolm Moos, who is president of the University of Minnesota but who was then an executive at the Ford Foundation, asked me to make a general investigation into the topic of violence. I had not previously engaged in any special studies qualifying me as an expert in this field, but perhaps Dr. Moos felt that this was in my favor. At least I had no preconceptions or predispositions toward one or another of the various contending schools of thought.

I did not want to look solely into the subject of ghetto riots—though obviously this would be one of the chief problems. Initially, I wanted to find out about all forms of violence: sporadic acts by assassins or snipers, such as that of the berserk student who mounted a tower at the University of Texas and shot down at people; the violence of the student demonstrators, both when directed against their universities and when directed against our nation's war; the hippies, who in one sense are waging a violent attack on the conventional morality of the established culture. Finally, I

Harvey Wheeler, "A Moral Equivalent for Riots," *Saturday Review*, May 11, 1968. Copyright 1968 Saturday Review, Inc.

wanted to study the various national liberation movements among the peoples of the third world.

I was given complete freedom to decide where to go, whom to seek out, and how to prepare the study. I visited Los Angeles, Stanford, Berkeley, Harvard, North Carolina, New York, London, Paris, Geneva, and many other places. I talked to famous leaders of the civil rights movement and to infamous leaders of street gangs; to philosophers, psychologists, sociologists, political scientists, reporters, public officials, and others. I taped more than 400 hours of interviews; my wife, who sat in on most of them, is only now completing the transcriptions.

First, a summary of the theories about violence held by my respondents:

1) Most respondents agreed that violence itself is not the thing to look at if one wants to understand it. That is, violence is a symptom rather than a cause, and if one wishes to reduce violence it will be of little avail to attack it directly as if it were something that could be cured or eliminated head on. Rather, one must try to get at the underlying causes or roots of what elicits violence.

2) Most respondents, in one way or another, believed violence to be an indelible part of human nature in some fundamental way. (This opinion was held by such otherwise diverse respondents as Hans J. Morgenthau and Martin Luther King, Jr.) So it is not possible, or even desirable, for us to achieve the complete elimination of violence. Rather, we may eliminate some of its most destructive manifestations, and perhaps divert it into more harmless, or even constructive, channels.

3) There was a tendency to point out that, while all societies are violent, and the United States is especially so, societies draw lines between what they consider "good" violence and "bad" violence. Many Southern whites, for example, consider violence against Negroes to be a good thing.

Many of those interviewed recently about Martin Luther King's assassination clearly betrayed the feeling that it was probably a good thing that he was shot. (I must relate that a close relative of mine, in a phone call the day after the assassination, mentioned that he thought the assassination a "blessing.") Such thoughts, though really quite horrifying, are harbored in the breasts of a large number of Americans, and we must face that fact.

The National Advisory Commission on Civil Disorders referred to the root of the problem as lying in a deepseated racism that permeates American society. Most of my respondents assented to this theory. It is very difficult, therefore, to distinguish between acts of violence that differ only in that some have our approval. We officially approve of search-and-destroy violence in the Vietnam war. We approvingly portray the battlefield results of this policy on TV each evening. Recall the ghastly scenes of on-the-spot executions, and the expulsion of a network reporter because he filmed a GI setting fire to native homes. Recall again that in most states we retain the death penalty. But more insidious is the kind of permissive violence of which we are scarcely aware. Negroes are aware of it, however, for it strikes against them daily.

4) One of my respondents referred to the problem as being one not of violence, but of "violation." Violence, he said, must be looked at in terms of the violation of the dignity of human beings. In those terms, violence is merely the sporadic counter-response when one's humanity and one's dignity has been violated. A culture in which human relationships are characterized by a great deal of violation will therefore produce a great deal of violence.

This country, as Edward Lurie has shown, has been a personality-violating culture since its birth. It has been unable to solve any of its greatest collective or internal problems without resort to violence. In addition, new cultural forces associated with the scientific revolution and with bureaucratization carry a special kind of violation. As these technological and organizational varieties of violation have increased, so has the incidence of counterviolation. And this latter more or less impersonal, or "systemic," violation helps account for the more or less impersonal, or "anti-system," violence of the reactions.

5) Respondents in the main agreed to another historical generalization. After the Civil War, the U.S. gave verbal, statutory, and even Constitutional expression to the principle of equal rights for Negroes. But at the same time it instituted an informal—in the South, quite formalized—racist culture in which Jim Crow regulations and practices of a most degrading (violating) type were enforced generally. We tend to think of Jim Crow as a Southern institution, but it often had its most cruel impact in the North.

The lovely little Northern town—let us call it "Elmstown"—where I grew up had two Negro families. One was headed by the kindly old "handkerchief-head darky" who was barber at the Elks Club, the other by a lady, apparently quite gracious, who served the community otherwise. The reason only two Negro families lived there was that the town had earlier chased the others out, posting signs at each road entering the town: NIGGER, DON'T LET THE SUN GO DOWN ON YOU IN ELMSTOWN. In the larger Northern cities, of course, the pattern of ghettoization—completely unknown at that time in Southern cities—was rigidly enforced.

The result of this uniform human violation was the creation of the myth of Negro inferiority—a myth which was accepted, with very few exceptions, by Negroes themselves. This official violation of Negroes' humanity then was turned inward, leading them to hate themselves and their blackness and their Negroid characteristics. They valued light skins over dark and violated their own natures—as in hair straighteners—in a perpetual effort to suppress their Negroism. Amos 'n' Andy, Stepin Fetchit, Rochester—white man's stereotypes of the good but slavish darky—were accepted by Negroes as their own heroes.

One result of the Negroes' inward turning of violence against themselves was the destruction of any possibility of maintaining an integral family structure. Negro women led all others in deprecating their men, contributing to the so-called emasculation of the Negro male about which we have heard so much. This internalization of violence, when it spilled out, took the form of the Negroes' physical attacks against one another in highly publicized brawls, cuttings, and wifebeatings that authorities reinforced by applying different law-enforcement standards for Negroes. Negroes were overpoliced in their relations to property and to whites; they were underpoliced in their relations to each other. It was all right for Negroes to knife other Negroes to death. But it was, in effect, a capital offense to even mildly affront a white. In short, Negroes not only internalized violence, taking it out against each other, but were "paid off" for doing so by the larger society.

The change came after 1954 with *Brown vs. Topeka.* Then, for the first time, Negroes began to turn violence outward against the white society that had violated them— first in the sit-ins and demonstrations, later in the riots. The result was a rebirth, perhaps an inauguration, of Negro self-respect. This assertion of self-respect has been the psychic power of the recent pattern of violence.

6) Sociologist Daniel Bell, in "Crime as an American Way of Life," has pointed out another variant of the tradition of violence. The Anglo-Saxon Protestant, Bell notes, got here first and monopolized all the official avenues to wealth and status. Then came the immigration waves; Irish, Middle Europeans, Jews, etc. Each was faced with a foreclosure of the normal avenues to participation in the

bourgeois bounties of the land. The Irish turned to politics and monopolized the party system, not only using it to gain office, but systematizing graft into a characteristically American kind of capital accumulation. When the Middle Europeans arrived later, not only business but also politics was closed to them. The result, says Bell, was a resort to crime as "an American Way of Life": crime as a way of becoming middle-class Americans.

But what of the Negro? Now we must consider the possibility that violence—direct action in the streets—has become the Negro version of this pattern of Americanization. All other avenues are closed; only direct action, sometimes issuing in violence, is left. This is the historic setting within which the Black Power movement must be understood. That being so, one must also look forward to the possibility that rioting and street demonstrations will become the institutionalized form of Americanization for Negroes.

7) We conclude that there is a large measure of truth to the Black Power charge that America is an imperialist culture. The imperialism with which America approaches the world outside is mirrored by a related form of imperialism that it turns against its own ethnic minorities. Hence, the charge that the Negro (and the Mexican-American, the Spanish-Indian, and others) lives in a colonial status in his own country. The rather transparent validity of this charge is what forges unity between the struggle of the Negro against domestic oppression and the international struggles of the third world against colonialism. Both are essentially anti-imperialist movements and both will have to apply generally similar tactics to achieve their goals. This does not necessarily mean violent tactics, but obviously the situation both at home and abroad is fraught with a very high violence potential. This is also why Mrs. Martin Luther King was right two years ago when she finally convinced her

husband that the struggle against racist despotism in
America would have to be linked with the struggle against
American imperialism abroad.

What is the source of our domestic imperialism? The
National Advisory Commission is right as far as it goes.
America *is* a racist culture. But the commission doesn't go
nearly far enough. Our internal form of despotism begins
innocuously, right at birth. The medical evidence is mounting that children who begin life in conditions of emotional
and nutritional deprivation develop physical and mental
deficiencies that are virtually irreversible, no matter how
healthful their conditions may later become. Now, of
course, this is a condition that afflicts all the poor. But
because of the proportional overconcentration of Negroes in
the so-called culture of poverty, the effects of deprivation
strike selectively against them. So they start life with
ineradicable chains dragging down their every step.

Even if this were not so, or even if it were eliminated
overnight, another cultural barrier still lies in the Negroes'
path, and it will prove to be the most difficult one to eradicate. This has to do with the acculturation process and the
way it relates to the educational process. We know that the
performance of children in schools is directly correlated
with the cultural and economic status of their parents. Children from highly educated, affluent homes will inevitably
make better grades, go to better schools, acquire higher
degrees, and ultimately find better jobs than those from
deprived homes. It is sometimes falsely concluded that this
means that education is the bootstrap by which all can pull
themselves out of deprivation and ascend the pinnacles of
white middle-class society. But that is transparently false, is
it not? One has to be middle class to *start* with, in order to
be middle class at the end. Education as such has little or
nothing to do with it.

The other side of this premise is that deprived boys
and girls, starting in school, have no cultural reinforcement

at home. They have no stimulus urging them toward cultural heights. They have limited verbal and reading skills to reinforce their schoolroom efforts. As a result they are automatically processed through what we call the "track" system, and what the English call "streaming." The track system means that even in schools that are technically desegregated, there is an internal segregation based upon test performance. Test performance is sometimes thought to represent innate intellectual ability. In fact, however, intelligence-test results merely reflect the conditions of one's cultural origins.

Under the track system, those from culturally deprived homes are automatically passed through the grades regardless of performance, until legal school-leaving age is reached. At that time they are dumped out on the streets, where they will spend the rest of their lives grubbing for existence through the offal of our cities. The second track is for those with low, but passable, achievement records. They are placed in the manual-arts, nonacademic track and are destined for the menial, semiskilled trades. The highest, of course, are put into the liberal-arts, college preparatory programs, and they inevitably will end up with college degrees and Establishment jobs. The point is that the track system reinforces—and even magnifies—the initial condition with which students begin life. Before the average child is ten years old the school system has already determined, beyond the child's ability to influence it, his entire lifetime career.

There are a few extremely rare cases in which the pattern is overcome, and we paternalistically display these with a great show of pride. This is the cruelest cultural despotism imaginable. It is also remorselessly violent. For who can argue with objective placement tests? What, then, is to be done about it? Shouldn't any sensible child—or any sensible high school student, when faced from the beginning of life with a predetermined second-class status, destined to last forever—react with violence to this ultimate violation of his innate talents?

8) An aspect of this same despotism reaches even middle-class children. Our culture has always been goaded on by the whiplash of the dollar. The threat of economic failure (absolutely or relatively) dogs our steps from birth to death. This is a burden that often becomes too much for even the seemingly well to do. But recently the whiplash of the dollar has become supplemented by that of the school. For each person's status—rich as well as poor—appears to depend upon his grade records. So the grade record becomes the whiplash of the young, terrorizing them from kindergarten on. And where the school stops, the parent takes up. So school (abetted by career-conscious parents) becomes a place of terror whose whiplash is the grade system and which reaches an apex for the hardy in the ultimate indignity of the College Board examinations. So there is little wonder that all students, black and white alike, are today in open rebellion against the school system.

The answer to one of our preliminary questions now begins to reveal itself: The systematic "violation" of our youth brings Negroes, hippies, and university students together into the same framework, struggling together in the same cause.

9) It was often remarked, two years ago, that Los Angeles was the most unlikely place for a riot to occur. Watts is not a ghetto in the normal sense of the word, for it abounds with single-family homes. I remember ten years ago hearing Eastern Negroes say that Los Angeles was the Negro's "heaven." "Man, *that's* where I want to go when I die." A second comment about Watts was that it was not technically a "race riot"; it was not against whites—at least not personally. So, Watts was the most affluent Negro community in the world, and its riot was directed against that very community. How can we explain this?

There is general agreement that the Watts pattern fits well what is known about *all* the revolutions of history. They do not start among those making up the dregs of society. Moreover, they do not occur when oppression and exploitation are at their worst. So-called revolutions of the belly are statistically rare in history, and when they occur they usually have little effect on the conditions of those in revolt— except death. Rather, revolutions typically occur among those who have experienced a definite, steady rise in their conditions of life, and *then* suffer a setback. Revolutions are made by rising classes rather than by declining classes. And this leads us to the current catch phrase about the "revolutions of rising expectations"; that is, the revolutions being carried out by all peoples in the world who want to enjoy the good things in life made famous by Americans.

There is general agreement that the Negro Revolution is another one of these revolutions of rising expectations. It is precisely because Negroes desperately want to enjoy the beneficences of the American way of life that they are in revolt. It is *Life* magazine, actively abetted by *Ebony* and multiplied a thousand-fold by television programs and commercials, that provides the real stimulus to the Negro revolution. And this is one reason why the revolts take the form of burning and looting. Revolutions destroy the physical symbols of deprivation; in the present case these are tenement houses and the gouging merchants. And then the rebels go on to looting, helping themselves to the gadgets and goodies the mass media have overstimulated them to desire.

10) Finally, there appears to be irrefutable physiological and anthropological evidence that the mere fact of physical overcrowding induces violence. Some anthropologists claim to be able to chart reliable curves of violence-potentials correlated with rates of congestion. Dramatic confirmation comes from experiments with monkeys. They are

normally quite peaceful creatures. At the most they engage
in their curious ritualized shouting wars in which violence
seldom if ever results. In one experiment a collection of
monkeys was loaded on a ship for transportation to an un-
inhabited Caribbean island—as an experimental refuge.
During the period of shipboard crowding they developed on
their own most of the typical maladies of human beings.
They learned how to fight each other, even to death. They
acquired coronary problems and they developed a full range
of mental diseases. But what is worse, their violent patterns
of behavior, once learned on shipboard, were continued
even after debarkation on an island where sufficient space
and food could have permitted the return to their traditional (presumably instinctual) ways of peace.

So, we have ten general propositions about violence. It
is apparent from them that the problem runs quite deep—
so deep that not even massive investments in the improvement of the physical conditions of the ghettos will resolve
them. A few propositions, however, can be derived from
what we have uncovered:

Self-Strengthening. One of the most important functions of the riots has been to permit Negroes to turn to
violence outward. Violence allowed them to sublimate the
self-destructive internalized aggression patterns of the post-
Civil War era. It has provided a way for them to build their
own self-respect. It has also given them avenues to power—
"riot power" as an American way of life. Seen from below,
riots are a "good" kind of violence. It is like the case of a
person with anemia who happens onto alcohol rather than
vitamins. He has to be provided with constructive and
creative solutions to his problem before he will give up those
that have pernicious side effects.

So, to paraphrase William James, what the Negro—
and the society in general—needs is the moral equivalent
of riots: officially provided self-strengthening institutions.

Not institutions *given* the Negro, ready-built by whites—especially not by white liberals, who commiserate today over being excluded from the "Movement." The white liberal today is one of the Negro's most serious obstacles to self-strengthening. For in wanting to help, and to participate, and remain a part of the Movement, the white liberal stands directly in the way of the indigenous self-strengthening the Negro must build for himself—just as he built his riots for himself. The liberal becomes, unwittingly, the most patronizing and the most dangerous Uncle Tom creator confronting the Negro today.

What can be done? Because the solutions must be as profound as the causes, we must have the faith to be innovative in spite of seeming danger:

1) We must facilitate the establishment of Negro *community corporations.* We must foster the creation and maturation of Black Power by enabling it: by providing the funds whereby Negroes may organize their communities for themselves. Milton Kotler of the Institute of Policy Studies has actually started such a community corporation in Columbus, Ohio, and the prospect for their spread is quite promising.

2) Just as the developing world insists upon achieving development on its own, expelling its former white masters and organizing and administering its affairs for itself, so also with our Negro communities. We can provide them with funds for sending representatives abroad to the most successful parts of the developing world where they can learn directly about the problems of cultural development. This means funding study programs for Negroes in Tanzania, Ghana, Israel, and even Cuba. The lessons learned can be applied not only to the problems of urban organization, but also, perhaps using the Israel kibbutz model, to the problems of agricultural development throughout the South. There is no reason why the government cannot finance cadres of Negroes to learn kibbutz

management in Israel, and then finance the acquisition of large tracts of Southern farm land where such cadres can develop creative, productive, and healthful farming communities. Integration, of a new sort, will come one day, but only after the self-strengthening process has been fulfilled.

3) Finally, programs for the autonomous development of Negro culture must be subsidized. One might compare this to the problem of providing cultural autonomy for previously suppressed non-Western cultures. It is, in a way, the problem facing most of the nations of the world today. There are three "nations" in Yugoslavia, and the Government facilitates the development of their cultural autonomy. The same is true of Czechoslovakia, of Scotland, of Vietnam, and so on throughout the world. In the near future the entire world is destined to produce increasing cultural articulation for national minorities. The Negro, like the French Canadian, is fully justified in insisting on having his own autonomy. This can find political representation in a new kind of nonterritorial federalism in which the institutions expressing Negro autonomy may be politically represented, as in a third legislative chamber: a black Congress.

Rioting as an American Way of Life. Direct action—the sort that now issues in violence too often—must be given fuller Constitutional protection. This is not because we fear that each summer will bring a new wave of rioting. On the contrary, riots appear to be like lightning—they are devastating but they don't strike twice in the same place. The self-respect they engender mitigates against their repetition. Moreover, a riot produces a strange alchemy of love. The same ghetto which before the riot seemed to be a prison of alienation is made into one's own by the act of rioting against it. And once Negroes feel they own their ghettos they'll never burn them down. But this being so, the need for a moral alternative becomes even more necessary for the post-riot future.

We must have a new Constitutional right to civil disobedience. It will involve reinterpretation of the First Amendment. It will require expanding the freedom of speech clause and the clause protecting the right to petition for redress of grievances. Qualifications and safeguards are needed, but we know how to apply them. We have already the clear-and-present-danger test. Long ago, union picketing was established as a right under the free speech clause of the First Amendment. Such actions as the Memphis garbage workers' protest, and even the Spock draft resistance protest, may lead the way to the moral equivalent for riots.

Cultural Deprivation. This is the most serious concern —the element at the root of the built-in despotism that hounds the poor into a lifetime of ingrown poverty and deprivation. We must facilitate the acquisition of a specially designed and consciously engendered supplementary culture. It must be provided to all who need it virtually from birth, so that the cultural deprivation of the ghetto can be overstepped and each child can be provided with a sufficiently supportive environment to enable him to spring to the highest possible cultural and intellectual attainments. This will require drastic programs:

1) *Cottage schools.* Blackboard jungles must be torn down and cottage boarding schools established in their place. Class sizes must be held down to something around twenty. Moreover, it must be possible for each child to look forward to progression through his entire primary and secondary school career in the same class. This means that it must be possible for the culturally deprived to live in these schools—in a good boarding school—and also to commute to his own school from across town, or even across

the nation, staying with his own class through graduation. If this sounds expensive, well, it is. It is like guaranteeing an Andover education to every child. And this is exactly what we must do.

2) *Multimedia homes*. This may provide the ultimate solution for the cultural deprivation of us all. Consider the technological possibilities we now possess. We have television, audiotapes, records, newspapers, magazines, encyclopedias, movie films—and computers to run them all. We have the possibility of integrating all these into a home-sized multimedia installation. This means that we can all "subscribe" to a total information, cultural, educational, and amusement "program," the way we now subscribe to separate newspapers and journals. Moreover, these programs can be specially designed for individual family needs, so that we can start with the most depressed family imaginable and design progressive, long-term multimedia cultural programs in much the way insurance consultants now design lifetime protection policies for their clients. Through such means it is technologically possible to bring even the most deprived person through all the stages of cultural development within a single lifetime.

The City. We know that megalopolis is not only obsolete; it is the breeding ground of cultural and physical disease. We also know that it is now technologically feasible to have any kind of city we wish. Today in the Midwest there is an exciting new plan for the construction of an autonomous urban community of not more than 250,000 people. The computer and other new technological advances now make such cultural and economic autonomy possible. They also make it possible for us to engage in what Robert Hutchins calls the "learning society," with the quest for creature comforts giving way to the quest for culture comforts. We shall have to build these new cities sooner or later. We might as well start now.

Dr. Hutchins likes to tell about the time Marshal Lyautey, who was the French Governor General of Morocco, asked his gardener about a beautiful tree he had seen, wishing to have more of them for his own garden. "But General," said the gardener, "that tree takes 200 years to reach maturity." "In that case," said Marshal Lyautey, "we have no time to lose. Plant them this afternoon."

We have less time to lose—and quicker and more beautiful results to expect. We must start planting the seeds of our new and more humane culture today.

QUESTIONS FOR DISCUSSION

1. *What are Wheeler's ten propositions about violence? Which of these have not been mentioned by previous authors?*
2. *What three solutions does Wheeler suggest?*
3. *What is the author advocating in the section entitled "Rioting as an American Way of Life"?*
4. *What are the three solutions he offers for cultural deprivation?*

5

Group Disturbances

"All we want is old-fashioned law and order
like we used to have down yere 30 years ago."

[----from *The Herblock Gallery* (Simon & Schuster, 1968).]

TO PEOPLE WANTING SOCIAL REFORM OR CHANGE IN THE structure of a society, violence is a valuable tool. A midwestern tale relates that a young farmer once bought a mule from his older neighbor after being assured that the animal would work well from simple, spoken commands. The next morning, after spending an hour or so unsuccessfully trying to talk the beast from its stall into the harness, the purchaser sought his neighbor's help. When the older man smashed a two-by-four over the mule's head and said quietly, "Get in harness," the mule immediately staggered out and complied. The young farmer protested, "But I thought you said I wouldn't have to beat him!" His neighbor smiled, "That's right, but first you have to attract his attention."

As an attention-getter, violence is effective. It serves as a lever under the existing society. We live in a culture that is tuned in to violence. It has found violence meaningful and useful. If those who want change use it, violence becomes acceptable to the establishment as patriotic counterattack, as a way of preserving laws, and as a way of maintaining the manners of a civilization. Acts of violence, especially by vigorous groups, disturb the tranquillity of the community. The establishment's failure to keep the peace puts doubts into the minds of many who have accepted things as they are. Their doubts frighten established groups into certain actions. One form of action is to bribe the violent faction with concessions so that order will be restored. Often these handouts under duress are sufficient and retard further questions from those portions of the society that are content with periodic minor modifications in the existing arrangements. Consequently, the violent movement may lose momentum, its leaders may be isolated and shunned, and its ideals more or less assimillated into the establishment.

A frequently more popular reaction by an established group is to meet the actions of the violent faction with equal or greater ferocity. The establishment's force is often met by still more force from other elements in the society. But when the establishment again replies in greater kind, either the escalation horrifies all observers and an uneasy truce settles upon the scene, or the repression temporarily stalls the violent faction. Smug in that feeling, the society sometimes goes further than necessary and sows the seeds of an even greater upheaval in the future.

Sometimes we forget that barnburners, klan members, "yippies," and others who object violently to certain conditions are not the only contributors to our violent history. Ranchers, industrialists and others who fail to see the need for change are equally guilty. Many recent disturbances have not burst suddenly upon the national scene. Some of them are aimed at abuses three hundred and fifty years in the making.

Since 1960, violence has generally appeared in urban areas, between racial or ethnic groups, and frequently involved a disproportionate number of young people. The articles selected for this section reflect these conditions. The National Advisory Commission on Civil Disorders and the National Commission on the Causes and Prevention of Violence both indicated that a class of violence exists that is distinctly between groups, regardless of the excuse used in a given setting. These authors are discussing principles that apply to all such group-to-group confrontations.

The element of change in the political and social structures of the United States has always been a source of fear, amazement, and amusement to the observers of our system. Changes have always been made with each election, with each generation. Yet, today a segment of our society is reluctant to make further political and social changes. Could this reluctance be due in part to the speed and amount of technological change?

In American politics, if no issue exists, invent one. If there is no trouble, manufacture some. Cloud the real, unacceptable issues with those that the people *will* accept and vote for—or against. It isn't what people think—it's what they *think* they think. When we deal with causes of violence we examine the violent act itself and fail to recognize the problems that really brought it about. We focus on the symptom rather than the sickness.

Writing of another period of violent and bloody civil disorder involving a basic crisis in American culture, Bruce Catton commented, "It was not an ending but a beginning . . . an opening chapter in the still unfinished story whose final outcome depends, somehow, on whether you and I really believe in the things which, as American citizens, we suppose we believe in." The generation of our great-grandfathers was not less fearful or less frustrated than we are. For their time, they met the challenges of their circumstances as well as they could. Once more, we have changes and challenges before us.

THE
AMERICAN
WAY

A SOCIAL
AND POLITICAL
HISTORY

BOOKMARKS

[Copyright © 1968, The Chicago *Sun-Times*. Reproduced by courtesy of Wil-Jo Associates, Inc., and Bill Mauldin.]

Rioting, Insurrection and Civil Disobedience

RALPH W. CONANT

Rioting is a spontaneous outburst of group violence characterized by excitement mixed with rage. The outburst is
usually directed against alleged perpetrators of injustice or
gross misusers of political power. The typical rioter has no
premeditated purpose, plan or direction, although systematic looting, arson and attack on persons may occur
once the riot is underway. Also, criminals and conspirators
may expand their routine activities in the wake of the riot
chaos. While it is quite clear that riots are unpremeditated
outbursts, they are not as a rule *senseless* outbursts. The
rage behind riots is a shared rage growing out of specific
rage-inducing experiences. In the United States, the rage
felt by Negroes (increasingly manifested in ghetto riots) is
based on centuries of oppression, and in latter times on dis-
criminatory practices that frustrate equal opportunity to
social, economic and political goals. While all riots stem
from conflicts in society similar to those that inspire civil
disobedience, they ordinarily do not develop directly from

Reprinted from *The American Scholar*, Volume 37, Number 3,
Summer 1968. Copyright © 1968 by the United Chapters of Phi Beta
Kappa. By permission of the publishers.

specific acts of civil disobedience. Yet repeated failures of civil disobedience to achieve sought-after goals can and often do result in frustrations that provide fertile ground for the violent outbursts we call riots.

The factors universally associated with the occurrence and course of any riot are the following: (1) preconditions, (2) riot phases, and (3) social control. The discussion here is drawn from a review of the literature of collective behavior as well as on studies currently underway at the Lemberg Center for the Study of Violence at Brandeis University.

I. THE PREDICTIONS OF RIOT: VALUE CONFLICTS

All riots stem from intense conflicts within the value systems that stabilize the social and political processes of a nation. The ghetto riot is a concrete case of a group attempt to restructure value conflicts and clarify social relationships in a short time by deviant methods.

There are two classes of value conflicts, each of which gives rise to a different kind of struggle. The first calls for normative readjustment in which the dominant values of a society are being inequitably applied. In this case, the aggrieved groups protest, and if protest fails to attain readjustment, they riot.

The anti-draft rioter at the time of the Civil War was protesting the plight of the common man who could not, like his wealthier compatriots, buy his way out of the draft. American egalitarian values were not being applied across the board. The readjustment came only after the intensity of the riots stimulated public concern to force a change.

The contemporary ghetto riots grow out of the failure of the civil rights movement to achieve normative readjustment for black people through nonviolent protest. This failure has produced lines of cleavage which, if intensified, will result in the second type of value conflict, namely, value readjustment.

In this case, the dominant values of the society are brought under severe pressure for change. The social movement that organizes the activities of an aggrieved sector of the population, having given up hope for benefiting from the going value system, sets up a new configuration of values. The movement becomes revolutionary. When Americans gave up hope of benefiting from the English institutions of the monarchy and the colonial system, they set up their own egalitarian value system and staged a revolution.

Now, Black Power and Black Nationalist leaders are beginning to move in the direction of value readjustment. They are talking about organizing their people on the basis of separatist and collectivist values and they are moving away from the melting pot, individualistic values of our country, which are not working for them.

The Hostile Belief System. An aggrieved population erupts into violence on the basis of a preexisting hostile belief. During the anti-Catholic riots in the early part of the nineteenth century, the rioters really believed that the Pope, in Rome, was trying to take over the country. The anti-Negro rioters in Chicago and East St. Louis (and even in Detroit in 1943) really believed that Negroes were trying to appropriate their jobs and rape their women and kill their men.

Today, many rioters in black ghettos really believe in the malevolence of white society, its duplicity, and its basic commitment to oppressing Negroes. An important component of the hostile belief system is that the expected behavior of the identified adversary is seen as *extraordinary*— that is, beyond the pale of accepted norms. In the black ghettos, people are convinced, for example, that the police will behave toward them with extraordinary verbal incivility and physical brutality, far beyond any incivility and brutality displayed toward whites in similar circumstances.

The hostile belief system is connected, on the one hand, with the value conflict, and, on the other, with the incident that precipitates a riot. It embodies the value conflict, giving it form, substance and energy. It sets the stage for the precipitating incident which then becomes a concrete illustration of the beliefs. A police officer shooting and killing a young black suspected car thief (as in San Francisco in September, 1966), or beating and bloodying a black taxi driver (as in Newark in July, 1967), confirms and dramatizes the expectations incorporated into the hostile beliefs and triggers the uprising.

Hostile beliefs bear varying relations to "reality." Their systemization means that in some aspects they are incorrect exaggerations; in others, very close to the truth. In the 1830's, the Catholic Church wanted more power and influence locally, but it did not, consciously, want to take over the country. Today, large numbers of white people want to keep Negroes where they are by allowing them to advance only gradually. But they do not, at least consciously, want to oppress them.

Relative Deprivation. An important and almost universal causal factor in riots is a perception of real or imagined deprivation in relation to other groups in the society. As James R. Hundley has put it, the aggrieved see a gap between the conditions in which they find themselves and what could be achieved given a set of opportunities. Ghetto residents in the United States use middle-class white suburban living as a comparative point, and they feel acutely deprived. The areas of relative deprivation for the black American are pervasively economic, political and social.

Obstacles to Change. Another universal causal factor behind riots is the lack of effective channels for bringing about change. Stanley Lieberson and Arnold Silverman, in their study of riots in United States cities between 1910 and 1961, note a correlation between cities in which riots have occurred and cities that elect officials at large rather than from wards. In this situation, Negroes are not likely to have adequate representation, if any. The result is that they feel deprived of a local political voice and are in fact deprived of a potential channel through which to air grievances. An aggrieved population with no access to grievance channels is bound to resort to rioting if one or more of their grievances become dramatized in a precipitating incident.

Hope of Reward. While riot participants do not ordinarily think much in advance about the possible outcome of a riot, still those who participate harbor hopes, however vague, that extreme and violent behavior may bring about desired changes. Certainly the contagion effect had a significant role in the crescendo of ghetto riots in the United States during 1967. Part of the spirit was that things could not be made much worse by rioting, and riots might achieve unexpected concessions from influential whites. Any hard-pressed people are riot-prone and the more so if they see others like themselves making gains from rioting. What happens is spontaneous, but hope raises the combustion potential.

Communication. Ease of communication among potential rioters is less a *precondition* of riot than a necessary condition to the spread of riot, once started. Riots tend to occur in cities during warm weather when people are likely to be congregated in the streets and disengaged from normal daily activities.

II. The Phases of a Riot

A riot is a dynamic process which goes through different stages of development. If the preconditions described above exist, if a value conflict intensifies, hostile beliefs flourish, an incident that exemplifies the hostile beliefs occurs, communications are inadequate and rumor inflames feelings of resentment to a fever pitch, the process will get started. How far it will go depends upon a further process of interaction between the local authorities and an aroused community.

There are four stages within the riot process. Not all local civil disturbances go through all four stages; in fact, the majority do not reach stage three. It is still not certain at what point in the process it is appropriate to use the word "riot" to describe the event. In fact more information is needed about the process and better reporting of the phase structure itself.

Phase 1. The Precipitating Incident. All riots begin with a precipitating event, which is usually a gesture, act or event by the adversary that is seen by the aggrieved community as concrete evidence of the injustice or relative deprivation that is the substance of the hostility and rage felt by the aggrieved. The incident is inflammatory because it is typical of the adversary's behavior toward the aggrieved and responsible for the conditions suffered by the aggrieved. The incident is also taken as an excuse for striking back with "justified" violence in behavior akin to rage. The event may be distorted by rumor and made to seem more inflammatory than it actually is. In communities where the level of grievances is high, a seemingly minor incident may set off a riot; conversely, when the grievance level is low, a more dramatic event may be required to touch off the trouble.

A significant aspect of the precipitating event, besides its inflammatory nature, is the fact that it draws together a large number of people. Hundley explains that some come out of curiosity; others because they have heard rumors about the precipitating event; still others because they happen to be in the vicinity. Some of the converging crowd are instigators or agitators who are attempting to get a riot started; others come to exploit the situation and use the crowd as a cover for deviant activities. Local officials, church and civic leaders come because they see it as their duty to try to control the violent outburst.

Phase 2. Confrontation. Following the instigating incident, the local population swarms to the scene. A process of "keynoting" begins to take place. Potential riot promoters begin to articulate the rage accumulating in the crowd and they vie with each other in suggesting violent courses of action. Others, frequently recognized ghetto leaders, suggest that the crowd disband to let tempers cool and to allow time for a more considered course of action. Law enforcement officers appear and try to disrupt the "key-noting" process by ordering and forcing the crowd to disperse. More often than not, their behavior, which will be discussed below, serves to elevate one or another hostile "keynoter" to a position of dominance, thus flipping the riot process into the next phase.

The outcome of phase 2 is clearly of crucial importance. The temper of the crowd may dissipate spontaneously, or escalate explosively. The response of civil authorities at this point is also crucial. If representatives of local authority appear, listen to complaints and suggest some responsive method for dealing with them, the agitation tends to subside; a "let's wait and see" attitude takes over. If they fail to show up and are represented only by the police, the level of agitation tends to rise.

How the news media handle phase 2 has a critical effect on the course of the riot. During the "sensationalizing" era of a few years ago in the United States, almost any street confrontation was likely to be reported as a "riot." In the current policy of "restraint," a street confrontation may not be reported at all. Neither policy is appropriate. A policy of "adequate communication" is needed. The grievances stemming from the precipitating incident and agitating the crowd should be identified. The response of local authorities should be described. The adversary relations and their possible resolutions, violent or nonviolent, should be laid out insofar as possible.

Phase 3. Roman Holiday. If hostile "keynoting" reaches a sufficient crescendo in urban ghetto riots, a quantum jump in the riot process occurs and the threshold of phase 3 is crossed. Usually the crowd leaves the scene of the street confrontation and reassembles elsewhere. Older persons drop out for the time being and young people take over the action. They display an angry intoxication indistinguishable from glee. They hurl rocks and bricks and bottles at white-owned stores and at cars containing whites or police, wildly cheering every "hit." They taunt law enforcement personnel, risk capture, and generally act out routine scenarios featuring the sortie, the ambush and the escape— the classic triad of violent action that they have seen whites go through endlessly on TV. They set the stage for looting, but are usually too involved in "the chase" and are too excited for systematic plunder. That action comes later in phase 3, when first younger, then older, adults, caught up on the Roman Holiday, and angered by tales of police brutality toward the kids, join in the spirit of righting ancient wrongs.

Phase 3 has a game structure. It is like a sport somehow gone astray but still subject to correction. Partly this openness derives from the "King-for-a-Day" carnival climate. Partly it is based on the intense ambivalence of black people toward the white system and its symbolic representatives; its hated stores and their beloved contents, its despised police and their admired weaponry, its unregenerate bigots and its exemplary civil rights advocates, now increasingly under suspicion. Because of the ambivalence, action and motive are unstable. Middle-class or upwardly mobile Negroes become militants overnight. Youths on the rampage one day put on white hats and armbands to "cool the neighborhood" the next. It is because of the ambivalence felt by Negroes, not only toward whites but toward violence itself, that so few phase 3 disturbances pass over into phase 4.

Phase 4. Siege. If a city's value conflict continues to be expressed by admonishment from local authorities and violent suppression of the Roman Holiday behavior in the ghetto, the riot process will be kicked over into phase 4. The adversary relations between ghetto dwellers and local and City Hall whites reach such a degree of polarization that no direct communications of any kind can be established. Communications, such as they are, consist of symbolic, warlike acts. State and federal military assistance is summoned for even more violent repression. A curfew is declared. The ghetto is subjected to a state of siege. Citizens can no longer move freely into and out of their neighborhoods. Forces within the ghetto, now increasingly composed of adults, throw fire bombs at white-owned establishments, and disrupt fire fighting. Snipers attack invading paramilitary forces. The siege runs its course, like a Greek tragedy, until both sides tire of this fruitless and devastating way of solving a conflict.

III. Social Control

Studies of past and present riots show that the collective hostility of a community breaks out as a result of inattention to the value conflict (the long-range causes) and as a result of failures in social control (immediate causation). These failures are of two sorts: under-control and over-control. In the condition of under-control, law-enforcement personnel are insufficiently active. Although the condition may be brought about in various ways, the effect is always the same. The dissident group, noting the weakness of the authorities, seizes the opportunity to express its hostility. The inactivity of the police functions as an invitation to act out long-suppressed feelings, free of the social consequences of illegal behavior.

In some communities, as in the 1967 Detroit riot, under-control during early phase 3 produces an efflorescence of looting and is then suddenly replaced with over-control. In other communities, over-control is instituted early, during phase 2. Local and state police are rushed to the scene of the confrontation and begin to manhandle everyone in sight. Since the action is out of proportion to the event, it generates an intense reaction. If over-control is sufficiently repressive, as in the 1967 Milwaukee riot, where a 24-hour curfew was ordered early in phase 3 and the National Guard summoned, the disturbances are quieted. In Milwaukee, the ghetto was placed under a state of siege as the Roman Holiday was beginning to take hold in the community. No "catharsis" occurred and there was no improvement in ghetto-City Hall communications. The consequences of such premature repression cannot yet be discerned. Short of the use of overwhelming force, over-control usually leads to increased violence. The black people in the ghetto see the police as violent and strike back with increasing intensity. Studies being conducted currently at the Lemberg Center show that in the majority of instances, police violence toward ghetto residents precedes and supersedes ghetto violence.

An adequate law-enforcement response requires an effective police presence when illegal activities, such as looting, take place. Arrests can and should be made, without cruelty. It is not necessary that all offenders be caught and arrested to show that authorities intend to maintain order. Crowds can be broken up or contained through a variety of techniques not based on clubbing or shooting.

The avoidance of both under- and over-control is a matter of police training for riot control. This was the deliberate pattern of police response in several cities (notably Pittsburgh) to the riots following the assassination of Martin Luther King in April.

Commenting on the interaction between a riot crowd and social control agencies, Hundley observes (1) that the presence of police tends to create an event, provide a focal point and draw people together for easy rumor transmittal; (2) that the result of too few police is uncontrolled deviant behavior; (3) that a legitimate police activity (from the standpoint of riot participants) will not escalate the incident, but even if the original police activity *is* seen as legitimate, policemen observed being rude, unfair or brutal at the scene may touch off a riot; (4) success of a police withdrawal *during* a riot depends upon officials contacting the legitimate leaders of the community and allowing them to exert social control; (5) when officials do not know the community leaders (or no effective ones are available), their withdrawal simply allows the instigators and exploiters to create or continue the riot; (6) the presence of police who do *not* exert control promotes the emergence of norms that encourage deviant activity.

Hundley adds these further observations on social control factors: (1) the sooner help comes from outside control agencies, the sooner the riot stops, although we think a riot can be stopped too soon, before catharsis or settlement of grievances can occur. Hundley's next point, however, takes this matter into account: (2) the sooner the larger community seeks out real ghetto leaders *and satisfies their grievances*, the sooner the riot stops. (3) The sooner the audience ceases watching the riot activity, the sooner the riot disappears. (4) The greater degree of "normalcy" maintained in the community during the riot, the more likely it is that the riot will remain small or cease.

IV. CIVIL INSURRECTION

When community grievances go unresolved for long periods of time and efforts at communication and/or negotiation seem unproductive or hopeless, despair in the aggrieved community may impel established, aspiring or self-appointed leaders to organize acts of rebellion against civil authorities. Such acts constitute insurrection and differ from riots in that the latter are largely spontaneous and unpremeditated. The exceptions are riots that are instigated by insurrectionists.

Although insurrection is deliberate rebellion, the aim of the insurrectionist, unlike that of the revolutionary, is to put down persons in power, to force abandonment of obnoxious policies or adoption of desirable ones. The insurrectionist is not out to overthrow the system. (The organizers of the Boston Tea Party were insurrectionists, they were not yet revolutionaries.) Like the civil disobedient (or the rioter), the insurrectionist will settle for some specific adjustment in the system, such as a change in political leadership, increased representation in the system, repeal of an objectionable law, or abandonment of an inequitable policy. The revolutionary has lost hope for any effective participation in the existing system (as had the American revolutionaries by 1776) and presses for a total overthrow.*

Civil insurrection is in effect a stage of *civil protest* that develops from the same set of conditions that inspire

---

* In the dictionary, insurgency is a condition of revolt against recognized government that does not reach the proportions of an organized revolutionary government and is not recognized as belligerency. This definition squares with my own as outlined above. An important distinction between insurrection (which I am using synonymously with insurgency) and revolution is the existence of a revolutionary government which is installed when the existing government is brought down.

acts of civil disobedience or riot. Riots do not turn into insurrection, although insurrectionists are often encouraged by riots to employ organized violence as a means to attain sought-after goals. The participants in acts of civil disobedience and riots are obviously seen by insurrectionists as potential participants in organized acts of violent protest. Indeed, the disobedients and the rioters may themselves be converted to insurrection tactics, not by existing insurrectionists, but by disillusionment and frustration in the other courses of action.

Civil disobedience and insurrection, both of which are deliberate acts, characteristically involve relatively few of the aggrieved population, because it is hard to get ordinary people to participate in planned disobedience of the law (and run the risk of punishment) or premeditated acts of violence (and run the double risk of physical harm and punishment). Also the various social control mechanisms, aside from the law-enforcement agencies, tend to keep most people from willful, premeditated violence and disobedience. Riots, on the other hand, may involve large numbers of people, many of whom are usually law-abiding, not because a riot is any more acceptable than insurrection or civil disobedience, but because these are irresistible elements of contagious emotion rooted in commonly shared and commonly repressed feelings of frustration and rage. These feelings of frustration and rage are linked to and grow out of hostile beliefs about the adversary, and in the early stages of a riot are inflamed by some incident that seems to be an example of the adversary's typical behavior. The incident becomes an excuse for an angry, concerted outburst, which can spread very rapidly in the aggrieved community and rationalize otherwise unacceptable acts. Law-abiding citizens who participate in a riot are not so easy to organize for insurrection. Persons who can be recruited for organized acts of violent protest are more likely to be those who have already become involved in some form of criminal activity as an individual, private (perhaps unconscious) protest against a hostile society. It may also be easier to organize insurrection in a community with an established tradition of either rioting or insurgency.

V. The Justification of Civil Protest

There is substantial agreement among legal and political thinkers that nonviolent challenges to the policies and laws of civil authority are an indispensable mechanism of corrective change in a democratic society. Insofar as possible, procedures for challenge which may involve open and deliberate disobedience should be built into the laws and policies of the system, for such procedures give the system a quality of resilience and flexibility, the capacity to absorb constructive attack from within.

As George Lakay has pointed out, one great strength of democratic institutions is that they build a degree of conflict into the decision-making structure just so that conflicts can be resolved publicly and without violence. Adequately designed democratic institutions deliberately reflect shifting views and power relations of interest groups and the normal workings of compromise and settlement, and equilibrium is usually maintained. Civil disobedience, and other forms of civil protest, are resorted to when political adversaries exhaust means of compromise in the political arena. Then the less powerful of the adversaries is forced to carry his challenge into a legal procedure or to the public in a show of protest.

Agreement on a policy of deliberate tolerance of peaceful challenge does not imply automatic agreement on what conditions *justify* challenges that involve disobedience. Moreover, agreement on a policy of tolerance toward nonviolent civil disobedience bears no necessary relationship at all to the question of the justification of civil protest involving violence, as riots and insurrection always do.

Nonviolent civil disobedience is justified under the following circumstances:

1) When an oppressed group is deprived of lawful channels for remedying its condition; conversely, a resort to civil disobedience is never politically legitimate where methods of due process in both the legal and political systems are available as remedies.

2) As a means of resisting or refusing to participate in an obvious and intolerable evil perpetrated by civil authorities (for example, a policy of genocide or enslavement).

3) When government takes or condones actions that are inconsistent with values on which the society and the political system are built, and thus violates the basic assumptions on which the regime's legitimacy rests.

4) When it is certain that the law or policy in question violates the constitution of the regime and, therefore, would be ruled unconstitutional by proper authority if challenged.

5) When a change in law or policy is demanded by social or economic need in the community and the normal procedures of law and politics are inadequate, obstructed or held captive by antilegal forces.

6) When the actions of government have become so obnoxious to one's own personal ethics (value system) that one would feel hypocritical in submitting to a law that enforces these actions: for example, the Fugitive Slave Law.

It seems to me that a citizen is justified in originating or participating in an act of civil disobedience under any of these circumstances, and, as Herbert Kelman has argued, that an act of civil disobedience in such circumstances should be generally regarded as *obligatory* in terms of the highest principles of citizenship. This does not mean that acts of civil disobedience should be ignored by civil authorities; on the contrary, aside from the damage such a policy would do to effectiveness of the act of civil disobedience, it must be considered the obligation of the regime to punish a law breaker *so long as the violated law is in force.* As William Buckley has argued, it is the individual's right to refuse to go along with his community, but the community, not the individual, must specify the consequences. For the regime to act otherwise would be to concede the right of personal veto over every act of government. At the same time, a conscientious challenge to civil authority (with full expectation of punishment) aimed at repairing a serious flaw in the system of justice is a step every citizen should know how *to decide* to take.

When is Civil Protest Involving Violence Justified? Americans like to think of themselves as a peace-loving people, yet violence is and always has been an important and sometimes indispensable instrument of social, economic and political change in our national history. We do not need to be reminded of the role it has played in United States foreign policy and in domestic relations.

The fact is that Americans are *both* peace-loving and willing to resort to violence when other avenues of goal achievement seem closed or ineffective. In our national history violence was the ultimate instrument in our conquest of the lands on the North American continent that now comprise the nation. Violence freed the American colonists from British rule and later insured freedom of the seas (1812–1815). Violence abolished slavery, established the bargaining rights of labor, twice put down threatening tyrannies in Europe and once in the Asian Pacific. In the present day, violence is the unintended instrument of black citizens to break through oppressive discrimination in housing, employment, education and political rights.

Americans have always taken the position that violence could be justified *as an instrument of last resort* in the achievement of critical national goals or in the face of external threat.

While it is true that we have always felt most comfortable about government-sponsored violence and especially violence in response to an external threat, we have often rationalized *post factum* the use of violence by aggrieved segments of the population *when the cause was regarded as a just one in terms of our deeply held egalitarian values.* The anti-draft riots during the Civil War are one example; labor strife that finally led to legitimizing workers' bargaining rights is another. Two or three generations from now, the ghetto riots (and even the spasmodic insurrection that is bound to follow) will be seen as having contributed to the perfection of our system of egalitarian values. Thus, I conclude that violence in the cause of hewing to our most cherished goals of freedom, justice and equal opportunity for all our citizens is and will remain as indispensable a corrective ingredient in our system as peaceful acts of civil disobedience. The sole qualification is that all other avenues of legitimate and peaceful change first be substantially closed, exhausted or ineffective.

When an aggrieved segment of the population finds it necessary to resist, riot, or commit deliberate acts of insurrection, the government must respond firmly to enforce the law, to protect people and property from the consequences of violence, but it must, with equal energy and dedication, seek out the causes of the outbursts and move speedily to rectify any injustices that are found at the root of the trouble.

QUESTIONS FOR DISCUSSION

1. *How does Conant define "rioting"? What does he mean when he says that riots "are not as a rule senseless outbursts?"*

2. What are the three factors "universally associated with the occurrence and course of any riot"?

3. What are the preconditions?

4. What is the "hostile belief system"?

5. What is "relative deprivation"?

6. What is the chief obstacle to change which Conant mentions?

7. What are the four stages in the riot process?

8. Explain those factors that can affect the second stage.

9. What are the two problems of social control that Conant mentions? What do they generally lead to?

10. What ten observations does Hundley make about the interaction between a riot crowd and social control agencies?

11. Explain the distinction between the insurrectionist and the revolutionary.

12. Under what circumstances is nonviolent civil disobedience justified?

13. What is the author's conclusion about the use of violence?

Excerpts From a Study to Determine the Characteristics of Negro Rioters

Following are excerpts from a study that was done for the National Advisory Commission on Civil Disorders on the characteristics of rioters:

In this report we have attempted to test the adequacy of three major themes of the "riffraff theory" of riot participation:

The first is that only 1 or 2 per cent of the Negro community actively participated in the riots. Our findings for six cities that experienced rioting in 1967 show, however, that about 18 per cent of the Negro residents in the riot areas, on the average, participated in the disorders.

The second theme is that the rioters were not representative of the Negro community, but were principally the riffraff and outside agitators. Our analysis reveals that the riot arrestees were not predominantly the riffraff elements, but were representative of the young adult Negro males in the urban ghetto.

Furthermore, we found no evidence of extensive participation in the riots by outsiders. On the contrary, only

1 per cent of the arrestees were out-of-state residents, 4 per cent lived in the state, but outside the city of the disturbance, and the remaining 95 per cent were residents of that city.

And the third theme holds that the overwhelming majority of the Negro community unequivocally opposed and deplored the riots. Our review of a number of surveys and polls taken recently in black communities throughout the country indicates that Negroes do not feel clearly one way or another about the rioting, but are ambivalent. While most of them disapprove of the violence, they, nevertheless, feel that the riots have beneficial consequences by increasing white society's concern to improve the Negro's condition.

RIFFRAFF THESIS POPULAR

Most public officials and, according to the opinion polls, most Americans have readily adopted the riffraff thesis to explain the riots since it focuses the blame on undesirable traits of individual rioters—and not on the inequities accorded minorities by the white institutions in the urban ghettos. Few of the adherents of this position, however, have offered solid supporting evidence. Too often, their opinions about the rioting were based upon casual observations, cursory soundings of moderate Negroes or the impressions of subordinates who had good reason to play down the disorders.

In this report, therefore, we have used arrest, survey, and census data, simultaneously, to aid us in making reliable estimates about the extent of riot participation and in drawing reasonable inferences about the characteristics of the actual rioters based upon the social composition of arrestees for several cities that experienced rioting in 1967.

Riot participation, by its nature, almost defies systematic analysis. Efforts to examine participation in riots have been based principally on two sources of data. Both types of data, however, suffer from serious methodological problems. With regard to the surveys, some of the problems are common to all survey research: are the samples random or biased? are the respondents honest or are they lying? Other problems are peculiar to surveys of reported deviant behavior: to what extent do ghetto residents under- or overestimate their participation in riots?

The major weakness of the arrest data, for our purposes, is that they have a social class bias: lower- and working-class persons—who disproportionately have riffraff traits—are more likely to be arrested than middle- and upper-class persons. Thus it was expected that the riffraff would be over-represented among the riot arrestees. Despite these limitations of survey and arrest data, however, we have found both types of data to be very useful throughout this report.

BASED ON SIX CITIES

Our estimates of riot participation are based on the six cities (Cincinnati, Dayton, Detroit, Grand Rapids, Newark, and New Haven) for which the National Advisory Commission on Civil Disorders provided us with census maps of their riot areas. In making our comparisons of the riot arrestee's profile with that of the riot area residents, we have used figures from four additional cities (Boston, Buffalo, Plainfield, and Phoenix). That the riots in all of these cities had been classified by the Commission as either "major" or "serious" disorders was a primary criterion for including these 10 cities in our analysis.

We have attempted to estimate the total number of rioters for the above-named six cities. In order to calculate these numbers, we used the age-eligible Negro population in the riot area, the neighborhood that experienced the rioting—not the city, nor even the poverty area—as the appropriate base figure. We operationally defined the age-eligible population or "potential rioters" as those Negro residents of the riot area between the ages of 10 and 59 inclusive. Thus, the infants and the elderly were excluded from the population of potential rioters.

The approach we used to derive our estimates of riot participation required two simple calculations. First, we obtained a "riot ratio" by dividing the number of potential rioters in a given age interval by the number of arrestees in the same age interval for the three cities (which are Detroit, Newark, and Los Angeles) where surveys of the riot areas had been taken. Second, we applied the average of these three ratios to the other cities by multiplying the average ratio times the total number of Negro arrestees in each city.

Using this approach, we obtained a riot ratio of 6 to 1 for Los Angeles, 5 to 1 for Newark, and 3 to 1 for Detroit. Since the 5-to-1 ratio was the average of the three ratios, it was arbitrarily applied to the remaining four cities.

PERCENTAGES OF PARTICIPATION

The application of these ratios yielded the following percentages of riot participation: in Cincinnati, 4 per cent of the Negro residents of the riot area participated in its June disturbance, while 26 per cent of the riot area residents participated in Dayton's June disorders. In Detroit, it was 11 per cent; Newark, 15 per cent; Grand Rapids, 16 per cent; and New Haven, 35 per cent.

Thus, we estimated that about 18 per cent of the riot area residents, on the average, took part in the disorders in these six cities. Also, we estimate that, on the average, four-fifths of those who rioted in these disturbances were not apprehended.

Our figures for the absolute number of rioters, however, which are based on 1960 census data, are conservative estimates of the minimum number of rioters for each city, since they do not reflect the rise in the Negro population of these cities since 1960.

In order to make inferences about the characteristics of the rioters, we have tried to determine which of the so-called riffraff traits—young, unattached, uprooted, unskilled, unemployed, and criminal—are overrepresented among the riot arrestees. We proceeded by comparing the profile of the Negro riot arrestee with that of the "potential rioters" (that is, those Negro residents of the riot areas between the ages of 10 and 59 inclusive). These comparisons resulted in the following findings:

[1]

Although the riot arrestees were predominantly male by 9 to 1, survey data indicated that a higher proportion of females participate in riots than are apprehended. For example, about 40 per cent of the rioters in the Detroit survey (conducted by Caplan and Paige of the University of Michigan's Survey Research Center) were females while only 10 per cent of those arrested for rioting in Detroit were females. Thus, although males are more likely to participate in riots than females, their differential rates of participation are much closer than arrest statistics indicate. The police, for one reason or another, are permitting large numbers of female rioters to go unapprehended.

[2]

The riots were not directed by the teen-agers. More than two-thirds of the arrestees in the nine cities for which we have comparative data were adults (that is, persons 18 years and older). And, among the riot area residents, or "potential rioters" more than four-fifths were adults. Eyewitness accounts of the riots, however, indicate that a higher proportion of juveniles take part in the rioting than is reflected in the arrest statistics.

[3]

Although juveniles were only a small minority of the arrestees, young adults between the ages of 15 and 34 constituted an overwhelming majority of the arrestees. Among the potential rioters, however, the proportion of persons in this age category was under 50 per cent.

[4]

More than twice as many arrestees as potential rioters were single. But in only two out of five cities did the single persons constitute a clear majority of the arrestees. Thus a plurality of the arrestees were single.

[5]

The arrestees were more likely to be Northern-born and natives of the state experiencing the riot than the potential rioters. Thus, the rioters are not newly arrived immigrants from the rural South.

[6]

About one and a half times as many arrestees as potential rioters held unskilled jobs. But almost as many arrestees as potential rioters held skilled or whitecollar jobs.

[7]

The overwhelming majority of rioters are employed. About three-fourth of the arrestees were found to be employed. Although unemployment is undoubtedly a factor in riot participation, it does not explain the involvement of the three-fourths who are employed.

[8]

Although from 40 to 90 per cent of the arrestees had prior criminal records, the criminal element was not found to be overrepresented. For criminologists estimate that from 50 to 90 per cent of the Negro males in the urban ghetto have criminal records. Thus to label most rioters as criminals is simply to brand the majority of Negro males in the urban ghettos as criminals.

[9]

The rioters, by no means, can be considered as outsiders. In seven of the nine cities considered, 97 per cent or more of the arrestees were residents of the city experiencing the riot.

Thus, the arrestees, as predicted by the riffraff theory, were more likely to be single and younger than the residents of the riot area. On the other hand, contrary to the riffraff thesis, the arrestees were less likely to be born outside the state, almost as likely to hold skilled or white-collar jobs and to be employed, and just as likely to have a criminal record as the residents of the riot areas. Consequently, over-all, our findings contradict the second component of the riffraff theory.

We continue our test of the second point of the riffraff thesis by examining the characteristics of the arrestees according to their booking offense, their day of arrest and the severity of the riot in which they were alleged to have participated.

[1]

We found that arsonists and looters were more likely to be older, Southern-born, and employed than assaulters

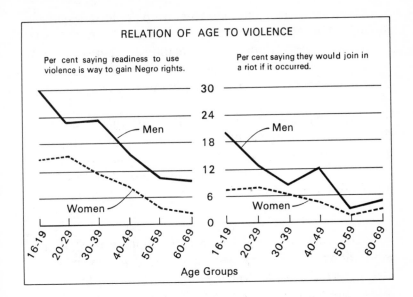

RELATION OF AGE TO VIOLENCE

Per cent saying readiness to use violence is way to gain Negro rights.

Per cent saying they would join in a riot if it occurred.

Men

Women

Men

Women

Age Groups

and disorderly persons. But the arsonists and disorderly persons were more likely to have a prior criminal record than assaulters and looters.

[2]

The younger, native-born persons were more likely to take part on the first day of rioting than the older, Southern-born individuals, who tend to become involved in the later phases of the riot. But, interestingly, males, the unemployed and those with prior criminal records participated to the same extent regardless of the stage of rioting.

[3]

Males, the young and unskilled were more likely to participate in the "less severe" disorders (like Buffalo's and Cincinnati's) than in the "more severe" disorders like Detroit's and Newark's.

Although the limited data suggest that the riffraff thesis may be more accurate for less serious disorders, it is not confirmed when the arrestees are examined according to their type offense and day of arrest. In our N.I.M.H. report, we intend to analyze the relationship between social characteristics of the arrestees and severity of the riot more systematically by including many more riot cities.

We considered the third theme of the riffraff theory— that the overwhelming majority of the Negro population unequivocally opposed and deplored the riots. Our conclusions, based upon an examination of recent surveys munity [sic] as follows:

[1]

The attitude of the Negro community toward rioting was ambivalent. According to a U.C.L.A. survey taken of Los Angeles Negroes after the riot in 1965, while most of them opposed the violence of the rioting, two-thirds believed that it would increase white America's awareness and improve the Negro's position.

[2]

It is possible that future riots may gain recruits from the more favorable segments of the Negro community. According to a Louis Harris poll of Negroes taken nationally in 1966, lower-middle, middle- and upper-middle-income Negroes were more likely to say that they would join a riot than the lower-income Negroes.

Thus the black community does not feel clearly one way or another about the rioting. While the overwhelming majority deplore the violence in the riots, a majority feel that the riots will have beneficial consequences for improving the Negro's social and economic conditions.

It is important to realize that the findings in this report are tentative; they are based solely upon the characteristics of those persons arrested in the more serious riots of 1967.

We do not know, at this time, the extent to which these findings can be generalized to earlier—or later riots. It is for this reason that our report has sought merely to describe its findings in relation to the three themes of the riffraff theory. For it is quite possible that the riffraff thesis may be more accurate for many of the earlier riots of the 1960's.

Therefore, we have not attempted to offer an alternative "theory" of riot participation in this report. For we feel that in order for it to be viable, such a "theory" should emerge after a systematic empirical analysis has been made of several of the major riots occurring between 1964 and 1967. We will attempt to move in this direction in our M.I.N.H. report.

QUESTIONS FOR DISCUSSION

1. *What are the three major themes of the "riffraff theory"?*
2. *Why have most public officials readily adopted this theory?*
3. *About what per cent of the riot area residents, on the average, took part in the disorders in the six cities studied?*
4. *According to this study, were many women involved in rioting? Were more women or men apprehended for their activities?*
5. *Do many teenagers direct or become involved in these riots?*
6. *What age group overwhelmingly constituted the majority of the arrestees?*
7. *Were the rioters newly arrived immigrants from the rural South?*
8. *What types of jobs did the rioters hold? How large a share of the rioters was unemployed? Was the criminal element overrepresented in the group?*
9. *What were the characteristics of the looters, the arsonists, the assaulters, and the disorderly?*

10. *Who participated earliest in the rioting? Who tended to become involved in the later phases of the riot?*

11. *How did the Negro community, as a whole, feel about rioting?*

12. *According to the Louis Harris poll of Negroes in 1966, what income groups were more likely to say that they would join a riot?*

Genesis of a Riot

MARK EDELSON

There has been an official interpretation for riots ever since they began in the summer of 1964 in central Harlem; one which has never wavered in its recriminations against the general society, and in its implied exculpation of the rioters. Since "studies" of these affairs all come out the same way (like a fixed fight) and since the deeper the study, the more general the self-recrimination, I felt this time I should see the seminal event "live" and not on tape a few hours old. A prejudice is a prejudice, I thought, and some are old and some are new. And these new ones against the society, which must be really, unusually evil to cause so many cities to burn, sound thinner and more mindless than the old ones, which produced the obscene English of "nigger" and "spic." And I understood that this oppressive, disparaged society had to be me. The indictment was not against the burners, but against those who did not burn, not against the looters, but against those who would not loot. Here, right at hand, lay an opportunity for a study truly in depth.

Mark Edelson, "Genesis of a Riot," *National Review*, June 30, 1968. Reprinted by permission of *National Review*, 150 East 35 Street, New York, N.Y. 10016.

It was Monday night, July 24, 1967. I entered East Harlem a little after 7:00 P.M., from 125th Street and Lexington Avenue, and found it under occupation. Moving south down Lexington, and then switching over to Madison, I saw police on all four corners of every intersection, usually in pairs, sometimes bunched up in threes and fours. Besides the heavy foot-force there was the cavalry of patrol cars and scooters. The force appeared to be almost 90 per cent white, a fact which has been grist to the mill of some anti-police writers, but which I found viscerally reassuring—an example, alas, of prejudice, but a very comforting one.

The occupiers, however, were not from another country, but merely another area, or areas, of the same city. If you want to postulate East Harlem as a different country in our midst (as do those white ideologues who follow the chic of calling it "El Barrio"), then it means that you are willing to concede a polyglot America, beginning in New York . . . a country which is not willing even to enforce a linguistic homogeneity, and is ready to overseer, or at least oversee, its own cultural fragmentation. If we no longer have an East Harlem, or even a "Spanish Harlem," but instead "El Barrio," then the city is giving itself away in pieces. Chinatown or Little Italy, after all, are linguistic indications of Americanization. "El Barrio" describes, not an oppressive but a tired society, one no longer willing to maintain even its most basic substructure. Then, America would really be Rome or Carthage—though just in the beginning stages.

The blue occupiers were notable for numbers, but even more for passivity. And this was to be their character and role all evening. They were a saturation, but a very quiet and inoffensive one. Unless the presence of an American peace force in an American city (East Harlem) is to be regarded in itself as offensive. The police, even the tactical force (who were off the streets filling the luncheonettes and pizza parlors), looked warm under all their equipment, and some were obviously tired, but I saw no pugnacity or quarrelsomeness on any of their faces. They are, of course, part of that oppressive enclosing society which the automatic partisans of all minorities recriminate in the wake of all rioting, but according to my experience (or prejudice, or both), if there was any easily definable group of good guys in that night's interaction, it could only have been these armed men.

It Takes One to Quarrel

As I moved downtown, switching every couple of blocks, westward toward Park and Madison or east to Third, I saw knots of adolescents and post-adolescents, just off the avenues and on the side streets, which themselves were generally unpoliced. In East Harlem, and Central Harlem also, this is not an unusual sight, particularly in season—the warm months. In the rapidly shrinking enclaves of white New York the people come out in summertime also, but the cluttered and pulsating street is a specific characteristic of the Negro and Puerto Rican areas. This time, however, there was a difference. Hostility was seen and felt on those side streets, just off the avenues. Whether this youth or that young man had undergone brutality at the hands of these other youths and men I do not know—that is a matter for real and careful proof, not easy apologetics for the underdog—but there could be no mistaking their sullen faces and mood to quarrel. It does not take two necessarily to make a quarrel. One can do it if he tries hard enough.

Of course, most of the people in the streets were not so predisposed. They were as pacific and unconcerned as the police. They were living out their early evening as casually as they had just lived out their day. Whether they, too, were the victims of a society which deserves to be recriminated by its own intellectuals, I cannot say—but the thought occurred to me that if it is so, then the Caribbean must breed a masochistic race—did not all these people come here as volunteers and write back signaling their relatives and friends to make the trip, too?

It was now past eight o'clock, and I was on Lexington Avenue below 116th Street, where the clutter of East Harlem is broken, as it so often is, by one of the landscaped and airy city housing projects. I had intended to get a container of coffee and drink it outside, in one of those unofficial little parks between the project buildings, when I noticed a movement of people. It was eastward toward Third, which I had left for Lexington at 116th Street. This was the first sight of something definite, so, giving up my plans, I became part of the movement, and came out on Third at 111th Street.

Almost a block away, I could already see it was the focal point of the argument. But you heard more than you saw. You heard the speaker, a hoarse, abrasive voice (in Spanish), and without knowing Spanish you knew it was not an address, but at the very least a harangue. You also heard the crowd, or parts of it, as animated as the speaker, already an organism, exhilarated by a preliminary victory.

The victory: control of the intersection of 111th Street and Third Avenue. The speaker was standing on what looked like an inverted city litter basket, not on the sidewalk, but where the four roads crossed. The crowd of two or three hundred was itself mostly in the intersection, and it knew as much as the speaker did that the intersection had been taken from the city and that the city had not reacted. It was a type of minor annexation—for New York, the government, had retreated a block and a half away. A block and a half north and a block and a half south on Third was again the characteristic governmental presence, large numbers of police, but passive and non-reactive. More than that, they were cooperative. Barriers had been placed across Third, and the normally busy traffic was police-directed away. That meant cars, trucks and the important Third Avenue bus route were all interrupted so that activists against the police could harangue a crowd. To emphasize the tone of the speeches, two people stood beside the platform and held up a large Puerto Rican flag—but there was no American flag, here at Third Avenue and 111th Street, to keep it company, and no one in the crowd seemed to mind.

SPEECHES RAN TRUE TO FORM

The speakers continued in English and in Spanish—someone in the crowd next to me translated the Spanish. There was a familar, almost formula list of complaints about housing, police and the schools, but the tone was not one of petition but one of truculence and, climactically, of ultimatum. Mayor Lindsay was told to come uptown and negotiate by ten o'clock (about an hour away) or the area would explode. It seemed reasonable, I thought, to be truculent. They had already annexed the street. They had cut off traffic. They had seen the city withdraw its authority a block and a half away. They had seen an allegiance to Puerto Rico (but not the United States) placed next to the speakers—and, there was no reaction.

Shortly after nine o'clock a police observer was spotted on one of the roofs overlooking the meeting, and the crowd, by now *itself* truculent and visibly exhilarated, shouted and shrieked to have him brought down on the obvious premise that this area belonged to them, and not to the government of New York City. The roof-observer did come down—he was ordered to do so by a police captain, who came into the insurgent area from his position a block and a half away. Then, both he and the roof-observer retreated to government territory. In one other incident, a patrol car coming into the intersection along 111th Street tried to drive carefully around the crowd, but it massed and rushed on the car, ordering it back out of the area; and it did go back, without contesting the intersection.

These capitulations did not relax or quiet the crowd, they visibly enlivened it—the concessions fed, not tranquility, but aggression. The police were becoming, obviously, not good guys, but small guys. The speeches had heated up the crowd, but I believe it was these small capitulations which pushed it over the line into riot.

It was shortly after the rooftop incident that the first bottle was thrown. It broke in the street without hurting anyone—but it made everyone turn his eyes, not toward the area from which it came but toward the police, just beyond the insurgency. The police, government itself, was being tested again. And, following the pattern, there was no reaction. Within a minute or two, the first bottle was followed by small barrages, not thrown at any person or group, but at the emptied street—the crowd had retreated from the avenue itself and were now along both sidewalks, a great part of it up against the building line. It was now possible to see that a knot of people had emerged from 112th Street, on the east side of the avenue, and that they had made the attack. At first it was a quick sally onto the avenue to throw, and then back into the darkness. But there was no police reaction. Having apparently collected every no-deposit bottle in East Harlem, they came out into the avenue itself. Then, standing in the light, they began throwing the bottles boldly at the buildings and store-fronts, and then at the quiescent policemen themselves.

There were no more speeches—and whether the bottle- and rock-throwers had once been in the audience was something I could not tell; but the violence began just after the harangues, and almost at the same point. Also, the audience which had so protested the police did not, as far as I could hear, protest the obvious brutality of the flying bottles. There were police now among the crowd, and then between it and what was now the start of the riot. They were still, the police, a quiet presence, not active against anyone. They were, in their new position, merely a new and easier target for the rioters. This made us targets, too. The crowd dissolved into doorways, store entrances, flattened against buildings, and moved off the avenue into the side streets. It was a victim of its own work.

The police had now infiltrated the area in strength, still avoiding large movements, always emphasizing presence instead of action. They were now targets, both for the rioters' bottles and the non-rioters' ridicule. Those who had listened to and applauded the repetitious statements of police brutality now taunted the inactive police. (I thought, "That was an awful lot for eight thousand dollars a year.") There was no retort from the police, now helmeted, but they were no longer relaxed. I saw many sullen faces. They were like cats ready to move, but they did not move. When the bottles came at them, now generally in clusters, they flattened as far as they could, against the building line, turning away their heads, taking the fire with their shoulders. It occurred to me: the preponderance of weapons is with the rioters. Because, though the police all have guns they don't use them. And the rounds of ammunition here were glass. It was becoming, as a matter of fact, a contest between armed and unarmed men.

To Bell a Cat

At this point the looting began. All evening, law and government had been probed, defied and repudiated, in measured steps. The key always seemed to be the nonreaction of authority. It seemed to occur this way now. The street and sidewalks were mainly broken glass. There had been no move against the people who had done this, and now they made their own greater move. The rioters moved from their point on the corner of the avenue and 112th Street, and pushing down the avenue itself a few feet, stalled in front of a supermarket boarded up along its whole length. It took almost ten minutes of heavy work to pry open the wooden slats—ten minutes of present but absent government. When the boards finally came off, the rioters stopped to cheer their work, and then began to smash in the plate glass. This, finally, was the point of contact. Squads of police, from several directions, moved in on the rioters—but did not rush them. Apparently they were being given time to get away. This particular store wasn't looted. The rioters broke very quickly and fled before the police, foiled but not captured.

It was now a little past ten o'clock, and for the next two hours I walked Third and Lexington Avenues, between 111th and 102nd Streets, part of the shapeless lump of anarchy that moved from block to block, reproduced itself, and proliferated in many directions. The shape of police, and thus of governmental action, beginning at the captured intersection of 111th and Third, was repeated many times and solidified into the pattern of government for that night. The first duty of government is not to dispense justice but to rule. And in that section of the United States that night, there was no rule, only the shapeless lump of anarchy, moving up and down the avenues and streets, often dispersed by the police, never suppressed.

The mob did not appear brave to me. It was an example of bluster, not of *machismo*—the bully, not the man. The mob always broke before the essentially unarmed police. In the cross section of riot I saw, I never observed one clubbing, and, though many shots were fired, often in volleys, it was always done for effect, harmlessly into the air.* The rioting never stopped or diminished because the

_____

* Bullets fired "harmlessly" into the air by a police force under lethal attack from glass and stone represent the optimum of restraint, caution and self-risk. But a city block is a confined place and can

rioters were never apprehended but merely dispersed, moment to moment, to continuously re-form, on other blocks, with the increasing awareness that they had achieved a supraequality before the law—they were now more equal than others.

The apologists for rioters who from a distance conclude our sympathies should be more with the lawless than the law, should be air-dropped into the middle of the next disturbance to find out from experience whether the flint of anarchy is deprivation or truculence. I saw no hollow cheeks, patched clothes or tragic eyes among the stone-throwers—but I did see continuously the liquor of power in all their faces—and I had the apprehension, as well as they did, of a declining, and even vanishing government. By midnight, when I left the zone, there was only a pinpoint of government left (though it was a heavily occupied area), not because a government was now despised—but because, through its own inactions, it was *properly* despised.

When an organism becomes unable to react, then we know it is dying. A government had become so obsessed with minority complaint that it had forgotten how to rule. There was so much intellectual self-reproach and quibble in its mind that it was unable anymore to express its own right to live. This erosion of power, though internal, has a telep-

---

give a bullet, no matter how harmlessly intended, two or three lives, and the first ricochet can bring a casualty, the result neither of intent nor recklessness. Two died that night of gunshot wounds, traced to police weapons. Both victims were apparently in the "audience" of the riot, which drew many, for many reasons. Though disturbing and repelling (at least to one member of the audience), it was a good show but it was a dangerous attraction. The tragedy of these affairs is that the innocent always get hurt. If the police ever aimed their shots specifically to kill, or even to wound, it was an anomaly of that evening, and not a characteristic. And, in that fairly comprehensive crosscut of the evening I observed, there was not even that anomaly.

athy which is apprehended as quickly as fear. And it is appetite to truculence. Whatever the quantum of social inequity there may be in New York—after decades of welfare-oriented administrations—still the major phenomenon of this city is not injustice but the decline of government. Self-recrimination and self-doubt, both cults now, have subtracted from the desire to live. The aftermaths of these riots are more damaging than the period of anarchy itself. If looting and arson are defined as a form of protest or petition, as the curious apologetics always run, then the society which supports and even subsidizes these apologetics is inviting itself to be dissolved, is yearning for its own death.

More dangerous than the exceptional periods of riot are the quieter interludes. For some time now, government has not existed in East Harlem (or Central Harlem) as it exists in Jackson Heights or Flatbush. The real constant in the Negro or Puerto Rican areas is not the police excess, and certainly not the police atrocity, but instead the great difficulty of making normal arrests. The real news is the number of minor mob actions against the police which are never news. The main problem in the various slums is the problem of restoring government itself to these areas. The withering away of the state has progressed further in parts of New York City than any Marxist covenant yet applied.

Someone must have been sacrificing to the rain gods during that night of suspended government, because a little after 2:00 A.M. a heavy downpour fell on the city, both the governed and the ungoverned parts, and a deteriorating situation was cured by weather. The next day, through a process of redefinition, what was palpably a riot to those who had been there was reduced to a "disturbance" by those who had not—part of the new alchemy of government. But a government (or quasi-government) that shuffles definitions to make things come out even must be more interested in theory than in fact. It may not always rain in time.

QUESTIONS FOR DISCUSSION

1. How does this assessment of violence differ from the previous studies by Conant and the National Advisory Commission on Civil Disorders?
2. Is one man's view of a situation as valid as a scientific study of a problem? How does Edelson counteract the fact that many people might criticize his view of violence?
3. Does the author really seem to be concerned about the cause for rebellion, or is he more interested in speaking out against violence?
4. How would the authors of previous articles react to this statement by Edelson: "The first duty of government is not to dispense justice but to rule"?

Money to Burn

ERNEST VAN DEN HAAG

The government, at various levels, is concerned with how to channel aid to riot-damaged areas. It also is considering programs to induce or compel (or substitute for) private insurance companies to insure property and businesses in areas in which riots have broken out and may again break out.

The intention—to help riot victims—is laudable; nonetheless such efforts would also help, or even subsidize, rioting, and thereby produce more riot victims. Further, if the Federal Government hands out subsidies, local authorities will see their liability to riot victims reduced. Ambitious politicians thus may, at times, be induced to let property be destroyed instead of protected: it may enhance their popularity with the group bent on destruction—and the Federal Government will compensate the owners of the destroyed property.

I believe that the proper policy should aim at discouraging riots, at encouraging police forces to protect life and property, and at encouraging stable neighborhood ele-

Ernest van den Haag, "Money to Burn," *National Review*, June 30, 1968.

ments to discourage rioters. It should be preventive rather than corrective, and, even after the fact, aim at prevention of recurrence more than at repair of damage.

This means that the Federal Government must not compensate any riot victims directly or indirectly. Compensation must be left entirely to local authorities. They are, after all, in charge of local protection. Secondly, property holders in riot-prone areas should be allowed to take out whatever insurance they can. But the Federal Government should not underwrite losses directly or indirectly by subsidizing insurance. To do so would be to tell in advance both the property owners and the rioters that the game will cost them nothing: it will be at the expense only of the taxpayers. Finally, areas in which riots have happened should not be rewarded by an influx of federal money to rebuild what rioters have destroyed.

These considerations lead me to suggest that the Congress should make a law prohibiting the expenditure of federal money for at least three years after the riot date in areas in which riots have happened. From this prohibition one might exclude only a few expenditures unrelated to riots, such as military expenditures or expenditures on roads —although here, too, one must make reasonably sure that no subsidy is sneaked in. By a riot area I would mean one so certified by police authorities or one in which looting has taken place since the date of the law, or an area in which policemen were wounded (so as to have to spend more than a week in a hospital) or killed, during civil unrest. It would be far too lengthy a business here to draft the kind of law I have in mind. I must therefore confine myself to suggesting it, and to attempting to justify it; let me indicate, though, that there is no technical obstacle to drafting such a law. Obviously, such a law would deprive not only rioters, but also residents who had nothing to do with the riots in their area, of the federal benefits they now enjoy. There might indeed be some hardship cases. I do not see, though, why these could not be taken care of at local and state government levels.

There is a twofold rationale for the proposed law. On the one hand, the neighborhood that has passively tolerated the riot will now find it in its interest to prevent another. Knowing as much, such a neighborhood may take preventive measures. Similar reasoning applies to the actions or inactions of local authorities.

To Understand Is Not to Justify

Secondly, the budding tendency of the Federal Government, so clearly suggested in the Kerner report, to, in effect, reward rioting will be effectively quashed. If we allow rioting to function as a reminder of the unfulfilled desires of the riot-neighborhood, and if as a result of the rioting we start to fulfill them, then, despite all denials, we justify the riot after the fact. Negro militants will, quite rightly, point out the advantages secured by the riot. They will be able to say, "If you riot you get it—look at what happened elsewhere—if you don't, you don't." The only way to counter this is to make clear that "if you riot you won't get what you would have got if you hadn't, and you will lose what you have got." It is not enough to say so; we must do so.

Negroes and the poor in general have many just grievances which should be acted upon. However, we should act upon these grievances where there have been no riots, and suspend action where there have been. Else we would reward riots and establish them as an effective grievance procedure. In effect we would say, "You can burn it up, baby, if you are mad, and we will replace it." Riots can be explained. But they cannot be justified. We must not act as though understanding the causes of riots implies condoning, accepting, or justifying them. Yet unless we act along the lines suggested above, that is what we are doing. (It need hardly be said that states and localities should reserve severe punishments for rioters and looters. As yet I know of no efforts even to recover looted goods or punish those who knowingly possess them.)

Often I can understand all too well why a man kills his wife. Sometimes one feels more sympathy for the murderer than for the victim. In many cases putting the murderer in jail is not going to help him or the murdered wife. It may not rehabilitate him, or he may not need rehabilitation (he may never remarry). Nonetheless, if he is not at the least jailed, other wives would not be safe. He is placed in jail, that is, to deter and discourage others, and to make sure that his act is unrewarding. For even the worst wife does not justify—though she may explain—murder. I think the case is sufficiently analogous to that of riots to take analogous action. And don't tell me that penalties have not prevented wife murders. Most wives—miraculously enough—survive. What other explanation could there be?

QUESTIONS FOR DISCUSSION

1. *Why does the author believe that the Federal Government must not compensate any riot victims directly or indirectly?*
2. *How would Conant, and the National Advisory Commission on Civil Disturbances react to van den Haag's proposal?*
3. *How do you react to the following statement by the author? "The only clear way to counter this is to make clear that 'if you riot you won't get what you would have got if you hadn't, and you will lose what you have got.'"*
4. *Is the author's analogy in the last paragraph sound?*

As Violence Spreads in High Schools...

Unrest and violence are sweeping through the high schools of urban America on an ever-widening scale.

The spread is now recognized as a national problem that is interrupting the education and endangering the safety of thousands of teen-age students. Some educators are convinced it will grow as big as the revolt on college campuses.

Every public school in Providence, R. I., and Trenton, N. J., was closed for several days when fights between black and white students got out of control late last month. Trenton's public-safety director said he did not have enough manpower to protect children in the schools. The city imposed a curfew to keep youngsters off the streets.

Since the autumn term began in September, schools in more than a dozen other cities have had to shut down temporarily because of student rampages.

There were a few bright spots, and some indications that school officials are learning by experience how to cope with unrest. Chicago and San Francisco were among cities reporting less disturbance this year than last.

Reprinted from *U.S. News & World Report*, November 30, 1970, pp. 18–20.

. . .

Root of Trouble. Racial antagonism is blamed as the basis of most of the unrest. But other issues frequently are causes. High-school students in many places are demanding a bigger voice in school affairs. They are challenging dress codes and calling for curriculum changes, including introduction of black studies.

Some authorities believe the trouble is being stirred up by outside agitators. Albert Shanker, president of the United Federation of Teachers in New York City, asserted on November 15 there is "an organized effort to bring about rule in schools by violence." He asked for a government investigation of "goon squads" which he said were traveling from school to school.

Officials in Houston, Tex., also suspect there is an organized effort to foment discord in their schools.

Two recent studies of disruption in American high schools found most of the conflict to be centered in racially mixed public schools.

Integration Blamed. A report from the National Association of Secondary School Principals stated, "The greatest incidence of conflict was in the mixed-black-and-white schools, of which 77 per cent said they had experienced it."

The second report, made by the Syracuse University Research Corporation, declared:

"Disruption is positively related to integration. Schools which are almost all white or all black are less likely to be disrupted. This might suggest a policy of apartheid as a solution to disruption, but this option is unavailable. Among other drawbacks, it is unconstitutional."

The Syracuse researchers also attributed disorders in high schools to the violence shown on TV screens that young people watch every day.

"Graphic and incessant TV publicity of disruptions in the whole society creates a climate which, in our opinion, makes disruptions in a high school much more likely," the researchers said.

The Syracuse research group also had this comment:

"It may be an unpleasant subject, but no honest observers of the urban high-school scene could bypass the phenomenon of black revenge. We found it sad but psychologically understandable when numbers of black high-school students told us one way or another that 'it's Whitey's turn to take some heat.' . . .

"We found that much of the physical fighting, the extortion, the bullying in and around schools had a clear racial basis. This was particularly apparent where the student mix was predominantly but not wholly black.

"White students are hesitant to express their fears on this subject, but those fears are very real and run very deep. Some were finally willing to tell us that they traveled only in large white groups, studiously avoiding physical proximity to black groups, and 'getting the hell out of there as fast as we can.' "

No Pat Answer. Nobody who has studied the high-school problem has come up with a clear-cut solution.

"If the causes of disruption in urban high-schools are complex, so are the cures," the Syracuse group said.

"Our investigations have led us to the conclusion that, short of a total moral conversion, the American society will continue to behave in such a way as to insure some degree of pathological unrest in our urban high schools for some time to come."

The Syracuse group did have some recommendations, however. Among them:

Younger teachers in central-city schools.

More black teachers in predominantly black schools.

More-tolerant social codes, including relaxed rules on dress and grooming.

Review of the grade requirements which now limit minority
participation in student government, athletics and other
extracurricular activities.

Security forces of neighborhood people who are not connected
with the faculty or police. Half of the principals interviewed
in the Syracuse survey agreed that "the mere presence of
uniformed police inside a school building is often a cause
rather than a deterrent of school disruption."

What Schoolmen Say. For a first-hand account of conditions in urban high schools, staff members of "U. S. News
& World Report" talked with school officials in cities all
over the country. Here is what they found in mid-Novem-
ber:

School officials in the Detroit area prefer to play down

SIGNS OF TURMOIL IN THE NATION'S SCHOOLS

*A survey by the Syracuse University Research Corpora-
tion found that, of nearly 700 urban high schools responding
to its questionnaires, the following percentages reported disruptions of various kinds during the past three years—*

Teacher boycott or strike	22%
Student boycott or strike	33%
Arson	21%
Other property damage	56%
Rioting	11%
Student attacks on teachers	29%
Picketing or parading	25%
Abnormal unruliness by students	33%
Unruly nonschool persons on campus	54%

All told, 85 per cent of the schools suffered some type of disruption. Many of the incidents were related to race.

the significance of violent incidents in high schools. However, in many cases, security forces are being strengthened.

After sit-ins or racial disturbances in four of its 22 high schools this autumn, the Detroit public-school system is adding 34 in-school security guards to its present staff of 20.

The principal security problem in Detroit high schools, according to Security Director Robert Potts, is keeping out "ne'er-do-wells, dropouts and intruders."

In Houston, parents have complained to the city council about "terror" in the public schools. Les Burton, security officer for the Houston school district, blamed most of the trouble on uncertainty and unrest among students and their parents after court-ordered redistricting for integration.

"The problem stems from the fact that many students —black and white—were forced to leave their old schools and go to schools where they didn't want to go," Mr. Burton said.

Fast-spreading rumors of shootings, stabbings and rapes in newly integrated high schools kept the Houston district in turmoil for weeks after school began this year. The rumors—most of them false—stopped after the FBI began an investigation into the possibility of a conspiracy to spread them.

Calm in California. A San Francisco school official, Myron Moskowitz, reported schools quieter than last year. The chief incident so far was a two-day closure of one high school after a fight.

Mr. Moskowitz said the narcotics problem among students is "no worse than last year, perhaps better." He added: "But any time a kid is hung up on drugs you are going to get a kid who is unaccountable for his actions."

Physical attacks on teachers and students in San Francisco have been numerous in past years, but no figures are available yet for this term. In junior high schools alone, during the last school year, there were 99 attacks on teachers and 444 attacks on students.

A report from Atlanta said violence in high schools in the Southeast has increased noticeably. Atlanta officials called this the most crucial year yet for integration. Blacks are often moved into formerly all-white high schools, and both races are tense. Schoolmen said the wonder is not that there is violence, but that the incidence of violence is so small.

Much of the fighting was described by Atlanta's school superintendent, John Letson, as normal schoolboy scuffling.

In Miami, Fla., School Board Chairman G. Holmes Braddock estimated there may be 200 to 300 "radicals" in a high-school population of around 250,000. One concession being made to students in this area is a liberalization of dress codes.

School or Jail. Las Vegas, Nev., is beginning to restore order with a policy of "go to school or go to jail." Last year the schools were shut down every time a disturbance broke out.

"We learned that won't do," said Charles Fleming, an official of the Clark County school district. "Only 5 per cent of the school body is out in the hall making trouble; the remainder is trying to get an education, and we run the schools for them."

Now Las Vegas school administrators do not hesitate to call police to high-school grounds. Once brought in, lawmen make arrests. In the disturbances last month, 163 young people were booked.

Mr. Fleming reported "some" evidence of outside agitation at high schools. He said narcotics are not considered a major factor in school disturbances.

Changed Attitudes. Chicago high schools have had a relatively quiet autumn, attributed to changes in school and security-guard attitudes rather than changes in student attitudes. Said Edward D. Brady, director of security for the Chicago board of education:

"We've had much less trouble this fall in the schools. I'd say it's been quieter than in the last two years. Last year we saw student protests break out in several schools a week. There have been very few incidents this fall—and most of them were parental protests against overcrowded conditions."

Mr. Brady said his security corps of 450 men has won more co-operation from students since it began trying to be "a preventive force, not an oppressive force."

Better communication between parents, students and schools also has made for a calmer autumn, officials said.

The situation was different in New York City.

Hands Tied. Henry T. Hillson, principal of Midwood High School in Brooklyn and president-elect of the New York City High School Principals Association, reported there was more trouble in New York high schools than ever before.

Among the 4,200 integrated students at his school, Mr. Hillson said, there aren't more than 40 troublemakers, but "these 40 are enough to keep us going night and day."

As a result of school policies, Mr. Hillson said, New York high schools are packed with students who have no interest in education. He explained:

"We have thousands of pupils, literally thousands, who pass no subject. Some have not passed a single subject in two full years. They roam the buildings at will. They come and go as they please, go to class or not, as they wish. They hang around in the toilets. They disturb classrooms. And we may not do anything about them unless they engage in an act of violence. We cannot even ask the superintendent for suspension. There is nothing anybody can do to get them out of school before they are 21, if they wish to stay."

Mr. Hillson made this prediction:

"Unless the board of education and the State legislature will take action in respect to some kind of control or some kind of special schooling for this disruptive group, within a limited period of years we won't have a good academic high school left in the city. And that goes for every big city in the country where they have a problem population."

QUESTIONS FOR DISCUSSION

1. *What is the basis of most of the unrest in our high schools? What are the other issues disturbing students?*
2. *Where has the greatest incidence of conflict occurred?*
3. *In what way do TV and "black revenge" affect the climate in high school?*
4. *What are some of the corrective recommendations made by the Syracuse research group?*
5. *Does the use of narcotics in some schools affect student behavior?*
6. *How may boredom or a disinterest in education relate to violence in New York high schools?*

How Not to Prevent Civil Disorders

ERNEST VAN DEN HAAG

The Report of the National Advisory Commission on Civil Disorders is so comprehensive as to be useless: the attempt to include everything makes it unselective, though for this very reason, unobjectionable. Nothing is left out, but there is no distinction between the desirable and the possible, and no priorities are given: all things—from changing personal attitudes to rebuilding cities—are to be done (by spending money) at once; wherefore none will be.

Although unwilling to give programmatic priorities, the Commission is unsparing with remonstrances and re-criminations addressed to whites; they amount to a mislead-ing "explanation" for last summer's riots. For, if all the grievances of the rioters were justified (and I think most are) they would not "explain" the riots; these were caused by the grievances as much, and no more, as the murder of Jews in Germany, or of capitalists in Russia, was "caused" by grievances against them.

Despite pale disclaimers—riots must not be regarded, after all, as rational or desirable remedies—the Commission

Ernest van den Haag, "How Not to Prevent Civil Disorders," *National Review*, March 26, 1968.

clearly suggests that the riots have come as a punishment for our sins, and are to be avoided in the future by repentance and repair. Undoubtedly a religiously orthodox explanation, but not a scientific one. Sins we have committed. Possibly we deserve everything we get and more—I won't argue the point. But the Commission confused sin and punishment with cause and effect: it assumed that whatever deserved punishment *ipso facto* was the cause of the riots, which are felt to be the punishment deserved. Such a theory of crime and punishment does not flow from information and analysis; it has nothing to do with the facts; it was dictated by the guilty consciences of the Commission's members. However, conscience is not a reliable guide to investigate and predict factual matters, nor to determine what means of control would be effective: conscience is a guide only to normative matters, to moral aims, not to the effectiveness of means or of causes.

Pangs of Conscience

There is not a shred of evidence indicating that the riots were caused by our sins—any more than that epidemics of bubonic plague, or the sack of Rome, were caused by the unquestioned sinfulness of the population. Now, if the Report had mentioned infection, or weakness—but it does not; it cannot, because it is part of both—a symptom rather than a diagnosis of the malaise it was to scrutinize. For the riots—the report notwithstanding—were caused less by our sinfulness than by our attempts to repent for it—to repair the harm done—and by the guilty conscience so dramatically manifested by the Commission.

The Commission believes in a secularized Marxist version of the crime (sin) and punishment theory. Riots occur because white society is rich and allows, or causes, Negroes to be poor in its midst. If the Commission had used more mundane means of investigation—it seems to have used moral generosity exclusively—it might have found that:

(a) the contrast between rich and poor (including Negroes) was greater in the past;

(b) the contrast is greater in most European countries;

(c) the U.S. riots did not occur where Negroes were least well treated;

(d) the contrast is greater in the Soviet Union (if one considers not theory, but consumption, power, and prestige differentials), and

(e) in India and South America.

Morally the contrast may be deplorable. But it neither "explains" nor "caused" the riots.

Negroes have certainly been discriminated against, beginning with slavery. They have suffered from deprivation and lack of opportunity, from unfulfilled promises, and, finally, from demoralization. Yet discrimination has diminished, and conditions have rapidly improved since the Second World War. There has been more improvement in the last twenty years than in the previous two hundred. Thus, the Commission, after stating that white incomes have risen faster than Negro incomes (true for the two aggregate groups, but not for each sub-group), finds (inconspicuously) that "the proportion of Negro families with incomes of $7,000 or more was double in 1966 (28 per cent) of what it was in 1960 [!] and four times greater than the proportion receiving such incomes in 1947" and that "the proportion of Negroes employed in high-skill, high-status and well-paying jobs, rose faster than the comparable proportion amog whites from 1960 to 1966." Further, "in 1947, 65 per cent of all Negro families made less than $3,000; in 1966 only thirty-two per cent." A more extended statistical presentation would confirm that, in all material respects, the fate of Negroes has improved faster than ever before, although, as one might expect, some groups benefited more than others.

The riots occurred not despite, but because of, this rapid improvement. The point has been made very well by Alexis de Tocqueville:

"It is natural that the love of equality should constantly increase together with equality itself, and that it should grow by what it feeds on. . . ." ". . . . When a people which has put up with an oppressive rule over a long period without protest suddenly finds the government relaxing its pressure, it takes up arms against it. . . ." ". . . . Experience teaches us that, generally speaking, the most perilous moment for a bad government is one when it seeks to mend its ways. . . ." ". . . . *The mere fact that certain abuses have been remedied draws attention to the others and they now appear more galling; people may suffer less, but their sensibility is exacerbated. . . .*"

Modern empirical research states these matters less succinctly and elegantly, but confirms them amply. The inevitable is tolerated, the inadequate is not: improvement as a process leads to more dissatisfaction than static misery, for aspiration fueled by the process of improvement pulls ahead of any possible fulfillment.

The Vicious Circle

Although they do not "explain" riots, many external causes for dissatisfaction among Negroes remain. Drawn by economic circumstances, Negroes have migrated to cities which lack facilities to house them. In turn they lack the skills which would allow them to earn a reasonable living there, even in the absence of discrimination. Unions make it both hard to acquire and to utilize skills; and our government does not like to enforce laws against unions. Immigration into the cities, indeed, propinquity—let alone integration—intensifies dissatisfaction by comparison with better-off neighbors. (Thus, Lander[1] states: "when other factors are held constant, delinquency rates are highest in areas of maximum racial heterogeneity," i.e., not in areas tenanted by whites, or by Negroes, and regardless of housing conditions etc.) Government welfare provisions are marvelously unintelligent: they disorganize Negro families, they cause many to spurn menial and low-paid jobs they could fill, and they humiliate everybody unnecessarily. Welfare provisions defeat any reasonable purpose, and perpetuate the welfare worker, his client, and the misery of both.

Many of these hardships are unavoidable on the way to improvement; other immigrant groups (Negroes, however native, are immigrants to our cities with no fewer problems of acculturation than, say, Italians) have overcome similar harships without assistance. But some hardships are much worse for Negroes than for other immigrant groups: they are different; and so are the circumstances. (Yet many might be avoided, not necessarily by more money, but by more intelligent ways of using it.)

These external causes—added to many internal ones—have caused Negroes to become more demoralized, hopeless and resentful than any immigrant group ever was. The Commission contributes to this demoralization. No other group has been told so often and so authoritatively what the Commission has now repeated *ex cathedra:* that all their misfortunes are due to others (who therefore must pay for all improvements); and that they are somehow entitled to dicharge (at least excused for discharging) their resentment against those who have what they want, by taking it away, or by destroying it.

[1] *Towards An Understanding of Juvenile Delinquency.* Columbia University Press, 1954.

Not only does the Commission blame the riots on those rioted against—it also proposes to make rioting more rewarding. The equation is: if there are riots, people are dissatisfied; let's satisfy them, for we must be at fault if they are dissatisfied. The conclusion, for anyone dissatisfied or resentful—for good or bad reasons—is obvious: if you riot, you get what you need or want fast; if you don't, you don't, and you may never. It should be obvious that grievances should be remedied according to their merits, but never so as to reward the aggrieved for expressing their resentment by injurious actions. However, it was not obvious to the Commission.

Full of good will and innocent naiveté, empty of historical or sociological knowledge, the Commission treats the riots as the rational phenomenon they are not. By now many Negroes want to fight, and win a victory—even if they could get more material benefits without fighting white authorities. The need to defy, to fight and to win, if you wish, to get things illegally and violently, has become independent of material effects, something desired for its own sake—probably the most important cause of the riots. This need, generated by feelings of humiliation and inadequacy, and by the consequent anger, cannot be satisfied by anything given—only by things taken; not by concessions, only by victories.

Indulgence Is Not the Remedy

Nothing is more pitiful therefore, and sillier, than the stance of the "white liberal": "I know we are at fault; I'll help you, I'll give you anything, just tell me what you want." Negroes are embarrassed. For what they—particularly young Negroes—feel they want, but cannot consciously articulate—though they certainly act it out—might be paraphrased: "We don't want to be given a damn thing by you. Stand up like a man, so we can fight you; we want to beat you up, to express our anger, not to bargain it away for any concessions. Whatever you offer we will ask for more—until you are ready to fight. For the benefits you offer cannot possibly match our fantasies, or make us feel powerful." Such a psychological condition requires specific remedies; indulgence is not among them. (Incidentally, the white liberal attitude is most apparent to Negroes in Jews—and it is a major cause of their antisemitism.)

One thing is certain: if the desire to fight whites, which many young Negroes feel, can be gratified without penalty, if it is rewarded and admired, and victory seems possible, it is not going to weaken. It is not impossible to divert such a desire into harmless, even into productive, channels, provided not only that these channels be made available, but, more important, provided that it be made entirely and credibly clear that the harmful channels are heavily penalized.

Although the demoralization, hysteria, and dissociation from reality of many Negroes is a reaction to external historical events, this reaction, and the attending evils, will not vanish if the external causes are simply removed: the phenomenon is now internal and largely independent of external changes. Meanwhile the demoralized must be prevented from inflicting harm on others or infecting them.

Considering remedies and preventives, it is essential to distinguish between what is immediately possible and necessary, and what might be useful in the long run. The Commission's remedies are not distinguished by originality, or imagination; nor are they accompanied by evidence of effectiveness, or estimates of feasibility. While some are known to be ineffective, others may be moderately helpful; but practically all are long-run remedies, and in the long run we are all going to be dead unless we provide for the short run first.

Riot Prevention Is Simple

The riots took those in charge of public order by surprise. Attempts to control them therefore were delayed, haphazard, inept, feeble and more harmful to the innocent than to the guilty. Legislation, organization, and, training of police departments easily can prevent riots. It is a silly canard that punishment "does not go to the causes of the crime." As the present Attorney General phrases this delusion, "in the long run only the elimination of the [social] causes of crime can make a significant and lasting difference in the incidence of crime."

Mr. Ramsey Clark's view suggests a fireman who declines fire-extinguishing apparatus by pointing out that "in the long run only the elimination of the causes of fire can make a significant and lasting difference in the incidence of fire," and that fire-fighting equipment does not eliminate "the causes"—except that such a fireman would probably not rise to fire chief. Actually, whether fires are checked depends on fire-fighting apparatus, and on the efforts of the firemen using it, no less than on the presence of "the causes": inflammable materials. So with riots. Laws, courts and police actions are no less important in restraining them, than "the causes" are in impelling them. If firemen (or attorneys general) pass the buck, and refuse to use the means available, we may all be burned while waiting for "the long run" and "the elimination of the causes."

Whether any activity—be it lawful or unlawful—takes place depends on whether the desire for it, or for whatever is to be secured by it, is stronger than the desire to avoid the costs involved. Accordingly people work, attend college, riot, go to the movies—or refrain from any of these activities. Attendance at a theater may be high because the show is entertaining and because the price of admission is low. Obviously the attendance depends on both—on the combination of expected gratification and cost. The wish, motive or impulse for doing anything—the experienced or expected gratification—is the cause of doing it; the wish to avoid the cost is the cause of not doing it. One is no more and no less "cause" than the other. Common speech supports this use of "cause" no less than logic. "Why did you go to Jamaica?" "Because it is such a beautiful place." "Why didn't you go to Jamaica?" "Because it is too expensive"— "Why do you read NATIONAL REVIEW?" "Because it is so lively and instructive." "Why don't you read NATIONAL REVIEW?" "Because it is too exasperating." In this sense, penalties (costs) are causes of lawfulness, or (if too low or uncertain) of unlawfulness, of crime, including riots or looting.

People commit crimes or riot because, given their condition, the desire for the satisfaction felt, or sought, prevails over the desire to avoid the risk of penalties. They refrain if the desire to avoid the cost prevails. Riots will increase if the penalties are reduced, or the desire is raised. Riots can be decreased by raising the cost, or by reducing the desire. The cost of riots to the rioters is more easily and swiftly changed than the conditions producing the inclination to riot. Costs are within the power of the government to change immediately, whereas the conditions producing the propensity to riot will necessarily take a long time to change; some may be altogether beyond the control of the government. The Commission's one-sided emphasis on these conditions, and its undue neglect of costs, will contribute to more riots.

What matters in riots is the immediate and stern enforcement of the law; those who initially engage in unlawful action must be used to deter others, by immediate apprehension, and if they refuse to surrender, immobilization by the most effective and least injurious means. To spare lives, it is very important that the police be armed with immobilizing non-lethel weapons, which permit the immediate apprehension of looters, stone-throwers, and snipers. Riots spread like fire and it is important to extinguish the first sparks even at a relatively high cost. Certainly there should be laws making looting, and incitement to looting, a specific crime and to punish severely anyone who knowingly disposes of looted goods. (I have not noticed among the Commission's proposals any referring to punishments meted out by the states for civil disorders.) The Commission's major idea for the police is to oppose "the indiscriminate and excessive use of force" (whoever favors anything "excessive"?) and to condemn "moves to equip police departments with automatic rifles, machine guns and tanks." Now, a police department should be able to do without these. However it is obviously reasonable to have such weapons in reserve. (Some sort of armored car—whether or not it is called a tank—would have been extremely useful in last year's riots.) Meanwhile it is important to have enough police, to organize them well, and to equip them with means to control crowds without lasting injury, so that riots will not get into the shooting stage.

In the Medium Run

Medium-run measures, which (mostly) will have effects only some years from now, include employment, housing, and—largely a long-run matter—acquisition of skills, and of motivation to acquire them and to seek employment.

Negro unemployment is twice as high as white unemployment and that of Negro adolescents is several times as high as that of white adolescents. This has little to do with present, though it has much to do with past, discrimination, which resulted in Negroes often being capable only of unreliable or unskilled work. It is not true, however, that unskilled work is not available. On the contrary, while unskilled workers and particular adolescents are unemployed, there are unfilled jobs these workers could fill. They cannot be hired, or they refuse to take these jobs, because what employers could pay for their services either is less than what minimum wage laws prescribe, or seems inadequate to maintain a worker properly by current standards. However, prescribing a minimum wage does not improve matters. It just causes the employer not to hire workers to whom he would have to pay more than they are worth to him.

Two measures are required:

1) Minimum wage laws which are at best useless, and often harmful to those supposed to be helped by them, should be eliminated.

2) Welfare payments should supplement inadequate incomes from work, and, above all, should not be reduced, so as to eliminate incentives to earn, once income from work becomes available. The Commission, as have others, makes timid suggestions in this direction but does not go far enough. Too little thought is given to incentives to make "unemployables" employable, and to cause employables to work; too much thought is based on the assumption that they cannot possibly contribute anything to their own welfare. They would, if they were helped to do so. Instead they are helped not to do so, and sometimes helped only on condition that they won't try.

Although noting the high percentage of fatherless families among Negroes and stressing that nearly half of all welfare recipients are dependent children, or those who take care of them, the Commission says nothing about the high fertility rates of the poor. Yet, if "the pill" were made available without prescription—there is no reason whatever not to do so—the fertility rates of the poor would approach those of the rich. I don't think this would foster illicit intercourse; but I'm sure it would reduce illicit conception.

The Commission indicts ghettoes (segregated housing) and slums (bad housing) as causes of riots. This confuses location and cause; it is as though hospitals were indicted as causes of illness. The original Jewish, and the present-day Chinese, ghettoes have not caused riots. There must be a specific element other than segregation, to produce riots in Negro ghettoes. Slums, bad housing, scarcely cause riots either. Surely housing has been worse, and remains so, in many parts of the world.

Nonetheless much could and should be done to improve housing. Yet the Commission proposes nothing that can be taken seriously. Its support for urban renewal (not unjustly nicknamed "Negro removal") is absurd: it is well known that this curious enterprise has destroyed far more dwellings—especially of the poor—than it has replaced.

Although admitting that the cost of building has made it impossible for the poor to find decent dwelling space, the Commission avoids asking why this nation, as it gets richer, seems less able to provide housing. However, the answer is obvious: unions have raised the cost of building so high that people cannot afford the necessary rent. Unions have done so largely by excluding the poor—specifically Negroes—from membership. Our laws, and their selective enforcement, foster and tolerate this monopolistic gouging. The political cost of better housing for the poor appears too high to the government. It would cost the taxpayer nothing. The immense expenses proposed by the Commission, on the other hand, would not begin to solve the problem.

On education the report of the Commission is highly misleading. The low school performance of Negro pupils is largely ascribed to bad textbooks, laboratories, libraries, and to segregation, even though the Coleman Report (which the Commission quotes misleadingly) states explicitly: "The data suggest that variations in school quality are not highly related to variations in achievement of pupils . . . ; the school appears unable to exert independent influence to make achievement levels less dependent on the child's background—and this is true within each ethnic group just as it is between groups" (p. 297). Elsewhere (*The Public Interest*, Fall 1967) James Coleman states: "Even in socially or racially integrated schools a child's family background shows a very high relation to his performance. The findings of the report are quite unambiguous on this score. Even if the school is integrated the heterogeneity of backgrounds with which children enter school is generally preserved in the heterogeneity of their performance when they finish."

Since Coleman wrote, it has become clearer that the deprivation in the background of Negro children is not the main cause of their low scholastic performance. Thus, Morris Gross tested "two Jewish middle class groups" and found that "marked differences in school work were apparent which resemble those uncovered in Negro-white studies . . . the differences between these two Jewish middle class groups parallel those found in different races and classes."[2] The two groups were equally prosperous. Hence deprivation, or, for that matter, race, cannot be mainly responsible. An elusive factor—the cultural home ideal— must bear major responsibility. Yet the Commission tirelessly repeats the old (and false) clichés about segregation and deprivation. . . . Another study, by Susan S. Stodolsky and Gerald Lesser, might be mentioned. The authors found: 1) "ethnicity has primary effects upon the organization of mental abilities. . ." 2) "social class variations within the ethnic group do not alter this."[3]

There are more things involved in differential educational achievement than the Commission has dreamt of.

Can anything be done about the whole mess? A great deal, I think. Some things can be done easily with immediate results. Others will take time and are difficult; still others require more research. I have had space only to suggest a few problems and solutions. However, one thing is clear; if we are to make progress we must look at the actual

[2] "Learning Readiness in Two Jewish Groups," Center for Urban Education, New York 1967.

[3] "Learning Patterns in the Disadvantaged," *Harvard Educational Review*, Fall 1967.

problems and forget about the pathetic handwringing, the pompous threats and reassurances, and the silly clichés the President's Commission has produced.

QUESTIONS FOR DISCUSSION

1. *Before or after reading this article, you should review an earlier one in this chapter: "Excerpts from a Study to Determine the Characteristics of Negro Rioters."*

2. *On what grounds does van den Haag criticize the Report of the National Advisory Commission on Civil Disorders?*

3. *How does the author react to this statement, supposedly made by the Commission: "Riots occur because white society is rich and allows, or causes, Negroes to be poor in its midst"?*

4. *What theory about violence is van den Haag ignoring?*

5. *The author believes that the feelings of young blacks can be paraphrased as follows: "We don't want to be given a damn thing by you. Stand up like a man, so we can fight you; we want to beat you up, to express our anger, not to bargain it away for any concessions." What does he think this means?*

6. *What are the author's criticisms of the Commission's remedies?*

7. *Is the author's analogy of riots and fires a fair one?*

8. *What would van den Haag stress to reduce the number of riots? What are the "medium-run measures" that he would pursue?*

9. *Why does van den Haag believe that better housing is not the answer to less rioting?*

10. *If deprivation in the background of Negro children is not the main cause of their low scholastic performance, what is?*

Violence: Left and Middle

Mary C. Segers

"It is necessary for every urban guerrilla to keep in mind always that he can only maintain his existence if he is disposed to kill the police and those dedicated to repression, and if he is determined to expropriate the wealth of the big capitalists, the latifundists and the imperialists."

> Carlos Marighella
> *Minimanual of the Urban Guerrilla*
> *Time* Nov. 2, 1970

"There are . . . advantages to political assassination, not that this can eliminate the function, but you know that the man will be replaced, and it has great educational value. It teaches the people to kill the enemy and hate the enemy. It would give me great satisfaction if Richard Nixon should be killed. I would consider that an excellent thing."

> Eldridge Cleaver
> "Cleaver Speaks", statement to
> Sanche de Gramont, *New York Times*
> *Magazine* November 1, 1970.

"Violence: Left and Middle," *Catholic World*, March 1971, pp. 307–311. Reprinted by permission of *Catholic World* and the author.

The rhetoric of violence fills the air; the above statements are simply two examples. Before we dismiss these statements as "rhetorical excess," or before we mesmerize ourselves into accepting them as grounds for action, perhaps we should try to clarify our thinking about the subject of violence. What follows are some considerations on the use of violence in political action.

Max Weber's definition of the state may be a fruitful starting point for any discussion of the use of violence as a political tactic. (I think here of internal strife within a polity and not of warfare in the international arena.) The distinguishing feature of the modern state, Weber asserts, is that it has a monopoly of the legitimate means of violence. The key word here is "legitimate." Certain members of a society (commonly called "criminal") may employ violence in the pursuit of their own ends, but such resort to violence is "illegitimate" since it is not employed in defense of, but against, the public interest. By contrast, the modern state is characterized as having a monopoly of the (legitimate) violence business, a monopoly justified by the necessity in any society of some institution to protect the lives and interests of the members of that society.

It is precisely Weber's recognition of the intimate connection between politics and violence that prompts some New Left adherents to justify the use of (what Weber might regard as "illegitimate") violence in America today. Briefly, their argument runs as follows: First, the concept of violence must be broadened to include not only physical but psychological violence; there is as much violence in prejudicial attitudes or in ideologically-skewed judges and juries as there is in more graphic and concrete cases of beatings with nightsticks. In fact, the American "power elite" has not only a monopoly of the legitimate means of physical violence; it also has a near monopoly of psychological force as well, since it "controls" the mass media and subtly yet effectively blocks lawful channels of social change. (It is for precisely this reason that H. Marcuse argues that universities should not be bombed; they constitute the last refuge of free inquiry in an otherwise controlled and repressive society.)

Secondly, it is argued that, since the American system has proved impervious to peaceful means of social change, both the overt and covert violence of American society today must be met with counter-violence (bombings are pretty fashionable, but conceivably the new tactics could include political kidnapping and political assassination). In other words, since evolution has failed in this country, its citizens had better prepare for terrorism and, ultimately, violent revolution.

Needless to say, the above argument requires empirical verification at certain key points (Is there in fact a "power elite"? Does it control the means of communication? Have we exhausted all peaceful means of social change?). Assuming for the moment, however, that the above argument constitutes an accurate description of this society, I would like to address myself to the problem of violence as an avenue of social change in the America of the seventies.

It seems to me that we can cull a few pearls of wisdom about the meaning of revolution from the conduct of certain radical factions in the New Left and from no less reputable a source than Aristotle. When Aristotle speaks of changing a constitution (and he thought of a constitution as a way of life as well as an arrangement of offices or distribution of power), he thinks of revolution as essentially a change in consciousness. People have different levels of consciousness, different conceptions of justice. What causes revolutions is the passion for equality: democrats think of free men as equals, oligarchs think of wealthy men as equals, aristocrats think of excellent (virtuous) men as equals. Each faction has a different conception of justice, a different criterion for the allocation of offices, honors, and merits in society. In order to see its conception realized, a faction has to change the consciousness of other members of the society; it must persuade them to accept its conception of a just and good society. When consciousness has been sufficiently broadened and developed, the requisite change in the constitution (a way of life and a distribution of power) will occur. That is essentially what revolution is about: changing consciousness.

If we examine the behavior of New Left factions, it should become clear that a revolution is already occurring in this society. It is no accident that the Vice-President criticizes the student movement for such "unimportant" accidentals as dress, hair-style, permissiveness, use of drugs, etc. Such accidentals are not trivial but may be essential to a new emerging life-style—one which values peace, dignity, freedom, spontaneity, authenticity, and fraternal respect for others over a success ethic which measures human worth in terms of acquisitions and the ability to compete well on the market. However, I do not wish to analyze the ideals of the New Left here; I simply wish to point out that they are revolutionary in the Aristotelian sense. They represent a new level of consciousness and are rightly regarded as threatening by the second-in-command of the present Administration. In a sense the revolution is taking place under our noses; it is taking place from within, where it cannot be defeated.

The problem for the New Left has been that of intensifying and extending the new consciousness—of integrating rather than alienating groups such as "the hardhats." How can the revolution be extended so as to include broader categories within the society? Here again, the Movement gives its own answer. Ask a Black Panther what his Afro hair-style means and he will respond that it has something to do with identity, self-conception, attitude, consciousness. Ask a member of the Progressive Labor Party what he is doing to further "the revolution," and he will undoubtedly reply: distributing newspapers, picketing, writing, propagandizing, "rapping." If you pursue the point, he will undoubtedly agree that he is talking only to the converted, the faithful. What the New Left adherent is doing, in other words, is developing his own self-consciousness and endeavoring to reinforce that of his fellow adherents—little more. Perhaps this self-absorption accounts in part for the intensity of ideological debate within the Movement as well as its tendency to factionalism.

One is entitled to ask what revolutionaries are doing in the way of truly political action. Are they merely talking to one another to gain psychological reinforcement of tenuous positions, or are they really endeavoring to reach that silent majority of which the Vice-President is so fond? Are they really revolutionary, that is, are they really seeking to change the consciousness of the "retrograde elements of the population"? Or are they a closed shop, an inner circle of the enlightened which delights in heaping abuse upon the unenlightened masses?

I would argue that the New Left has not exhausted peaceful means of social change because it has not yet focused on its main target: Middle America. I would argue, further, that sporadic bombing is not the most intelligent method of winning converts from the ranks of the Silent Majority. Revolutionizing this sector of the population requires not only a critique of present social arrangements but the presentation of alternative solutions to the problems which beset us. For one thing, the Movement must present an image of a future society which is satisfying *and* plausible. Vague allusions to "participatory democracy" in a "non-repressive society" will satisfy neither white collar administrators who know the difficulties inherent in running large-scale programs nor economists who are aware of the interdependent character of regional and national economies. Too often, the utopian character of New Left solutions alienates both white and blue collar workers whose work experience equips them with a knowledge of human nature not to be gained from books in a university setting. Perhaps a renewed effort at reaching the Silent Majority through intelligent presentation of constructive alternatives must be tried before embarking on the path of violence.

Let us assume, however, that peaceful means have been exhausted and that escalation to violent tactics is now felt to be in order. This is my real concern in this essay and, at the outset, I must confess to no clear-cut position on this harrowing question. What follows, then, are some exploratory thoughts on the use of violence as a political tactic in America today.

First, the argument that resort to violence will dramatically illustrate the inherently repressive character of American society (by inducing repression from the Right) seems to me to be irrelevant to the larger concerns of the New Left. Indeed, this type of argument in favor of escalation strikes me as both crude and paranoid. In such a projected bloodbath, the Movement would be destroyed (it is still a minority in the country), but there would be no positive gains to offset this loss. Furthermore, in any such confrontation between extremists of both Left and Right, the crucial question is always the direction of the Middle, those moderates who have property and a stake in the system and who are emotionally resistant to violence as a means of social change. I suspect that violent provocation initiated by the New Left will simply drive moderates to the Right (one reason I am against the current rash of bombings). In other words, resorting to violence to dramatize the inherently repressive character of the system is self-defeating on two counts: the Left would be destroyed and the Middle would be lost to the Right.

Secondly, effecting a revolution in any society means changing the consciousness of a majority and thereby gaining public support for a new order, a new distribution of power, and a new allocation of goods. To seize power without public support (that is, without the requisite change in consciousness) is to stage a *coup d'état*, not a revolution. And to govern without public support is to rely heavily on the instruments of coercion, terror and violence (as the Bolsheviks did in 1917 and the Brazilian and Greek governments do today). Such a continual reliance on violence to both seize and retain power suggests an elitism which, on the face of it, would vitiate the very ideals (*e.g.*, participatory democracy) which the New Left holds dear.

I have deliberately refrained from mentioning anything about the value of human life in the above paragraphs because I mean to stress the calculative aspect of any decision to employ violence. The revolutionary (as well as the statesman or government official) is duty-bound, in my opinion, to attempt to calculate the consequences of his actions. This is especially true of violent actions. Rather than subscribe to a Sorelian exaltation of violence as the cataclysmic encounter which will purge society of its evils, the revolutionary had better re-think Weber's distinction between an ethics of consequences (in which one has to give an account of the foreseeable results of one's action) and an ethics of ultimate ends (in which one must conform to a set of unconditional norms, no matter what the consequences). The apocalyptic use of violence may in fact be diabolical.

In the two arguments cited above, I maintain that the consequences of resorting to violence would be self-defeating for the New Left. What of the consequences of violent actions for those other than the New Left revolutionaries? This involves a shift from pragmatic arguments regarding correct tactics to principled arguments about the use of violence in general. In the *Brothers Karamazov*, Dostoevsky poses the problem directly when he asks whether the sacrifice of one human life for the sake of the Utilitarian's "greatest happiness of the greatest number" is ever justified. This is much too broad a question to treat within the scope of this essay; here again, therefore, I would simply offer some exploratory comments.

First, most of us reject in principle the wanton taking of innocent life in the name of some abstract higher ideal. We reject this because we have an instinctive sense of the problematic character of human existence. Human life is fraught with the factor of unintended consequences: "the best laid plans of mice and men" have a habit of coming to nought or, at least, going awry. In political philosophy, this is nothing other than the means-end problem, which is always critical in individual and political decision-making, but which assumes monumental proportions when the decision concerns the use of violence. As Hannah Arendt remarks, "The very substance of violent action is ruled by the means-end category, whose chief characteristic, if applied to human affairs, has always been that the end is in danger of being overwhelmed by the means which it justifies and which are needed to reach it. Since the end of human action, as distinct from the end products of fabrication (art), can never be reliably predicted, the means used to achieve political goals are more often than not of greater relevance to the future world than the intended goals."

In other words, the means employed does not necessarily assure the end desired. Who among the "old Bolsheviks" could have foreseen—and would have condoned—the Purges of the thirties? Not only are the results of men's actions beyond the actors' control; violence as a specific means also "harbors within itself an additional element of abitrariness: nowhere does Fortuna, good or ill luck, play a more fateful role in human affairs than on the battlefield." (Arendt) The factor of the unintended, the accidental, the utterly unexpected looms particularly large in any decision to use violence. The death of a researcher in the bombing of the Math Building at the University of Wisconsin was clearly accidental, unforeseen and unplanned. The point is: such unforeseen "accidents" tend to multiply when violence is employed.

Considerations such as these should foster in any revolutionary a reluctance to embark on the path of violent revolution. However, an additional consideration must be stressed, one which directly concerns the individual involved in any decision to employ violence as a political tactic. I speak here of the factor of motivation. If there is anything we have learned from Freudian (and post-Freudian) psychology, it is that human beings are rationalizing (not rational) animals and that our actions are often prompted by a mixture of noble and ignoble motives. Consciously, we may mean well; unconsciously, we may really desire to "do in" the other for a variety of less worthy reasons or even, perhaps, for reasons that have nothing to do with the existence of the other. Aggressive tendencies within the human psyche are not to be unleashed without the gravest provocation. As Freud himself remarked, civilization (admittedly based on the renunciation of instinctual satisfaction) is a hard-won achievement, a fragile, delicate fabric not to be heedlessly tampered with or treated lightly —since the alternative to civilization is barbarism and anarchy.

In short, I am arguing that the New Left should resist the temptation to plunge mindlessly into direct violent action. Not without reason did Weber characterize politics as "a strong and slow boring of hard boards." Political action requires both passion and perspective as well as the ability to tolerate and live with the frustration involved in "the slow boring of hard boards." Violent action, by contrast, destroys the sense of trust and tolerance on which a community's survival depends.

I have said that the New Left has yet to make an all-out frontal assault on the Middle American hinterlands. I think particularly of the white New Left for whom the Silent Majority is a natural constituency (blacks and Third World revolutionaries have their own natural constituencies). To date, two things have prevented the white New Left from effectively reaching its own constituency: its rhetoric and its style. Its rhetoric has invoked "We-They" categories extensively and intensively: it's "Us" (the good guys) against "Them" (the bad guys) and "ne'er the twain shall meet." Such language imposes artificial categories on experience, categories of distortion which then become bases for action. Thinking in distorted categories results in the erection of artificial barriers to communication between people. Indeed, such categorical language is a rhetoric of exclusion and serves to keep the New Left a marginal group, locked into conversation with itself instead of with groups in the larger society (needless to say, this very same rhetoric of exclusion and division characterized almost all Administration utterances in the recent campaign).

Similarly, in the style it adopts, the New Left seems to aim more at alienating than converting silent majoritarians. In the 1930's George Orwell criticized his fellow socialists for their nonconformist habits and tastes (libertinism and vegetarianism) which only served to alienate the British working class. Rosemary Ruether echoes Orwell in her criticism of today's Left:

> It is obvious that the Left, if it had real imagination and access to middle Americans, could make an enormous impact simply by working on the native conservative values of localism and anti-interventionalism and linking up these conservative and deeply-held traits of mind of the American mainstream with a sane international policy. Nixon's policies operate on an elaborate obscurantism of American conservatism, yet the Left, instead of demythologizing this obscurantism, continually creates rhetoric and tactics designed to play right into its hands! Nothing could be better for the Right than for the Left to posture,

quite unnecessarily, as anarchists, Communists and sex and drug freakouts all at the same time, in the face of a terrified Middle America, already deeply bred with visions of international Communist conspiracy and breakdown of moral values. The Left, year by year, builds up its symbiosis with the Right on lines that couldn't be better if they had been written by the CIA, and the possibility of getting across the real messages that need to be communicated retreats farther and farther from the scene. (*Commonweal*, Nov. 6, 1970.)

The communications gap in this country between the Left and the Middle must be bridged. Before the Left gives up on politics and resorts to violent action, one final effort must be made to reach Nixon's constituency and communicate to them a critical message in a tone and style they can relate to, rather than one which needlessly turns them off from the content of the message. Bombing will turn them off; so will a rhetoric of exclusion and a flamboyant life-style deliberately flaunted. What will turn them on are some carefully thought-out alternative solutions to existing problems and a viable image of a future society. Perhaps they will really respond if the Peace Movement lives its ideal.

QUESTIONS FOR DISCUSSION

1. *Is this article strictly about violence as a political tactic?*
2. *How does the author justify "legitimate" violence?*
3. *According to Segers, how does the New Left justify "illegitimate" violence?*
4. *What causes revolutions?*
5. *What must a faction do to change the consciousness of other members of society?*
6. *What is the problem for the New Left of "intensifying and extending the new consciousness"?*

7. What could be the main target of the New Left?

8. Why is violence not the way to convert the Silent Majority?

9. How does the author refute the New Left argument that "resort to violence will dramatically illustrate the inherently repressive character of American society"?

10. What is wrong with seizing power without public support?

11. Why must the revolutionary try to calculate the consequences of his act?

12. What does the author mean when he says, "the means employed does not necessarily assure the end desired"?

13. According to the author, what two things have prevented the white New Left from effectively reaching its own constituency?

14. Why must the communications gap between the Left and Middle be bridged?

Epilogue

ROBERT M. FOGELSON

A year after the Kerner Commission issued its report Urban America and the Urban Coalition made a survey of the country's response to the commission's recommendations and the racial crisis. They called it *One Year Later*. The survey found a few minor improvements. Employment and income had increased somewhat in the black ghettos; school desegregation had proceeded ahead in a few small and medium-size cities; and fair housing legislation had gained passage in the Congress. But otherwise the survey found little change. Poverty was pervasive in the ghetto, job discrimination was widespread outside, and the hard-core unemployed were untouched by nationwide prosperity; nothing was done to reform the welfare system either. Federal implementation of school desegregation was lagging; so were local efforts to improve education; and the ghetto schools, racked by the controversies over decentralization, were failing the children. Congress had not appropriated adequate funds to implement the 1968 Housing Act

(or to enforce its open housing provisions); housing rehabilitation had not fulfilled its promise, and model cities had
not yet had much impact. In sum, the survey concluded,
the country has not made "a serious start toward the
changes in national priorities, programs, and institutions
advocated by the Commission."[1]

Nor, in all likelihood, will it do so in the foreseeable
future. The Nixon Administration is more concerned
about the profits of defense industries than the survival of
ghetto residents; witness its positions on the antiballistic
missile and welfare reform. The Congress is reluctant to
deal with the conditions underlying the ghetto's grievances;
and in view of the character of the House of Representatives, it is probably just as well. The Supreme Court may
assume a more passive role under its new Chief Justice;
and besides, the problems plaguing the black ghettos are
not particularly susceptible to judicial solution.[2] Prospects
are highly inauspicious on the local level, too. The munici-
pal bureaucracies and public employee unions are hostile
to black demands; and they can count on substantial support among middle-class liberals as well as working-class
conservatives. To aggravate this situation several capable
mayors, notably Jerome P. Cavanagh of Detroit, have
retired, and several others, including John V. Lindsay of
New York, have barely won re-election. So even if the
Kerner Commission's recommendations would assure the
blacks a greater share of the national wealth and a greater
voice in local decisions, which is highly unlikely, they would
probably not be implemented.[3]

Turning from conditions to attitudes, the survey found
a few reassuring signs. Few blacks were prepared to follow
militant leaders toward separatism and violence; and many
whites were moved by the commission's report and the
assassination of Dr. Martin Luther King, Jr. But otherwise
the survey found the situation extremely ominous. The militants were exerting increasing influence in the ghettos,

particularly among the young blacks who are growing more and more proud of their racial heritage. At the same time pressure for "law and order" was undermining sympathy for domestic reform among whites; and white resistance to black demands was gaining momentum virtually everywhere. White and black perceptions of civil disorders (which have recently erupted not only in the ghettos but also, on a smaller scale, in the universities and high schools) have become increasingly divergent. And despite the virtual halt in black migration, the segregation of the races has not diminished; nor, in spite of (or perhaps because of) these patterns, have the authorities changed the prevailing policy of drift. All in all, Urban America and the Urban Coalition concluded, the country is "a year closer to being two societies, black and white, increasingly separate and scarcely less unequal."[4]

And, in all probability, it will be even closer two years, five years, or ten years later. The blacks and particularly the upcoming generation of blacks born and raised in the northern ghettos who reached maturity in the 1950s and 1960s will not settle for token concessions; they are determined to eliminate the ghetto's grievances. They intend to carry this struggle not only to the Capitol but to city hall and the ghetto, not only to corporations but to unions, and not only to politicians but to policemen, teachers, caseworkers, highway engineers, and other civil servants.[5] In the process the blacks will probably antagonize many working-class, first- and second-generation whites who believe that the blacks are demanding (and, even worse, receiving) too much too soon—and at their expense. And if, as appears likely, the blacks insist on community control, they will probably alienate many middle-class, native-American whites who are strongly committed to the centralization, professionalization, and bureaucratization of urban institutions.[6] To put it bluntly, a return to the relative harmony of the civil rights movement of the late 1950s is out of the question: for better or worse, racial confrontation is probably inevitable in the foreseeable future.

But whether riots are also inevitable is another issue. Indeed, some observers have insisted that the 1960s riots, as exemplified by the Los Angeles, Newark, and Detroit riots, have already run their course. Much can be said in favor of this position. By most measures, the intensity of the riots has declined since the Washington and Chicago riots of spring 1968 (and possibly even the Newark and Detroit riots of summer 1967). Also, most ghettos have already experienced riots; and, if it turns out that no ghetto will suffer more than one major riot, the number of riots may decrease too.[7] What is more, many blacks have realized that blacks, not whites, suffer the worst personal casualties (though not the most property damage) in the disorders. And many militants have decided that the group's interests can best be advanced by encouraging self-help, pressing for community control, and avoiding violent confrontations. And, as if this were not enough, the police, National Guard, and federal troops have devised fairly sophisticated and highly effective riot-control tactics over the past few years.[8] From this perspective, the 1960s riots are a transitory, if highly dramatic, episode in the history of American race relations.

But much can be said against this position. Although none of the 1969 riots matched the Washington and Chicago riots of 1968, none of the 1966 riots equaled the Los Angeles riots of 1965; and yet the Newark and Detroit riots erupted in 1967 anyway. One relatively quiet summer does not make a long-term trend. Also, though few ghettos have experienced more than one major riot, many ghettos, notably Chicago's West Side and south-central Los Angeles, have suffered several riots of varying intensity. And the pressures which generated the early riots are building up again. If the public opinion polls are reliable, a large segment of the black community believes that the disorders were beneficial and an even larger segment holds that they are inevitable. A significant minority intends to join in them, too.[9] Also, thus far very few militants have gained the loyalties or formed the organizations which would enable them to head off future rioting in the ghettos. Besides, not all the militants are determined to avoid confrontation. And, notwithstanding improved riot-control tactics, neither the police, the National Guard nor the federal troops can keep the ghetto under full-time surveillance. They can contain the riots, but they cannot prevent them. Hence the blacks will probably resort to violent protest in the years ahead.

Whether they will also resort to disruption and terrorism is another matter. From time to time over the past few years the country has been warned that cadres of blacks are planning to block highways and subways, poison water supplies, dynamite banks and department stores, and ambush white patrolmen. These warnings have been issued by black militants, seeking to strengthen their bargaining position vis-à-vis white authorities, and by law enforcement officials, trying to legitimize repressive legislation and increased appropriations.[10] Moreover, a few developments have enhanced the credibility of these warnings. Some militant organizations, including the Revolutionary Action Movement, have taken the stance that only through disruption and terrorism can the blacks overcome white racism. Many ordinary blacks, and especially young blacks in the northern ghettos, have expressed doubts that American society will respond to nonviolent protest. And according to Brandeis University's Lemberg Center for the Study of Violence, scattered incidents of disruption and terrorism have occurred recently in several large cities.[11] If these warnings are accurate, insurrectionary activity will supplant violent protest in the black ghettos in the near future.

But these warnings are probably premature. Very few blacks have engaged in disruption or terrorism; and, though obviously no one can be certain, not many more are planning to do so. Besides, most militant organizations are not cohesive enough to maintain the secrecy essential for these activities. Very few blacks are so disaffected with American society that they are ready to offer the militants the tacit support that the Algerians gave the F.L.N. And without this support guerrilla tactics are, as Che Guevara found out in Bolivia, all but hopeless. What is more, the whites are not so divided in their loyalties that the authorities would be prevented from vigorously suppressing disruption or terrorism. In the face of these activities virtually all whites would quickly rally to the support of the government. Lastly, most black militants apparently realize that, as Barrington Moore, Jr., recently observed, the United States is not in a revolutionary (or even a prerevolutionary) situation.[12] It is hard to tell how long the realization will restrain them. But it is safe to say that the blacks will probably not resort to disruption and terrorism in the near future—or at any rate not unless they are driven to it.

Shortly after the 1967 riots it seemed that they might be. Throughout the country local, state, and federal law enforcement officials were, in the phrase of *Esquire* reporter Gary Wills, "arming for armageddon." The F.B.I., I.D.A., and other government (or quasi-government) agencies were designing contingency plans and devising riot-control tactics; so were local police departments, National Guard units, and regular army divisions. To the benefit of General Ordnance and other weapons manufacturers, the police and the military were also building up arsenals of carbines, submachine guns, bazookas, tanks, helicopters, and MACE and teaching their personnel how to use them. Moreover, local, state, and federal intelligence units were compiling dossiers on thousands of black militants and placing H. Rap Brown and other conspicuous militant leaders under exceedingly close surveillance. And in the meantime white civilians were not only buying guns and rifles in record numbers in Los Angeles, Detroit, and Chicago but also forming vigilante organizations in the ethnic neighborhoods of Newark. Everywhere, it seemed, the authorities were drawing the line very tightly—indeed so tightly that after completing a survey of the racial crisis Wills wrote a book predicting a second civil war.[13]

Events took a different course, however. The official response to the Washington, Baltimore, Chicago, and other riots which followed the assassination of Martin Luther King in the spring of 1968 was exceptionally quick, tightly disciplined, and admirably restrained. The authorities restored order in most of these cities with relatively few casualties and relatively little resentment—a far cry from the performance of the Newark police or the Michigan National Guard in the 1967 riots.[14] Apparently the Kerner Commission deserves a good deal of the credit. In response to testimony by Cyrus R. Vance, President Johnson's personal emissary to the Detroit riots, the commission persuaded the President to call a conference of mayors, city managers, and police chiefs to discuss the problem of riot control. The Justice Department and International Association of Chiefs of Police jointly sponsored it. At the meetings, held later in the year, the commission and the administration prevailed upon local authorities to adopt the policies of prior planning, professional supervision, and deliberate restraint recommended in the appendix to the commission's report.[15] The authorities rapidly implemented these policies, successfully employed them in the spring disorders, and presumably will do so in any future riots.

These policies suggest that the nation—or at any rate its public officials—has learned a few valuable things about the 1960s riots. One, that the riots are not revolutionary uprisings against American society but violent protests against its abuses; hence it is incumbent upon the authorities to avoid resorting to overwhelming and indiscriminate force at all costs. Two, that violent protest can best be understood not in terms of a simple dichotomy between violence and nonviolence but in terms of a political continuum ranging from apathy, at one end, to insurrectionary activity, at the other. And three, that the country can survive riots, even riots on the scale of the Los Angeles and Detroit riots; but it cannot survive disruption, terrorism, or guerrilla warfare, at least not as a pluralistic democracy under civilian rule. By following the Kerner Commission's guidelines the authorities signaled to the blacks that though they could not riot with impunity they could riot and that they need not turn to more serious and less visible forms of violence. And by so doing the authorities honored the unwritten rule (the internal morality, so to speak) of the riots, which is that violent protest and official repression are tolerable only so long as they are restrained and selective.

But, in light of the white reaction in Chicago and a few other cities to the official response to the 1968 riots, it is not clear whether the local authorities will be restrained in the near future. Nor, in view of the increasing militancy of the upcoming generation of blacks, and particularly the black teen-agers, is it clear whether the militant blacks will be restrained in the years ahead. Hence the situation is, to say the least, quite precarious; and, in all likelihood, it will remain so until American society responds to the protest delivered in the 1960s riots. The authorities must not only design sophisticated riot-control tactics; they must also provide the blacks with a greater share of the nation's wealth and a greater voice in the city's decisions. For, in the final analysis, the problem is less the 1960s riots than the black ghettos and less the black ghettos than the American society (and especially its existing institutional arrangements). Indeed, a redistribution of national income or increase in black participation will, as I have already pointed out, require fundamental changes in America's political and economic institutions. And thus far the American people have displayed little understanding of this problem and even less determination to resolve it.

NOTES

1. Urban America, Inc., and The Urban Coalition, *One Year Later* (1969), 4–62.
2. New York *Times*, June 5, August 9, 1969.
3. For an attempt to place their problem in a national perspective, see James Q. Wilson and Harold R. Wilde, "The Urban Mood," *Commentary*, October 1969, 52–61.
4. Urban America, Inc., and The Urban Coalition, *One Year Later*, 66–118.
5. "Report from Black America," *Newsweek*, June 30, 1969, 17–35.
6. "The Troubled American," *ibid.*, October 6, 1969, 29–73.
7. Morris Janowitz, "Patterns of Collective Racial Violence," in Hugh Davis Graham and Ted Robert Gurr, *Violence in America*, a report to the National Commission on the Causes and Prevention of Violence (New York, 1969), 408–11.
8. Professional Standards Division, International Association of Chiefs of Police, *Civil Disorders: After-Action Reports Spring 1968*, a report to the Attorney General of the United States, chapters 1–4.
9. Angus Campbell and Howard Schuman, "Racial Attitudes in Fifteen American Cities," in *Supplemental Studies for the National Advisory Commission on Civil Disorders* (Washington, D.C., 1968), chapter 5.
10. For a sample of these warnings, see *Hearings Before the Permanent Subcommittee on Investigations of the Committee on Government Operations: United States Senate, Ninety-First Congress, First Session* (Washington, D.C., 1969), part 20, 4175–4498.

11. "Sniping Incidents—a New Pattern of Violence," in Lemberg Center for the Study of Violence, Brandeis University, *Riot Data Review*, February 1969. See also Louis H. Masotti and Jerome R. Corsi, *Shoot-out in Cleveland*, a report to the National Commission on the Causes and Prevention of Violence (New York, 1969).

12. Barrington Moore, Jr., "Revolution in America," *The New York Review of Books*, January 30, 1969, 6–12. See also Martin Oppenheimer, *The Urban Guerrilla* (Chicago, 1969), chapters 4 and 5.

13. Gary Wills, *The Second Civil War* (New York, 1968). The Federal Bureau of Investigation's *Prevention and Control of Mobs and Riots* (Washington, D.C., 1965) and the Department of the Army's *Civil Disturbances and Disasters* (Washington, D.C., 1968) are quite revealing too.

14. Tom Hayden, *Rebellion in Newark* (New York, 1967), chapter 4; *Hearings Before Special Subcommittee to Inquire into the Capability of the National Guard to Cope with Civil Disturbances: Committee on Armed Services, House of Representatives, Ninetieth Congress, First Session* (Washington, D.C., 1967), 6122–33; Urban America, Inc., and The Urban Coalition, *One Year Later*, 68–70.

15. *Report of the National Advisory Commission on Civil Disorders* (New York, 1968), 484–527; Urban America, Inc., and The Urban Coalition, *One Year Later*, 67–68.

QUESTIONS FOR DISCUSSION

1. *What improvements did the Urban America and the Urban Coalition's survey find since the Kerner Commission issued its report? What conditions remained the same?*

2. *Why doesn't Fogelson see many changes coming shortly?*

3. *What were some of the reassuring attitudes discovered by the survey?*

4. *Does Fogelson anticipate a return to the harmony of the civil rights movement of the late 1950's? Why may riots decrease? Why may they increase?*

5. *What evidence does Fogelson supply that the blacks may be driven to further violence?*

6. *What has the nation learned, according to Fogelson, from the riots of the 1960's?*

7. *What does the author mean by the last two sentences in the essay?*